Analysis and reform of cultural heritage policies in South-East Europe

Directorate of Culture and Cultural and Natural Heritage
Regional Co-operation Division

Council of Europe Publishing

The opinions expressed in this work are the responsibility of the author(s) and do not necessarily reflect the official policy of the Council of Europe.

All rights reserved. No part of this publication may be translated, reproduced or transmitted, in any form or by any means, electronic (CD-Rom, Internet, etc.) or mechanical, including photocopying, recording or any information storage or retrieval system, without the prior permission in writing from the Public Information and Publishing Division, Directorate of Communication (F-67075 Strasbourg Cedex or publishing@coe.int).

Cover design: Graphic Design Studio, Council of Europe

Cover photos:
Albania – The fortress of Kruja (Council of Europe)
Bosnia and Herzegovina – Bridge of Mehmed Pasha Sokolović (Council of Europe)
Bulgaria – Thracian Tomb Alexandrovo ("Center for the Study of Democracy", Sofia)
Croatia – Veliki Tabor, Kosnicki Hum, Desinić (Council of Europe)
Kosovo/UNMIK – Woman spinning, Deçan (Woman's Society, BESA)
Montenegro – Roman Mosaics, Risinium (Ministry of Culture and Media of Montenegro)
Romania – The Latin School (Council of Europe)
Serbia – Vernacular architecture of the old shephard's village Pticje Polje (The Bird Field), Western Serbia (Mr B Šurdić, photographer)
"The former Yugoslav Republic of Macedonia" – The decorated mosque in Tetovo, erected in 1833/34 (National Conservation Center)

Layout: Desktop Publishing Unit, Council of Europe

Council of Europe Publishing
F-67075 Strasbourg Cedex
http://book.coe.int

ISBN 978-92-871-6265-6
© Council of Europe, January 2008
Printed at the Council of Europe

Dedication

This publication is dedicated to the memory of our dear colleague, Pierre-Laurent Frier, who, between 1996 and 2005, provided an important contribution to many countries seeking assistance from the Council of Europe in reforming legal and policy issues concerning their cultural heritage and its integration with other disciplines.

Colophon

Director of the publication: Robert Palmer (Director of Culture and Cultural and Natural Heritage, DGIV)

Co-ordination: Mikhaël de Thyse (Regional Co-operation Division, DGIV)

Editor: Robert Pickard (Expert consultant, Co-ordinator of the Legislative Support Task Force)

Texts:

The National Reports identified in Part 1 of this publication were prepared by the Programme Co-ordinators for the Regional Programme for Cultural and Natural Heritage in South-East Europe or other representatives of the countries: Florent Çeliku (Albania), Amra Hadžimuhamedović (Bosnia and Herzegovina), Peter Miladinov (Bulgaria), Nada Duic-Kowalsky and Tamara Ganoci Frisch (Croatia), Gjejlane Hohxa (Kosovo/UNMIK), Milorad Ivovic (Montenegro), Ioan Opris (Romania), Borislav Šurdić (Serbia), Biljana Prentoska ("the former Yugoslav Republic of Macedonia"). The comparative summary of issues arising from the National Reports was written by Myriam Goblet.

The eight themes in Part 2 were written by individual members of the Legislative Support Task Force, an ad hoc group of experts within the Technical Co-operation and Consultancy Programme: Pierre-Laurent Frier, France (themes 6 and 7), Myriam Goblet, Belgium (themes 2 and 5), Carsten Lund, Denmark (theme 8) and Robert Pickard, United Kingdom (themes 1, 3 and 4), with case studies by country representatives and the presentation of issues and responses raised by the participants in this study.

Conclusions in Parts 3 and 4 were prepared by Robert Pickard.

Contents

Foreward 7
Introduction 9

Part 1 – State of cultural heritage policies in South-East Europe

1. Albania 15
2. Bosnia and Herzegovina 25
3. Bulgaria 39
4. Croatia 53
5. Kosovo (UNMIK) 61
6. Montenegro 71
7. Romania 81
8. Serbia 91
9. "The former Yugoslav Republic of Macedonia" 99
10. Comparative summary 111

Part 2 – Eight themes and corresponding debates

Theme 1: Purpose of law, harmonisation of terms, categorisation
of protected items and the link to inventories/registers 121

Theme 2: Integrated conservation systems 141

Theme 3: Institutional reform – a new role for private owners and enterprises
and their professional advisers 159

Theme 4: Financial and other incentives, sanctions and coercive measures 177

Theme 5: The living heritage: a sustainable approach 201

Theme 6: Classification of museums and the status of collections 213

Theme 7: The circulation and restitution of cultural goods 227

Theme 8: Archaeological sites and research 239

Part 3 – Operational conclusions and key issues

1. Coherence and clarity in legal language, guidance and advice 257
2. Methodologies for selection, categorisation, identification and valorisation 259
3. Linking the cultural and natural heritage 263
4. Cultural impact assessment 264
5. Integrated conservation and sustainable development 265
6. Funding mechanisms 267
7. Institutional reform and partnership with the private sector 268
8. Sanctions and enforcement measures 269
9. Museums and the movable heritage 270

Part 4 – The next stage

1. The use of digital information systems 275
2. Cultural landscapes 276
3. Integrated conservation systems 278
4. Financial policy and funding measures 279
5. Sustainable development 280
6. Human resources and institutional reform 281

Foreword

As part of its contribution to ensuring democratic stability in South-East Europe, the Council of Europe proposed the Regional Programme for Cultural and Natural Heritage in South-East Europe to Albania, Bosnia and Herzegovina, Bulgaria, Croatia, Kosovo/UNMIK, Montenegro, Romania, Serbia and "the former Yugoslav Republic of Macedonia". The programme is conceived as a specific contribution to the development of democratic, peaceful and open societies in South-East Europe, in which the active participation of all citizens is promoted irrespective of religion, language, gender or ethnicity.

The regional programme includes three main complementary components: an Institutional Capacity Building Plan, an Integrated Rehabilitation Project Plan/Survey on the Architectural and Archaeological Heritage and the proposed development of Local Development Pilot Projects.

The Institutional Capacity Building Plan concentrates on the provision of policy and legal advice with the aim of establishing appropriate legislative frameworks, administrative reforms and national and local cultural heritage policies. It also considers the development of management tools and human resource development in relation to the provision and use of inventories and documentation, institutional co-ordination, integrated heritage conservation, enhancement of urban and land use planning decisions and provision of realistic strategies for development.

Within the context of this plan a series of international debates has been organised by the Council of Europe in association with different host countries. This book is the first to be published as a result of these multilateral activities and addresses issues concerning the reform of cultural heritage policies through the presentation of national reports, expert presentations and debates.

Introduction

Part 1 of this publication provides a number of national reports which summarise the state of the cultural heritage policies pursued by the nine countries participating in the Regional Programme for Cultural and Natural Heritage of South-East Europe. These include Albania, Bosnia and Herzegovina, Bulgaria, Croatia, Kosovo/UNMIK, Montenegro, Romania, Serbia and "the former Yugoslav Republic of Macedonia".

The national reports are based on three types of document:

– *Survey of the Architectural and Archaeological Heritage* (December 2003), prepared for each partner country by the Council of Europe and the European Union (EU), in connection with the launching of the Integrated Rehabilitation Project Plan (IRPP) (component B of the Regional Programme for Cultural and Natural Heritage of South-East Europe);

– *Interim Report on Legislative Reform in the field of Cultural Heritage,* detailing progress made with legislative reform in each partner country in connection with the Institutional Capacity-Building Plan (component A of the regional programme);

– various *reports on legislative assistance missions* to these countries, prepared by the Legislative Support Task Force (LSTF) of the Council of Europe's Technical Co-operation and Field Action Unit, particularly in connection with the Institutional Capacity Building Plan.

The information provided is limited, in that it has been provided by the national partners only since the regional programme was launched in 2003, and so makes no claim to be exhaustive. Some issues are thus covered in greater detail by certain countries than by others depending on their current concerns and problems.

Each country is dealt with by reference to eight subject areas: the historical context, heritage, political strategy, legislation, institutions, funding, documentation and ethnicity and community. Finally, a comparative summary of the national reports analyses these countries in terms of the five types of action which the Council of Europe sees as holding the key to improving their cultural heritage policies: reforming laws, strengthening institutions, encouraging civil society participation, increasing financial resources and devising and implementing sustainable political strategies.

Part 2 of this publication introduces eight themes identified by members of the LSTF as key issues for the reform of heritage legislation after consideration of various draft laws. This ad hoc group of experts was set up in 1997 to respond to formal requests made to the Secretariat of the Council of Europe (Cultural Heritage Department – Technical

Co-operation and Consultancy Programme) for expert opinions or advice on legislation and administration of cultural heritage protection.

Theme 1 covers the purpose of law, the harmonisation of terms to be used in legal texts in the context of Council of Europe conventions, interest factors and criteria for the selection of items of the immovable heritage to be protected, categories and levels of protection and the use of inventory standards.

Theme 2 explains the principle of integrated conservation and the practical implications for implementing this principle within heritage policies. It further considers the problems of transposing integrated mechanisms at legislative, institutional and political levels and provides examples of good practice.

Theme 3 considers the need for the reform of the roles of institutions dealing with heritage protection and management including the involvement of private owners, enterprises and their professional advisers in the heritage management process.

Theme 4 covers problems faced by countries within the regional programme in providing financial incentives and other forms of assistance and deals with issues relating to sanctions and coercive measures. It identifies a number of different measures which may be utilised to raise finance in support of the heritage and identifies a number of actions and procedures that may be considered in order to provide necessary statutory protection measures.

Theme 5 considers the introduction of the concept of sustainable development within heritage policies and addresses issues concerning economic development, social cohesion and the protection and enhancement of the environment, as well as good practice examples concerning the drafting of development plans, urban rehabilitation and rural development programmes, technical support and co-ordination measures.

Theme 6 examines the classification, rights and obligations of museums, the status of collections and the protection of items of the movable heritage.

Theme 7 scrutinises issues concerning the circulation and restitution of cultural goods including regulations to be adopted for professional dealers and methods of combating illicit trade in cultural objects.

Theme 8 investigates issues concerning the archaeological heritage including the use of inventories, ownership issues, the identification of monuments, sites, protective zones and archaeological reserves, integrated protection mechanisms, the underwater heritage, maintenance and restoration principles, public access, the archaeological profession and enforcement measures.

Following each theme there is a corresponding presentation relating to the specific issues raised and concerning the situation in one of the countries included within the regional programme. This is subsequently followed by issues which arose in the debate that followed each of the theme presentations.

Part 3 of this publication presents the operational conclusions and key issues that arose from this study. These cover the need for coherence and clarity in legal language, guidance and advice; methodologies for selecting heritage assets to be protected and their categorisation, identification and valorisation; links between the cultural and natural heritage; cultural impact assessments; integrated conservation and sustainable development; funding mechanisms; institutional reform and partnership with the private sector; sanctions and enforcement measures; and museums and the movable heritage.

Finally Part 4 of this publication identifies further subject areas that the participants in the debate identified for subsequent international activities which the Council of Europe, with different host countries, has undertaken to organise. The subject areas proposed are: the use of digital information systems; cultural landscapes; integrated conservation systems; cultural heritage and sustainable development; financial policy and funding mechanisms; and human resources for the management of the cultural heritage.

PART 1

STATE OF CULTURAL HERITAGE POLICIES IN SOUTH-EAST EUROPE

1. Albania

Historical context

Albania is a mountainous country of natural beauty, lying on the west (Adriatic) coast of the Balkan peninsula, bounded by Greece, "the former Yugoslav Republic of Macedonia", Kosovo/UNMIK and the Republic of Montenegro.

From Palaeolithic times onwards there has been human settlement in Albania as well as Neolithic (around 6000-2600 BC), Bronze Age (2600-1000 BC) and, from 1000 BC, early Iron Age settlements. It was the Illyrians, autochthonous tribes, who developed a common language and culture and were the ancestors of the modern Albanians: the name "Albania" derives from the Illyrian "Albani" tribe.

The Albanian language belongs to the family of Indo-European languages but it constitutes a separate branch in this family of languages. It is one of the ancient languages of the Balkans, but its written records, just like the Romanian language, date back only to the 15th century. The first written records were the formula of baptism in AD 1462.

Albanians are descendants of ancient Illyrians, who have appeared as inhabitants of eastern regions of the Balkan Peninsula since the dawn of European history. About the middle of the first millennium BC, the Illyrians followed the path of urban civilisation and established their separate states. This interpretation of sources is backed up by archaeological, linguistic and anthropological data. Sources mentioning Illyrian tribes may be found in the earliest works of Hellenic literature, in Homer and Hesiod's poems and Polybius and Strabon also give some precise data about them. In contrast, historical records appear to be limited during the first centuries AD, but some early recorded data in the Middle Ages (such as archaeological and linguistic evidence) provide a basis for reconstructing the history of Arbërs as descendants of Illyrians.

The Greek influence (4th century BC) is present in architectural style and city planning, evidence of a Greco-Illyrian culture in trade, social intercourse and religion. Greek colonisation was followed by the arrival of the Romans in the 3rd century BC, when the Albanian coast became an important bridgehead for Roman armies operating in the Balkan Peninsula. The arrival of Rome put an end to the independence of the country and brought the Pax Romana, which produced a flourishing urban life. The Romans built the Via Egnatia with its two branches, from Apollonia and Dyrrachium to Thessaloníki and Byzantium (Epidamnus). During this period the cities were increasingly exposed to Roman influence.

Towards the end of the 3rd century AD, with the division of the Roman Empire, Albania became part of the Byzantine Empire. The long Byzantine rule was punctuated by invasions of barbarians, Slavs, Bulgarians, Normans, Angevins and Serbs. During these centuries, only once did the Albanians have the opportunity to emancipate themselves politically and this occurred in the late 12th century with the formation of the Principality of Arbër that was also short-lived. The influence of Christianity had a powerful impact on art and architecture: monasteries, churches, frescoes and icons show a predominantly Byzantine style.

After the fall of Constantinople (1453), Albanian lands came under Ottoman rule. Albanian resistance culminated in 25 years under the leadership of Skanderbeg, who, in Lezhe on 2 March 1444, ensured the creation of an Albanian independent state which extended from the Devoll and Seman rivers in the south to Dukagjini highlands in the north, from the Adriatic in the west to the Drini i Zi valley in the east. This state had all the characteristics found in any state at that time and, along with secular law, both religious and customary laws also existed. After the fall of Albania to the Ottomans, a feudal military regime was established in the country. The majority of Albanians converted to Islam and a new artistic influence began with monumental mosques, palaces, bazaars *(besestenies)*, private houses, hammams and an excellent traditional architecture in the cities and in rural settlements.

From the 18th century onwards, the steady weakening of Ottoman authority allowed the Albanian feudal lords *(beys)*, to rely more on their own personal power. Part of the Albanian feudal class broke away from the Ottoman class and established separate political districts known as *pashaliks* (military districts) within the Ottoman state, thus embarking on the road to autonomy. The largest were those of Shkodwr, Kosovo, Berat and Ali Pashë Tepelena. The collapse of Albanian *pashaliks* (1831) marked the beginning of a new period in the history of Albanian people called the Albanian National Resistance, a movement aiming to liberate the country from the Ottoman invaders, uniting all Albanian territories in a single independent state and advancing Albanian language and culture.

In 1908, a congress of Albanian distinguished patriots adopted the Latin alphabet. In 1912, Albania was declared an independent sovereign state. The successful democratic movement of the 1921 to 1924 period was crowned with the arrival of the democratic government headed by Noli. In 1925 Albania was declared a republic with Ahmet Zogu as President for a seven-year term. In September 1928, Albania was declared a monarchy with Zogu as the King of Albania. During these years he introduced the Penal Code, the Civil Code and the Trade Code.

In 1939, Mussolini's ultimatum demanding Italian protectorate status meant the virtual end of Albanian sovereignty. The antifascist war was a liberating war and Albania aligned itself with the Allies. Afterwards, the country passed into communist rule in 1944, under the direction of Enver Hoxha. The first multiparty elections were held in 1991 and a new democratic regime was established in Albania in 1992. Despite the enormous difficulties, Albania has managed to progress towards further democratic standards, aiming to join the EU and the North Atlantic Treaty Organisation (NATO).

The house of Iljaz Babameto (Council of Europe)

Heritage

The Albanian heritage reflects the thousands of years of Albanian history. It consists of archaeological ruins or inhabited built constructions. They date back from the prehistoric period up to the last century. It includes a wide range of constructions which for the purpose of this study are divided as follows:

- antique and mediaeval monuments including protective constructions such as castles, archaeological sites, social, engineering and religious structures;

- popular constructions such as bazaars or ensembles;

- historical monuments concerning specific historical events or characters.

The construction of a place of worship for the orthodox religion (churches and basilicas) is characterised by decorations and wood carvings. Mosaics in monochrome or polychrome are typical in Palaeo-Christian churches and basilicas. In the Byzantine period we can observe the use of ceramics in vaults, frames, arches and walls, as well as different symbols in facades, unlike the post-Byzantine period. The churches and basilicas are decorated, for example, with carved wooden iconostases, frescoes, wooden decorated ceilings, use of *tchatma* in the guest rooms of monasteries and roofs covered in stone slabs.

The most important types of building are protective constructions and those for worship and habitation. The most significant types of ensembles are archaeological sites, historical centres and museum cities. The most threatened heritages are inhabited buildings due to urban development and new modern constructions such as in Gjirokastra or Berat city.

Tirana is a typical example of a post-communist Balkan city which is coming to terms with the market economy. Modern skyscrapers in metal and glass are antagonistically juxtaposed with older structures of wood and stone, but some islands of traditional ensembles remain intact.

Elsewhere, for example Berat, a well-preserved Ottoman city, and Gjirokastra, a city which is a candidate for World Heritage Site status, the original function of the buildings has been remarkably well maintained.

Political strategy

During the communist regime, Albanian cultural life was centralised by the state. Cultural events were mostly organised in the capital, Tirana, which was also home of the opera and ballet theatre, popular theatre, the state variety show hall, the Palace of Culture concert hall and the High Institute of Arts hall. There was considerable artistic and social progress and a cultural infrastructure was built up. For example, in 1964 the first Albanian art school was founded and artists created their first professional organisation – the Albanian Writers and Artists League – in 1952. A few years later, in 1954, the first national art gallery was opened which was an important institution to promote and protect the artistic heritage of both native and foreign artists. Despite limits placed on artistic freedom and freedom of movement, many young artists completed their studies and produced a variety of monuments and other monumental works in painting, sculpture, design, photography or the applied arts.

The collapse of communism in eastern European countries during the early 1990s led to the free movement of citizens and thus enabled Albanian artists to have direct contact with the art world outside Albania. In 1991 the Ministry of Culture, Youth and Sport was created by the President of the Republic, aiming to bring the Albanian cultural and sporting institutions into line with European standards. A new cultural policy was created to help recover and develop Albanian culture based on the right of citizens to participate in cultural life. The most important reforms in the field of culture took place after 1997.

Decentralisation is regarded as one of the priorities of Albania's transition towards a market economy. Local cultural commissions have been set up and are attached to local assemblies. Efforts for decentralisation in the cultural field are being concentrated in the field of cinema, theatre and literature. In 1998, the Council of Ministers approved a list of institutions which fall under the responsibility of the municipalities. These include, for example, cultural centres, cultural houses, local libraries, local art galleries, museums and cinemas.

In July 2000, a guide to the cultural policy of the Albanian state was produced by the Ministry of Culture, Youth and Sport to establish new goals for the country. Emphasis was placed on national heritage as well as on the wider goal of modernising Albanian society.

The Department of Cultural Heritage within the Ministry of Culture, Youth and Sport reflects the increasing importance of this sector in terms of policy making and programme development. Its main objectives are:

- to protect and conserve the cultural heritage, bearing in mind the modernisation and economic developments of the country, as well as the tourism industry;
- to involve outside specialists who are distinguished for their work in the field;
- to raise awareness and inform citizens about legislation and policy developments in the field;
- to establish and strengthen international co-operation;
- to find financing solutions.

Efforts have intensified in recent years to collect information about the state of protected buildings. Some of the major projects include the reconstruction of the administrative district in the centre of Tirana, restoration of the independent monuments in Vlora, urban restoration in Gjirokastra and the Butrint ecological project in the middle of a natural park, an Albanian site on the UNESCO World Heritage List.

The institutions responsible for conservation and excavation promote their work through publications, media and exhibitions. There does, however, need to be closer co-operation with institutions in charge of education, to organise awareness-raising programmes in schools on the heritage and to arrange visits to sites. The task of selling the heritage to the public is a difficult one, given other pressing concerns. In the future, it will be necessary to explain the positive impact of the restoration of monuments, transmitting evidence to forthcoming generations, strengthening areas economically and affirming Albanian identity as part of the pan-European identity.

Legislation

Historical overview

The very first legislative act relating to the cultural heritage of Albania was passed in 1889, namely the "Inner Rules of the Royal Museum". Another law for the protection of monuments dates back to 1912.

In 1922, the first Circulatory Act of the Ministry of Education in Albania, concerning the protection and enrichment of properties, was completed by the law on protection of national monuments.

In 1974 the Council of Ministers of Albania approved the decision for the discovery and protection of popular buildings, followed by many orders for the protection of a national list of monuments of culture.

The Law on the Protection of Movable and Immovable Cultural Properties, approved by the Albanian Parliament on 10 December 1994, has for a decade been the corner stone in the field of national heritage, but limiting itself only to material property and not including spiritual heritage.

For the past five years, the main focus of reform has been on developing legislation. The Albanian Parliament has approved some important laws on cinema, theatres, libraries and heritage.

Other laws and decisions which brought about innovative and revolutionary change in the field of national heritage in Albania were as follows:

- the Law on the Protection of National Symbols;
- decisions of the Council of Ministers regarding different subjects under protection (10 decisions);
- five orders of the Minister of Culture for the establishment of necessary mechanisms to implement the national policy for the protection of cultural heritage;
- two international conventions ratified by the Republic of Albania, specifically covering cultural heritage.

The Government of Albania has embarked on a proposal to develop new laws to bring procedures into line with European standards.

New law

As of April 2003, the new Law on Cultural Heritage (Law No. 9048) has been in force, although some acts remain to be passed. The intention of this law, which takes Council of Europe guidelines into account, is to legalise the preservation and conservation of the heritage and also to regulate the relationship between individuals, organisations, and central and local government. Prepared by the Ministry of Culture, Youth and Sport, it has taken into account the views of other ministries where interests overlap. The new law, which is available in both Albanian and English, includes five chapters:

1. General provisions classifying objects of cultural heritage into material and non-material, as well as criteria for their evaluation.
2. Movable property and problems of legal relations between owners and the state.
3. The various categories of cultural heritage: special attention is given to monuments discovered in archaeological excavations, including their protection.
4. Offences with regard to cultural heritage values.
5. Temporary and final provisions regarding law enforcement and the issuing of other legal acts for this purpose.

Heritage management is in a transitory phase, due mainly to the implementation of the new law on heritage, which was approved by the Albanian Parliament in April 2003 but is not yet fully effective. The present law on movable and immovable heritage dates from 1994.

Link with spatial and urban planning

There is also legal protection of cultural heritage against new construction in the Law on City Planning (No. 8405), but this has not always been effective since there have been problems with illegal construction in historical centres. According to the new law (Article 14), there will be protection against this: in cases where historical buildings are demolished or destroyed by fire, reconstruction will be allowed only over the previous land surface and volume, and strictly in accordance with the category and type of the damaged monument. Should an inhabited monument be demolished, the owner will be required to pay 50% of the restoration costs, the other 50% being met by the state.

In order to ensure appropriate links between planning and heritage, the Minister of Culture is also a member of the Council of Territorial Planning while the Director of the Institute of Monuments of Culture is a member of the technical secretariat of the Council. Proposals are studied by specialists who give opinions, and the local directorates of the Institute of Monuments oversee intervention. Restoration projects proposed by third parties (companies, associations, NGOs, etc.) are studied by the National Council of Restoration which is responsible for deciding whether to approve them.

Institutions

There are two institutions responsible for the built heritage: the Ministry of Culture, Youth and Sport and the Academy of Sciences.

– within the Ministry of Culture, Youth and Sport, the Department of Cultural Heritage oversees the Institute of Monuments, the nine national museums and the Centre of Registration of Cultural Property as well. The Institute of Monuments is responsible for every restoration and has eight regional departments and workshops, and through them surveys every intervention undertaken. Owners are obliged to record cultural heritage items in their possession and receive a certification passport from the Centre of Registration of Cultural Property. Changes of ownership must also be registered.

- the Academy of Sciences has institutes relating to specific scientific fields, including the Institute of Archaeology (responsible for archaeological excavations) and the Institute of Popular Culture (which mainly deals with questions of folklore). The Academy of Sciences is partly responsible for the protection of the national environment.

The institutes co-operate closely concerning all monuments, irrespective of religious or ethnic category.

In accordance with their fields of expertise or areas of interest, the Ministry of Culture, Youth and Sport, the Academy of Sciences, the General Directorate of State Archives, the universities and the local governing bodies research, protect and restore monuments, and also compile inventories.

There are insufficient staff members in restoration, project management and database compilation to cover all the protection needs, although there is a small number of experts and executives in the Institute of Monuments and the Institute of Archaeology with a high level of knowledge and experience in their profession. Professional training is currently inadequate and there is an obvious need for training courses in practical issues. Further specialised training abroad or joint initiatives in restoration work involving local trainees and foreign restorers could both be very helpful. Such specialised training that has been carried out – for example the training of Albanian specialists in the restoration of Byzantine icons in Thessaloníki at the Museum of Byzantine Culture – has been very successful and mutually beneficial.

Financing

The funding for intervention is made solely through the state budget, irrespective of the original source of the money. According to the law, the cultural heritage funds are allocated, on an annual basis, from the state to the Ministry of Culture, Youth and Sport, from revenues accrued from any legal source, including domestic or foreign, governmental or private foundations.

Even donations by individuals are directed along this same route. The institutes are then responsible for the implementation of projects, supervising restoration works and monitoring the allocation of the funds which must be used entirely for the restoration and maintenance of the monuments.

The National Council of Restoration and the Scientific Council, with the Institute of Monuments of Culture, discuss and approve all proposed restoration projects, deciding the terms of contracts.

A further positive contribution is made by the Albanian Orthodox Church, which has a large number of monuments in its care, as well as a professional restoration nucleus which can be called upon for expert advice. As a non-profit organisation, the Albanian Orthodox Church has funded several restoration projects in Orthodox churches. There is a very good relationship with the representatives of the Institute of Monuments of Culture in designing restoration projects, and furthermore a member of the Albanian Orthodox Church participates in the National Council of Restoration, within the Institute of Monuments of Culture.

Currently, there are a number of international funding bodies working in Albania: the German Embassy is funding the restoration of the basilica in Lin; Patrimoine sans frontières is working on the restoration of churches in Voskopoja; the American Embassy has funded restoration work in the castle of Lezha; the EU (through the INTERREG initiative) is funding restoration of the churches in Gjirokastra.

The Institute of Archaeology is also collaborating with several international universities, with the Israeli Government and with the Packard Foundation on numerous survey and excavation projects.

The Butrint archaeological and restoration project, in the middle of a natural park, is receiving support from a host of partners including UNESCO, the EU, the World Bank and the English Butrint Foundation. This is an interesting example of national governmental and non-governmental co-operation in this field.

Documentation

There is a general Directorate of Archives and a Centre for the Inventory of Cultural Properties within the Institute of Monuments of Culture and the Institute of Archaeology. These maintain the documentation and the whole activity is ongoing. The Centre for the Inventory of Cultural Properties is responsible for the computerised cataloguing of cultural properties and the national inventory for buildings and sites. The main criteria for inclusion are date and historical significance. The purpose is preservation, restoration and management. The index partly follows the Council of Europe's Core Data Index to Historic Buildings and Monuments of the Architectural Heritage; it includes ensembles and also lists them as individual monuments. It is indexed but not yet electronically retrievable. The documentation is not yet available to the public.

There is full professional access to documentation, but there is a need for staff training and also for an increase in expertise, particularly at a local level.

The Directorate of Archives possesses documents related to history of ownership. Local cadastres maintain maps which show ownership up to 1946 and some have been updated to reflect changes in ownership. The cartographic documents are kept in the Central Technical Archive.

Ethnicity and community

In Albania the main minorities – Greeks, Macedonians and Montenegrins – are considered as national minorities and the Roma and the Armenians (Vlachs) as linguistic minorities. All minorities are respected according to their common characteristics, language, religion and culture, and in the preservation of their heritage. The Office for Minorities was established in the Ministry of Foreign Affairs in 2000 in order to ensure the fulfilment of international obligations and commitments on the rights of minorities, supporting and promoting lawful activities and bringing problems or complaints to the attention of the government.

The Constitution of the Republic considers the national minorities to be an indivisible part of Albanian society, with full equality before the law and other fundamental rights which include the right to the preservation of their heritage and the exercise of their religion. The three official religions in Albania are Islam, Orthodox Christianity and Catholicism. Albania has generally been known historically for its religious tolerance.

2. Bosnia and Herzegovina

Historical context

The name Bosnia and Herzegovina is relatively new, coming into official use after the 1878 Congress of Berlin conferred on Austria-Hungary the mandate to occupy this former province of the Ottoman Empire.

Bosnia and Herzegovina has a rich architectural and archaeological heritage, inherited from various human occupations since the Palaeolithic period. All the prehistoric periods are represented there: Palaeolithic, Mesolithic, Neolithic and Eneolithic – the Copper, Iron and Bronze Ages.

In the second half of the 5th century the region was ruled for 40 years by the Ostrogoths, who left extensive evidence of their culture, recognisable in archaeological finds. This was followed by the period of Slav immigration and permanent settlement in the region in the second half of the 6th and the 7th centuries. At least a century before the earliest reference to the famous Bosnian – Ban Borić (1154-1163), Bosnia had already become a distinct early feudal state, extending from the source of the River Bosnia to the Vranduk pass in the north, and from the upper Drina to Borova Glava running east-west. At this time, Bosnia and Hum (later Herzegovina) were each evolving politically along their own lines, but by the early decades of the 14th century they had become part of a single polity. Mediaeval Bosnia reached its peak of political development in 1377 when Tvrtko I. Kotromanić was proclaimed king. As an independent political entity, maintaining contacts with many of the states of Europe of the day, and with its own schismatic Bosnian Church independent in jurisdiction from both the Catholic and Orthodox Churches, the Bosnian Kingdom lasted until 1463, when most of the country was conquered by the Ottoman Empire. The most striking economic and cultural feature of this period is the emergence of towns and cities and of links between them. Almost every town and city in Bosnia and Herzegovina dates back to this period, either based on a village, a crossroads, or built on an entirely new site. Widespread urbanisation was made possible thanks to the establishment of the institutions of the *vakuf* or perpetual endowment, which determined how towns would evolve and funded their development. The basic layout was that of the oriental town, with its division into a business quarter known as the *čaršija* and residential quarters called *mahalas,* but always based on previous Bosnian characteristics. Numerous religious and public edifices were built, as well as residential buildings.

Ottoman rule was replaced by the Austro-Hungarian administration in 1878, lasting until 1918 when Bosnia and Herzegovina became part of the state of Serbs, Croats and Slovenes (later to become the Kingdom of Yugoslavia). In 1945, Bosnia and Herzegovina became one of the republics of the newly formed socialist Yugoslavia, and in 1992 it gained international recognition.

Heritage

Dating from prehistoric times to the modern day, Bosnia and Herzegovina has a plethora of cultural riches of various provenances: prehistoric, Greek, Illyrio-Roman, Gothic, early Slav, mediaeval, Ottoman, Austro-Hungarian and Yugoslav.

Heritage inventory and protection

The inventory of the architectural heritage drawn up by the Statistics Institute of the Republic of Bosnia and Herzegovina provides details of the situation as of 31 December 1986. The 1986 inventory included 727 registered properties, of which 507 are individual monuments and 220 are complexes or ensembles. Forty-six of the registered monuments are part of registered ensembles. On the basis of the inventory data, the area under protection was 272 hectares or 0.31% of the total inhabited area of Bosnia and Herzegovina. The inventory included 162 religious buildings, 52 residential buildings and ensembles, and 36 commercial and civil engineering properties, most of which were military buildings and ensembles.

The 2002 Spatial Plan for Bosnia and Herzegovina refers to the fact that the country has 8 800 immovable properties of cultural interest, of which 2 267 have been listed as national monuments.

In accordance with its authority regulated by Annex 8 of the General Framework Agreement for Peace in Bosnia and Herzegovina (Dayton Peace Agreement), the Commission to Preserve National Monuments issues decisions designating property as a national monument. Up until March 2004, the commission had designated 157 properties as national monuments. The Provisional List of National Monuments of Bosnia and Herzegovina, which was adopted in 2000 (*Bosnia and Herzegovina Official Gazette*, No. 33/02), listed 777 individual properties. The commission issues decisions on designation as a national monument for each of the individual properties on the provisional list. The procedure for this is initiated by a petition or motion, which may be filed by any person or legal entity. In the period July 2002 to October 2003, 858 petitions were submitted.

The classification criteria used by the commission for designation of properties as national monuments varies according to the object as it may belong to different categories. Among the properties of cultural interest, there is movable cultural property (individual items or collections), immovable cultural property (monuments or ensembles) and sites. Immovable property can be residential (urban, rural, castles, etc.), religious (churches, mosques, monasteries, etc.), educational (*medresas, mektebs*, schools, etc.), administrative, public (inns and caravanserais, hospitals, hammams – public baths, etc.), commercial, infrastructural (water supplies, bridges, etc.), military (fortresses, towers, etc.), funerary (necropolises) agricultural, industrial and so on. The sites are urban, rural, archaeological, historic, industrial, cultural and natural sites related to certain rituals or traditions, natural, scientific or mixed.

Destruction during the 1992-95 war

Bosnia and Herzegovina's architectural heritage was systematically destroyed during the 1992-95 war. According to the data, which is as yet incomplete, gathered by the Institute for the Protection of the Cultural, Historical and Natural Heritage of Bosnia and Herzegovina, by November 1995, 2 771 architectural heritage properties had been demolished or damaged, 713 of them were totally destroyed and 554 were burned down and are unusable. These data are based partly on on-site inspections, partly on reports from individual organisations, religious communities and suchlike. The numbers in the reports, although incomplete, indicate the extensive state of devastation of the heritage of Bosnia and Herzegovina. Monuments from the 15th to the 19th century, followed by those of the Austro-Hungarian period, suffered the worst destruction.

The urban nuclei of Sarajevo, Mostar and Jajce were devastated, along with many individual buildings that the Spatial Plan for Bosnia and Herzegovina had assessed as heritage of international significance. The centres of Stolac, Banja Luka and Foca were also destroyed. The centres of Trebinje, Tesanj, Maglaj, Bihac, Travnik, Derventa and Livno were very badly damaged. Thus, out of a total of 60 valuable urban nuclei, 49 were destroyed or very badly damaged. All 9 valuable urban-rural ensembles were seriously damaged, with Pocitelj, Blagaj, Prusac, Jelec, Jezero and Kraljeva Sutjeska suffering the worst damage.

Out of the 58 most valuable mosques and *tekkes*, 22 were totally demolished, including 13 listed as Category One buildings. All the other *tekkes* and mosques were damaged. Out of the 40 most valuable churches and Orthodox and Catholic monasteries dating from the 15th to the 19th century, 5 were destroyed and 4 damaged (destroyed: the Orthodox monastery of Zitomislici, the Church of the Nativity of the Blessed Mother of God in the Bjelusine district of Mostar, the Orthodox Church of the Transfiguration of Christ in the village of Klepci near Capljina, the Orthodox Church of St Nicholas in the village of Trijebanj, and the Catholic monastery in Plehan near Derventa). The Catholic Church of St John in Podmilacje, an important pilgrimage site from the 15th century whose main church building dated from 1910, was also completely destroyed. The two synagogues in Sarajevo dating from the Ottoman period (the Old Sephardi Synagogue and the New Ashkenazi Synagogue) were partly damaged.

Many cemeteries and funeral monuments also suffered major damage, and some of those listed as Category One were totally destroyed. The cemetery of the Sinan-beg mosque in Cajnice, the Sinan-beg *turbe* (mausoleum) in Cajnice, the *turbe* of members of the Sinan-beg family in Cajnice, the *turbe* of Ibrahim in Foca, the *turbe* of Hasan Sheikh Kaimi-baba in Zvornik, three *turbes* alongside the Ferhad-pasa mosque in Banja Luka, the Halil-pasa *turbe* in Banja Luka, the Sephardi graveyard in Sarajevo, the old

Orthodox graveyard in Bjelusine (Mostar), and the chapel of the Orthodox graveyard in Kosevo (Sarajevo) were damaged.

The Old Bridge in Mostar, a monument of international importance, was destroyed. The Mehmed-pasa Sokolovic Bridge in Višegrad was damaged and its pillars are in danger as no steps have been taken to protect it following the construction of a hydroelectric power station and dam on the river Drina upstream from the bridge.

Sixteen Category One buildings dating from the Austro-Hungarian period were damaged and four destroyed (the *Vijecnica*, or town hall, housing the National and University Library, the Post Office in Sarajevo and the Baths and the Neretva Hotel in Mostar).

The heritage that was either damaged or destroyed during the war and faces further damage due to lack of maintenance, illegal reconstruction and the inability to carry out repairs is under the greatest threat.

Political strategy

A new vision of heritage after the war

The destruction of the heritage that took place side by side with the forced expulsions and killing demonstrated the importance of the heritage as the focus of cultural memory in the processes of both the destruction and the maintenance of community.

- Heritage evaluation became a more complex process, in which the non-material – the symbolic and ontological – value of the heritage carried more weight than the material. The very definition of heritage, as well as its significance, changed – its function in maintaining social patterns and the distinctive features of society became as important as its cultural and economic value.

- Wherever crimes against humanity were perpetrated in Bosnia and Herzegovina, so too was the heritage destroyed. Wherever those who were forced to leave their homes have been welcomed back, the first sign of their being able once again to enjoy their fundamental human rights has been the opportunity to renovate the buildings or groups of buildings of moderate or great significance in the town or village in question. The connection between the heritage and human rights has become a fact that cannot be ignored even at the global level.

- The heritage has been used both as a means of establishing durable peace and as a way of prolonging conflict. When the aim was to prevent refugees and displaced persons from exercising their right to return home, the heritage was invested with multi-faceted historical meaning that was interpreted as evidence of hostility and the impossibility of reconciliation. A modern law must develop objective mechanisms to prevent the misuse of the heritage and the disregard of, or preference for, any of its strata or expressions.

- When the heritage is ravaged and vandalised, each separate piece of a demolished monument becomes a monument in itself – reconstruction becomes a legitimate and desirable aim, ensuring that the urban landscape is preserved along with material documents and social patterns; it ensures that the birthplace or home of those returning from forced exile is preserved. The approach to heritage protection must be reconsidered at both the scientific and the legislative level.

Weaknesses and challenges

There is no official comprehensive strategy for the future management of monuments at the state level but one should be in place following the adoption of the state-level law on the protection and preservation of cultural monuments in Bosnia and Herzegovina.

The institutions responsible for the protection of the cultural heritage also suffer from insufficient numbers of qualified staff and are poorly equipped. In general, owing to a shortage of funds, it has not been possible to provide the conditions necessary to carry out a survey and evaluation of present heritage at any level.

The absence of a law for the protection of the heritage at the state level contributes to a non-systematic and non-synchronised process of protection. The weakness of post-war legislative arrangements is also a problem when it comes to preventing illegal construction, inexpert reconstruction, lack of maintenance or other forms of destruction. Funds should be made available in the budgets of the administrative authorities at all levels (local and state) for the removal of illegal constructions that endanger the cultural heritage. As part of this priority, it is essential to include certain regulations on the cultural heritage in sectoral laws (housing, urban planning, traffic, education, etc.).

Another weakness in heritage management is the lack of adequate documentation, most of which was destroyed during the war. In addition, the state of the heritage changed during the 1992-95 war.

The main obstacles are, however, the disparity between the very large number of endangered properties and the funds available for the protection and restoration of cultural heritage. Furthermore, the religious communities that own properties are very often reluctant to co-operate with the heritage protection institutions and fail to act in accordance with the professional advice given by the latter.

Bosnia and Herzegovina has come up against a great many unresolved issues from the past (laws on concessions, property restitution, ownership, etc.). It is encumbered both by established practice and inertia standing in the way of change and by the many new challenges to which there is no simple answer.

Legislation

Historical overview

Historically, the first proof of interest in the preservation of the heritage in Bosnia and Herzegovina is portrayed in a letter from the Grand Vizier dated 1874, ordering state officials not to permit the demolition of old buildings. The first heritage protection bill was drawn up just before First World War in 1914.

The law of 1985, which remained in force until the 1992 war (and in some parts of Bosnia and Herzegovina is still being applied), was part of an unbroken tradition in the approach to heritage protection in Bosnia and Herzegovina dating back to 1947. This approach was based on the principle that the heritage is public property. In line with this, a central system of heritage protection was set up, with authorities at professional, administrative and various co-ordinating levels concentrated mainly inside the institutes – one central and four regional. Matters of property ownership (by the federal and republican authorities, private and other persons) were clearly laid down. The law did not govern the generation of revenue for, and operation of the institutes, but in the light of their management and supervisory role, they did not operate on a commercial basis but were treated in the same way as the state's administrative authorities. The law stipulated the requirement to determine the boundaries of each property and those of its grounds or precincts within which particular restrictive measures relating to the protection of the property were to be implemented, as well as the requirement to provide financial assistance to the owner of the property. The law governed both the natural and the cultural heritage, incorporating the approach set forth in the Convention for the Protection of the Architectural Heritage of Europe (ETS No. 121 – Granada Convention) and the heritage categorisation criteria agreed at the third assembly.

During the war, Bosnia and Herzegovina was faced with efforts to dismantle the state system in every domain. After the war, a legal vacuum was created in parts of the country and legal chaos in others.

Current situation

There are currently 10 sets of regulations directly governing heritage issues in force in Bosnia and Herzegovina – 19, if those that imply heritage are counted.

The only one that applies to Bosnia and Herzegovina as a whole is the Dayton Peace Agreement, Annex 8 – Agreement on the Commission to Preserve National Monuments, 1995. This annex established the Commission to Preserve National Monuments – an institution responsible for legal heritage protection with the highest state-level authority.

The Dayton Peace Agreement defines in separate appendices the obligations at the different administrative levels (state level: the Republic of Bosnia and Herzegovina; the entity levels: the Federation of Bosnia and Herzegovina, Republika Srpska; and the District of Brčko).

The main legislation reference texts for the heritage are:

- in the Federation of Bosnia and Herzegovina: the 1985 Law on the Protection and Preservation of the Cultural, Historical and Natural Heritage, as amended in 1987, 1993 and 1994, in force and implemented in the cantons that do not have their own rules (only three cantons have adopted the heritage laws: Sarajevo, Zapadnohercegovački and Zenicko-Dobojski);
- in Republika Srpska: the Law on Cultural Property, 1995 (*Official Gazette of Republika Srpska* No.11/95);
- the Decision of the Presidency of Bosnia and Herzegovina on the Commission to Preserve National Monuments, 2001 (*Bosnia and Herzegovina Official Gazette*, Nos. 1/02 and 10/02);
- the Rules on the Activities of the Commission to Preserve National Monuments with respect to International Co-operation, 2002 (*Bosnia and Herzegovina Official Gazette*, No. 29/02);
- the Criteria for the Designation of Property as National Monuments, 2002/2003 (*Bosnia and Herzegovina Official Gazette*, Nos. 33/02 and 15/03; *Official Gazette of the Federation of Bosnia and Herzegovina*, No. 59/02; *Official Gazette of Republika Srpska*, No. 79/02);
- the Law on the Implementation of Decisions of the Commission to Preserve National Monuments Established Pursuant to Annex 8 of the Dayton Peace Agreement, 2002, adopted by the Federation of Bosnia and Herzegovina (*Official Gazette of the Federation of Bosnia and Herzegovina*, Nos. 2/02 and 27/02). This law defines monuments, the rehabilitation of monuments and co-operation between the bodies responsible;
- the Law on the Implementation of Decisions of the Commission to Preserve National Monuments Established Pursuant to Annex 8 of the Dayton Peace Agreement, 2002, adopted by the Republika Srpska (*Official Gazette of Republika Srpska*, No. 9/02);
- the Law on the Implementation of Decisions of the Commission to Preserve National Monuments Established Pursuant to Annex 8 of the Dayton Peace Agreement, 2002, adopted by the District of Brčko (*Official Gazette of the District of Brčko*, No. 2/02);
- the Federation of Bosnia and Herzegovina Law on Spatial Planning, 2002 (*Official Gazette of the Federation of Bosnia and Herzegovina*, No. 52/02);
- the Republika Srpska Law on Spatial Planning, 2002 (*Official Gazette of Republika Srpska*, No. 79/02).

These laws and regulations are published in the official gazettes in the local language (Bosnian, Serb, Croatian), and are available on the Web page of the commission. The legal framework and regulations are also available on the Web page of the commission in English.

New draft law at the state level

However, the many new questions arising from the post-war reconstruction period, a period of transition and of the adoption of European standards, compelled the Commission to Preserve National Monuments to designate, as its priority, the drafting of a legislative framework to govern heritage management at the state level.

A first draft of proposed new legislation on the protection and preservation of cultural monuments in Bosnia and Herzegovina was formulated in 2004, consisting of:

> Introduction
> Part I – General provisions
> Part II – Types of Bosnia and Herzegovina heritage
> Part III – Heritage protection in Bosnia and Herzegovina
> Part IV – Use of the Bosnia and Herzegovina heritage
> Part V – Financing heritage protection in Bosnia and Herzegovina
> Part VI – Supervision
> Part VII – Penal provisions
> Part VIII – Transitional arrangements.

Link with spatial and urban planning

With a view to improving relations between the heritage protection and town planning organisations, the proposal of the Federal Ministry for Spatial Planning should ensure a unified methodology, as specified in the Federation of Bosnia and Herzegovina Law on Spatial Planning, 2002. According to this law, spatial planning must be co-ordinated by means of special regulations on the protection of the cultural, historical and natural heritage. It also requires a list of the buildings and areas of architectural and natural heritage designated as national monuments by the Commission to Preserve National Monuments. Similar decisions are applied in Republika Srpska.

The Law on Spatial Planning also regulates that the cultural and historical heritage must come under special protection. The protected sites are determined by the commission in its decisions and by regional and town plans and they are governed by regulatory plans. In response to the Council of Europe's recommendations on measures to assess and protect the cultural heritage, the Bosnia and Herzegovina spatial plan includes a list of the most valuable archaeological and architectural heritage assets and classifies them into four categories.

Under the Law on the Implementation of the Decisions of the Commission to Preserve National Monuments and Annex 8 of the Dayton Peace Agreement, responsibility for enforcing the commission's decisions lies with the entity governments and the ministries responsible for regional planning. All executive and planning acts which are not in accordance with the provisions of the decisions should be revoked. The authorities in charge of urban planning and land registry matters are notified of the decisions in order to carry out the measures stipulated, and the competent municipal courts are informed for the purposes of registration in the Land Register.

Institutions

The Commission to Preserve National Monuments is an institution of the state of Bosnia and Herzegovina set up in accordance with Annex 8 of the Dayton Peace Agreement. The 2001 Decision of the Presidency of Bosnia and Herzegovina on the Commission to Preserve National Monuments resulted in the appointment of five members of the commission, three national and two foreign experts (Sweden and Turkey) to serve a five-year term. One of the local experts works in a full-time capacity in the commission. The three national members of the commission rotate in the post of chairperson every six months.

The commission's decisions are final and are enforced in accordance with the Laws on the Implementation of Decisions of the Commission to Preserve National Monuments Established Pursuant to Annex 8 of the Dayton Agreement, which provide national monuments with the highest degree of protection.

The commission has drawn up standard forms of petition by type of property and has lodged them with all the municipalities of Bosnia and Herzegovina, the institutions dealing with the protection of the cultural and historical heritage, religious communities and other institutions. The petition may also be submitted through the on-line form published on the official Web page of the commission. Within one year, starting from the date when a petition is submitted, the commission should make a decision on a property. In the absence of a specific request, the commission also issues decisions on designation as a national monument for each of the individual properties on the Provisional List of National Monuments of Bosnia and Herzegovina.

The commission monitors and considers the present situation and activities relating to national monuments endangered by illegal construction, inexpert reconstruction, lack of maintenance or other forms of destruction. In specific cases, it notifies the relevant entity or other authorities that a monument is endangered and proposes measures for its protection in accordance with the law, including the filing of criminal charges with the relevant authorities under the provisions of the Code of Criminal Procedure. The commission provides a list of the endangered monuments, and recommends priorities for protection to the responsible governments.

The commission is also authorised to engage international co-operation in the protection of the historical and cultural heritage.

The commission establishes regular co-operation with the institutions of Bosnia and Herzegovina, the entities, the towns and cities, the cantons and the municipalities, ministries responsible for culture and for spatial planning, museums, universities, archives, libraries, religious communities (Islamic, Catholic, Greek Orthodox, and Jewish) and NGOs concerning heritage matters.

The three entity/regional governments (Government of the Federation of Bosnia and Herzegovina, the Government of Republika Srpska and the Government of the District of Brčko) are responsible for ensuring and providing the financial, administrative, technical, scientific and legal resources necessary to protect, preserve, present and restore the national monuments. The governments must provide the resources for drawing up the necessary technical documentation for the restoration of the national monument and for implementing its provisions. The institutions for the protection of the heritage at entity level are financed from the entities' budgets via the entities' ministries responsible for culture. In response to the commission's decisions on designating properties as national monuments, the relevant ministries of the Federation of Bosnia and Herzegovina, the Republika Srpska and the District of Brčko should earmark funds for work on monuments, including endangered national monuments, both private and state-owned.

Responsibility for the enforcement of the commission's decisions lies with the entity/regional governments and the ministries responsible for regional planning. The institutions for the protection of the cultural, historical and natural heritage at the level of the entities in Republika Srpska and the Federation of Bosnia and Herzegovina are responsible for the implementation of the laws, and the Department for Education's Commission to Protect Heritage at the level of the District of Brčko. In addition, in the Federation of Bosnia and Herzegovina there are local institutions in Tuzla, Mostar and in the Canton of Sarajevo.

The Law on the Implementation of Decisions of the Commission to Preserve National Monuments lays down the responsibilities of, and relationship between, the departments, organisations or institutes responsible for heritage management.

- Everyone, in particular the competent authorities of the entities, the District of Brčko, cantons, and urban and municipal authorities, must refrain from any action that might endanger the national monuments or jeopardise their protection and restoration.
- Entity ministries responsible for spatial planning issue permits for the display and restoration of national heritage. The institutions responsible for the protection of the heritage provide expertise on restoration projects and expert supervision of restoration work.

– The entity governments, spatial planning ministry, heritage protection institutes and municipal authorities in charge of urban planning and land registry matters, are notified of the commission's decisions in order to carry out the legal measures and the competent municipal court is notified for the purposes of registration in the Land Register.

Historical Necropolis Radimlja (Council of Europe)

Financing

In the last two years, it has been possible to finance a number of restoration projects from the budget of the Government of the Federation of Bosnia and Herzegovina, the Government of the Canton of Sarajevo and the Government of the Canton of Zenica-Doboj.

In 2003, the Government of Republika Srpska did not establish a budget line for heritage. However, some projects financed by religious communities, private foundations and NGOs have been carried out on the territory of Republika Srpska.

The commission is authorised by the Rules on the Activities of the Commission to Preserve National Monuments with respect to International Co-operation, to engage in international co-operation on the preservation of national monuments. It must represent the interests of Bosnia and Herzegovina when it comes to sign and implement international conventions, to place national monuments on UNESCO's World Heritage List and the

World Monuments Watch List of the 100 Most Endangered Sites, to co-operate with Interpol, other international organisations and countries in the case of the disappearance of movable national property (procedural issues relating to the export of movable national property and the question of guarantees for their safekeeping in the event of their temporary export).

The international bodies working in the country and able to finance restoration projects are NGOs – Cultural Heritage without Borders (Sweden), Crossroads and SIDA (Sweden), the Aga Khan Trust for Culture (Geneva), World Monuments Fund (New York), UNESCO, IRCICA (Research Centre for Islamic History, Art and Culture) – the governments of Turkey, Italy, Sweden, Croatia, the Council of Europe, the Council of Europe Development Bank, the European Commission and the World Bank.

Documentation

The institutions involved in the protection of cultural and historical monuments have their own archives. In most cases these archives are not in electronic form, and in some cases access to them is difficult without specific references. In some regions of the country, the maps are not up to date and it is not possible to link land registry data with information on owners. In addition, in some parts of Bosnia and Herzegovina, books containing ownership information were destroyed during the Second World War and the 1992-95 war.

There is a national inventory of buildings and sites. The Statistical Institute of the Republic of Bosnia and Herzegovina held a census of immovable heritage in 1986. The Institute for Protection of Cultural, Historical and Natural Heritage of Bosnia and Herzegovina (that ceased to exist in 2003) conducted the inventory which had been exposed to partial devastation during the war. The purpose of the inventory is to ensure protection and registration as a national monument. It does not follow the Council of Europe's Core Data Standard for Archaeological Sites and Monuments. It includes both ordinary buildings and major monuments and is an ongoing activity.

The commission has prepared a proposal for an electronic archive of the heritage of Bosnia and Herzegovina which is designed to be a single documentation centre and will include national, entity, cantonal and municipal institutions. When data is entered into the archive, institutions involved with the cultural and historical heritage will be consulted. Part of the cultural and historical heritage has been covered at various levels by different institutional bodies.

There are experts at the local level and they originate from different ethnic communities. Access is available to planning information that could influence the prioritisation of buildings and sites. It is also possible to access expertise to assess damage and the costs of repairs. There is adequate photographic equipment.

The bodies holding the materials compiled are the commission itself, together with various local entities, national and international institutions and bodies involved directly or indirectly with the cultural and historical heritage in Bosnia and Herzegovina. At a state and at a local level, these institutions and bodies include the Ministry of Foreign Affairs; the Ministry of Foreign Trade and Economic Relations; the Ministry of Education, Science, Culture and Sport; the Ministry of Regional Planning and the Environment; the Ministry of Finance of both entities; the Ministry of Transport and Communications of both entities; and other institutions responsible for heritage issues in Bosnia and Herzegovina, such as museums, archives, galleries and universities, as well as NGOs.

Ethnicity and community

In the procedure for designating a given property as a national monument, the commission has drawn up standard forms based on the type of property and has sent them to all the municipalities, the institutions involved with the protection of the cultural and historical heritage, religious communities and other institutions. Properties belonging to the heritage of all the ethnic and religious groups have been designated as national monuments. Owners and political criteria are irrelevant for designation of property as a national monument (the Criteria for the Designation of Property as National Monuments, 2002/2003).

Priority is given to endangered monuments and monuments of great importance for the preservation of the identity of the state of Bosnia and Herzegovina. Annex 8 of the Dayton Peace Agreement explains that designations of national monuments are based upon their cultural, historical, religious and ethnic importance. The designation rules also regulate other criteria, including those of a symbolic nature (ontological, sacred, traditional, relating to rituals or traditions or significant for the identity of a group of people). The Presidency of Bosnia and Herzegovina has issued a formal decision on the appointment of the members of the commission, which consists of two foreign experts (from Sweden and Turkey) and three national experts, one from each of the constituent ethnic groups. Annex 8 also states that the officials and bodies of the parties must fully co-operate with the commission. The High Representative is authorised to impose decisions to revoke the appointment of representatives of the authorities who prevent the implementation of the Dayton Peace Agreement, including Annex 8.

3. Bulgaria

Historical context

Bulgaria has a rich architectural and archaeological heritage. It is the crossroads of civilisations, where political, economic and cultural influences of the West and the East have intersected.

Archaeological remains of human settlements date back to the Palaeolithic period (40 000 years BC). By the end of the third millennium BC, the Thracians had settled there, followed by the Hellenes and the Romans.

Bulgaria was founded as one of the oldest European states in 681, the First Kingdom lasting until 1018 when the lands were conquered by Byzantium. The Second Kingdom lasted from 1185 until 1396 and the coming of the Turks who remained in control until 1878 when a historical liberation took place, which is still celebrated as a national holiday as if it were the recent past. The Third Kingdom then lasted until 1944 when a totalitarian system of government was introduced, lasting until 1989.

The country is still coming to terms with its recent history and its future as a member of the EU.

Heritage

Typology and characteristics

All of these periods have left significant evidence of their cultures: Neolithic sites and necropolises; Thracian tombs and sanctuaries; Greek settlements from the 5th century BC; Roman camps and fortifications, amphitheatres, stadiums, baths, and so forth; Byzantine basilicas; mediaeval churches and monasteries; Ottoman mosques; icons and mural paintings; houses, inns, bridges and fountains; as well as modern houses and housing, public buildings and industrial monuments, including the Kokaliane hydroelectric plant, the first to be constructed in the Balkans.

The main characteristics of the Bulgarian heritage highlight the symbiosis between two major fundamental artistic trends:

> "…[o]n the one hand, concern, knowledge and 'open-mindedness' to dominant conceptual and artistic trends, well established in large cultural centres of the respective periods, and on the other, the expressed artistic individuality marked by local attitudes, traditions and practices, which stem from an enormous spatial canvas and go back deep down in history. At the same time, because of its geographical situation, Bulgaria has been the crossroads of various civilisations, cultures and religions, which

have had their impact on the overall cultural process in Bulgarian lands since antiquity. It is these complex interactions that form the background of the exceptional wealth, originality, diversity and the intricate stratification of Bulgarian archaeological and architectural heritage, whose best achievements during individual periods in turn have become models and a source of cultural influences in the region…" (Professor Dr Todor Krastev, ICOMOS Bulgaria).

Categorisation

Monuments in Bulgaria are categorised according to cultural and historical value as being of "world", "national" or "local" importance, of "ensemble" importance or just "for information".

In addition to the individual types of monuments noted above, there are a large number of significant ensembles including: Thracian tombs and sanctuaries; the remains of Roman towns; the complexes associated with monasteries and mosques; and protected zones – urban, rural and infrastructural.

Much of this rich heritage is threatened, particularly those archaeological sites away from urban centres which are difficult to research, conserve and protect and are subject to systematic pillaging with sophisticated equipment. Within the urban realm, the archaeology is threatened by infrastructural developments and the overall environment is threatened by building projects which maximise density and height at the expense of the urban scale. Also at significant risk are mural paintings in churches from the mediaeval to modern periods.

Protection

There are currently two types of protection: provisional and permanent – *inscrits* and *classés*. There are almost 40 000 monuments in the two groups, including those which are individually noted and those which form part of protected zones. These include monuments of art, architecture, archaeology, history, parks and cultural landscapes. There are 503 buildings and 45 ensembles which are categorised as being of "national importance". These have the status of "reserves" and include locations such as Veliko Tarnovo; the old parts of Plovdiv, Nessebar and Sozopol; the villages of Bozhentsi and Zheravna; and the ancient and mediaeval fortress of Kaliakra. All of these are well inventoried and documented, although the documentation needs to be updated.

In total there are 15 549 archaeological monuments currently listed (although there are believed to be approximately 100 000 archaeological sites in all); 15 495 architectural monuments; 1 762 monuments of art; 2 622 monuments of history and 61 parks and cultural landscapes. These larger statistics must, however, be treated with caution since some monuments may not have been properly assessed, and others have not been visited for 20 years.

Currently, the cut-off date for the protection of monuments is the Second World War. The proposal of candidates for protection is the task of the National Institute for Monuments of Culture, which both proposes candidates itself and assesses the proposals of others. It must then canvass the opinion of the relevant municipality. The institute carries out systematic programmes of work by annual territorial investigation (which is limited because of the available budget) and at times of agricultural, planning or civil works. The institute then compiles the necessary documentation, putting the monument under provisional protection until more detailed studies confirm its cultural historical value and social importance, the criteria, which apply to both individual monuments and ensembles, being: authenticity and level of conservation, age and technique, scientific and artistic value, relationship with the environment and social significance. Confirmation of the recommendation for this permanent level of protection is the responsibility of the Ministry of Culture, advised by an inter-institutional commission which reviews the documentation, collaborating where appropriate with the Ministry for the Environment and the Ministry of Regional and Urban Development. Problems concerning the heritage where ministerial functions overlap, as for example in defining the limits of reserves (where regional development, environment and agriculture might all have an interest), may be solved by inter-ministerial committees.

Religious heritage

There are a very large number of important Orthodox monuments: the Church has been an ever-present factor in Bulgarian life since the adoption of Orthodox Christianity as the official state religion in AD 865. In addition to the monuments, their contents and their surroundings, there is a vast collection of artefacts in the National Church Historical and Archaeological Museum in Sofia which holds 10 000 relics, icons, archives, sculptures and suchlike. The collection was begun in 1878, partly in order to prevent foreign removal; it was institutionalised as a museum in 1921. The museum has no role in maintaining church buildings, but it may provide advice and, given financial assistance, would be able to participate in restoration work if it expanded its currently small restoration workshop. Church buildings which are not in use may become "monuments", in which case they are the responsibility of the Ministry of Culture and the National Institute for Monuments of Culture. Those in use are the responsibility of the Synod, although the ministry has a continuing responsibility in matters of restoration. The authorities are supposed to ask the institute for advice about the buildings in their care but they do not always do so – interventions have been carried out without benefit of specialist guidance. It is also alleged that the income which the Church receives following the restitution of property from the state does not appear to benefit the buildings in their care. Such opinions on the Church's administration of its finances are not specific to this Bulgarian situation. They may be heard in many parts of Europe where there is anticlericalism, or at least scepticism, arising from the perceived tensions in the Church's prioritisation of limited resources. Such attitudes stem from potentially divergent imperatives: the Church's role as fount of divine expression and its obligations as curator of those major national monuments which play a fundamental role in the creation and celebration of national identity, over and above their primary religious function.

A contrast is drawn by some commentators on the situation with Islamic monuments and Jewish synagogues, where both types of building have received money from abroad for purposes of restoration which has been carried out with the approval of the monitoring authorities. While non-religious Islamic buildings are the business of the state, the mosques in use are administered by the central Islamic office, and twelve regional "mufti" offices. During the communist period, only the central mosque in Sofia was in occasional use; others have come back into use over the last decade. There has been rapid progress in restoring old mosques and building new ones. The state finances some conservation and restoration projects for mosques which have the status of monuments of national value but are not used for religious purposes. In 1999 Bulgaria and Turkey drew up a bilateral agreement for financing the restoration of historical monuments – Bulgarian churches in Turkey and mosques in Bulgaria. The local populations contribute money and there is also assistance from overseas. The institute has provided advice and permission and works are fully documented. Here as elsewhere, however, there is a difficulty in finding qualified craftsmen. Some do exist but they are not concentrated together in professional organisations or private companies specialising in restoration work. A non-profit-making organisation (the Association for Bulgarian Cultural and Historical Heritage) was set up very recently, in late 2003, and its membership includes architects, engineers and craftsmen from the private sector.

Political strategy

The penetrating social and economic changes which happened in recent years in the region have left a profound imprint on all spheres of social life, including culture. This is particularly relevant to the cultural and historical heritage, which is of strategic priority and even part of national security. The new conditions present a social perspective which is directly connected with the general improvement and betterment of lifestyle. New methods and approaches are being explored regarding the organisation and management of heritage and also to solve a number of problems related to its preservation and recognition.

Priorities for the heritage are considered to be the vigorous enactment of new legislation with an appropriately decentralised system of protection and the allocation of resources commensurate with the task and the acceptance of wider European best practice in protection, management and funding of the heritage.

The built heritage management policy is embodied in the legislation and in the system of institutes. The Ministry of Culture is in overall charge of all activities. Since times have changed dramatically over the eight years since the publication of *Bulgarian Cultural Policy 1990-95*, there is a clear and pressing need for a new heritage management strategy which should be accessible at a number of levels in order to answer the needs of professionals, politicians, funding bodies and the general public. This would supplement the current National Plans for Regional Development.

The absence of adequate resources for the heritage also influences the degree to which it can be advertised, popularised and made available to the wider public. Nevertheless, the level of publicity given to it is not as low as all that. Bulgaria is, for example, actively involved in the Council of Europe's "European Heritage Days". However, it is important to step up efforts because, if the public shows a desire for the heritage to be protected and accessible, then the government can be influenced in that direction. This would be significantly helped by the involvement of professional staff from the Ministry of Culture and the institutes, perhaps in association with members of the equivalent educational institutions and with the possible involvement of the media, in educational programmes, exhibitions, publications and guided visits. This requires resourcing but is surely achievable with limited resources if partners can be found.

The Holy Transfiguration Monastery, founded in 11th century ("Center for the Study of Democracy" Sofia)

Legislation

Historical overview

Institutional awareness of the value of the Bulgarian cultural heritage and the need to place it under legal protection emerged in the mid-19th century. Legal regulations followed as early as 1888, with further laws in the early decades of the 20th century: "Bulgaria became one of the first European countries to initiate a modern system for the preservation of the cultural heritage based on appropriate principles, rules and legal regulations; on an effective institutional organisation; and on stimulating public interest in the problems of the cultural heritage" (*Bulgarian Cultural Policy*). It is this original spirit, now much eroded following over half a century of changing political and economic circumstances and social upheaval, which must be recaptured if the heritage is to regain its rightful place as a fundamental component of contemporary Bulgarian life.

In the period between 1957 and 1985 heritage protection was well organised and widely funded. This protection needs to be resuscitated and adapted to the new economic and political context. Bulgaria is in need of a sophisticated legislative framework for the heritage with associated changes to the Criminal Code.

Current situation

There are a number of relevant laws in current use:

- the Law of Cultural Monuments and Museums (1969, with later amendments and supplements);
- the Law on Cultural Protection and Development (1999);
- Regulation No. 5 of the Ministry of Culture (1998) on listing monuments of built heritage;
- the Law on the Protected Territories (1998);
- international documents which Bulgaria has ratified, such as the 1970 UNESCO Convention on the Means of Prohibiting and Preventing the Illicit Import, Export and Transfer of Ownership of Cultural Property, the European Cultural Convention (ETS No. 18), the Convention for the Protection of the Architectural Heritage of Europe (ETS No. 121 – Granada Convention) and the European Convention on the Protection of the Archaeological Heritage (ETS No. 143 – the Valletta Convention).

The heritage legislation is developing based on two main principles: general accessibility and restriction regime. They guarantee the observation of the established constitutional standards regarding the cultural and historical heritage in Bulgaria. Another, quite typical, characteristic of the listed normative documents is that they pay attention to the entire process from exploration and discovery to the promotion of cultural monuments and to the institutional problems of organisations.

The Law of Cultural Monuments and Museums (LCMM) regulates the legal relationships in the cultural and historical heritage sector. Unfortunately, it is one of dozens among the currently effective laws and thus a considerable part of its texts have lost their actuality.

An attempt for partial modernisation was made through the acts for amendment and supplement to the LCMM after 1989. The definition of a cultural monument was significantly extended with the last amendment after 2004. At the same time, many of the articles have changed relating to the tasks and functions of the museums; the conditions for the creation of museums are regulated; the legal basis for creation of private museums has been set up; a new museums network has been set up in the country; and matters related to financing of museums have been dealt with. Details are regulated, including the declaration and registration of movable monuments and ownership declarations by either judicial bodies or civilians, which ensure that obligations are met in respect of the preservation of cultural monuments.

Despite these changes, a considerable range of problems are still outstanding and require solutions. Firstly, there is a problem with the lack of correlation between the specialised legislation in the cultural and historical heritage sector and the directly related peripheral laws – which in some degree relate to the heritage. Secondly, there are problems related to the preservation and recognition of cultural monuments, which in the majority of cases are a result of the insufficient financing of such activities. In addition, the law – instead of envisaging incentives and relief for the private owners of cultural monuments – has imposed several obligations on them, including the obligation to maintain the monuments in good condition, and to allow access to them.

Directly linked to the question of financing is the ownership of various types of cultural valuables. The state owns the majority of items, leaving a very small percentage in other ownership. Immovable monuments are mainly public property and the lack of specialised state authorities in the regions does not create the right conditions for more efficient management of artefacts.

Closely connected with this problem is the controversial question concerning concessions on cultural monuments. One of the most crucial current questions in this sector concerns illegal excavations – against which the existing specialised and indirect legislation cannot guarantee successful action.

In its current form the LCMM does not create the right conditions regarding the market of cultural valuables. Furthermore, one of the main principles established by the EU is the free movement of goods, services, persons and capital. For instance, in the last text amending and supplementing the LCMM, the main provisions of Regulation No. 3911/92 were incorporated into Bulgarian legislation regarding the export of cultural valuables. A new chapter was also created on "Export and temporary export of movable cultural monuments" which defines the procedures for issuing permits for export and temporary export of movable cultural monuments. At the same time the export of movable cultural monuments was prohibited as they are considered part of the national wealth – except for limited export, which requires special permission from the Minister of Culture. In a separate appendix there is a listing of the categories of movable cultural monuments that are not subject to export and temporary export. There is also a listing which defines the value of cultural monuments for which an export permit is required.

Parallel with these changes, the establishment of the Cultural Heritage Inspectorate is already under way, and this, in practice, will introduce the aforementioned regulations into the sector. There is one more addendum to the recent law, which is a novelty in the Bulgarian legal system, on the regulation and prohibition of the reproduction of cultural monuments and copies.

According to the experts in the field of cultural heritage, it is clear that all these changes provide only a partial resolution to the problems and in fact, in some cases, they are confusing and ambiguous. Therefore, a new law on cultural monuments and museums has been in preparation for several years now, but, for various reasons, has not yet been launched.

New draft law

A new law for the monuments of culture is currently being drafted in order to update and adapt the law to the new social and economic environment, and to bring it into line with wider European heritage legislation. The draft law is divided into seven chapters:

    Chapter 1 – General provisions
    Chapter 2 – Types of monuments of culture
    Chapter 3 – Protection of monuments
    Chapter 4 – Promotion of monuments of culture
    Chapter 5 – Ownership, financing
    Chapter 6 – Dissemination
    Chapter 7 – Administrative penal measures

The enactment of the new law will be a starting point. There will need to be further legislation, for example on penalties for unauthorised works and illegal trafficking in antiquities. There are problems with illegal construction, but there is no wording in the Law on the Structure of the Territories which covers illegal intervention in the built heritage, so it is currently impossible to regulate and prevent such action. So, illegal building works continue, although there are numerous strategies employed to combat it: spreading the word about the benefits of conservation as widely as possible; using historical building experts for consultation in planning; encouraging municipalities to use their existing powers to control developments; refusing to allow the demolition of buildings just because they are not in good condition or well built; creating a national list of evaluated, priority interventions; evaluating in each case the standard of intervention and the extent of the control required; and finding alternative forms of finance in order to lighten the load on the owner of the building.

Link with spatial planning and development

Since 1989, the privatisation of the Bulgarian economy and the embracing of new financial models has accelerated and exacerbated the inherent tensions between protection and development, and between conservation/preservation and the free movement of goods, as in all countries in the process of transition.

The privileging of financial interests had a most damaging legislative outcome in the passing in 2003 of the Law for the Amendments and Supplements to the Law on the Structure of the Territories, as these do not adequately address the question of the preservation of monuments when considering "layout plans" and "investment projects". The law covers protected areas of historical and cultural value, which, from the standpoint of layout plans and investment projects, are governed by provisions in other laws such as the Law on Cultural Monuments and Museums and the Order on Investment Projects of the Ministry of Regional and Urban Development.

As a result, local authorities have, to a certain extent, become disengaged from the process of heritage protection and there is no insistence on consultation with the National Institute for Monuments of Culture: reconstruction is treated in the same way as new construction. An attempt will be made to modify this situation in the new law and in any consequent regulatory legislation since it conflicts with the previous dispensation which allowed for a close working relationship between heritage concerns and planning, particularly in historically rich areas. Representatives of the national institute participate in municipal expert councils when layout schemes with a potential impact on historic monuments are discussed.

Institutions

The National Institute for Monuments of Culture, the Archaeological Institute, the Archaeological Museum and the regional historical museums come under the overall direction of the Ministry of Culture.

The heritage is understaffed considering the numbers of monuments and the pressures which they are under: there are only 61 full-time members of staff (researchers, experts and inspectors) in the National Institute for Monuments of Culture. The national institute makes recommendations for protection and control, manages architectural projects, monitors the built heritage, prepares evaluations, creates and maintains documentation. There are only 128 full-time staff in the Archaeological Institute, which carries out research and excavations, and documents and publishes the results. The regional museums and the municipal departments of culture are also very understaffed in view of their large role in preserving monuments and in tracing, documenting, investigating and popularising the cultural and historical heritage of their regions.

Expertise is now concentrated in the national institutes (for architecture and archaeology) which are rightly regarded as one of the strengths of the Bulgarian system, although, given their current funding, that strength may be potential rather than actual. Many employees left to join the free market after 1990 and new, young recruits are inhibited from joining the organisations due to the low salaries. Thus numbers have fallen and the average age has risen. Consequently, there are not enough staff to allow for significant structural change. There are, however, enough staff with the ability to manage freelance experts, provided that money is available to pay them. A register of such experts has been created recently.

The 12 permanent staff may be supplemented by up to 120 for specific projects, for example on architectural facades, wall paintings, gilding and restoration, as well as new civil works. In these circumstances, the ministry contracts the work out and then monitors the results through a commission of experts. The company provides documentation and analysis, supplying copies to the investor and to the national institute. Outside such companies, the majority of restoration workers are now freelance working on small contracts. In such circumstances, the craft skills which used to be developed within the climate of continuity provided by tradition, training and security of tenure within the institute are being lost. Five or six students a year may be trained in restoration techniques in the National Academy of Fine Arts, but this is far fewer than the numbers needed. There is a great need for more training in this traditional area as well as in such newer disciplines as database creation and project management.

There is a disabling lack of resources to support the professional staff engaged in heritage management; training in craft and restoration techniques is fairly limited and there are inevitable difficulties and tensions involved in the shift towards a privatised, contract-based economy.

The relationship between the centre and the regions, which was supported in the past by adequate funding, has been weakened since 1990 by a lack of resources to support the necessary links, thereby disabling the controls which used to be operated in partnership between the centre and the regions. The closure of the Cultural and Historic Heritage County Directorates has removed the direct link between the Ministry of Culture (and the National Institute for Monuments of Culture) and the county (provincial) municipalities so the range of activities – prevention, protection, rehabilitation, conservation – has been disrupted. For instance, when restoration of a historical building is proposed, the relationship is supposed to work as follows: the chief architect of the town issues a visa for works which then goes to the national institute, acting on behalf of the Ministry of Culture, for comment in the light of constraints and regulations. The owner will then outline a project which must be approved first by the institute and then by the municipality. This gives the municipality the possibility of varying the institute's recommendations, and indeed the municipalities often issue visas for works without reference to the institute at all. There appears to be no current mechanism for stopping such quasi-illegal works, despite the legislation which ought to pertain.

On the other hand, there is good co-operation with architectural and archaeological professionals from the University of Architecture, Civil Engineering and Geodesy, Sofia, and from the Academy of Science and the Academy of Fine Arts. It is incumbent upon the national institute, by law, to draw on such external expertise for advice. Meetings, seminars and conferences are held occasionally. Archaeological finds from official excavations overseen by the Archaeological Institute are, as a rule, deposited in the national museum, with copies in the local museum, the work of study and documentation being carried out with the help of students from the university, with whom there has been productive collaboration since 1990. Since the spring of 2003, there has been partnership between the architecture department of the University of Sofia and some schools of architecture in France concerning the management of the picturesque and historical village of Arbanasi, high on a plateau north of Veliko Tarnovo. The Archaeological Institute offers methodological support to museums, universities and other institutions and has regular partnerships with the regional museums of history. Specialists from the Archaeological Institute are currently participating in 16 international archaeological research projects. An established mechanism for the approval or the assessment of works proposed by international organisations is set out in Article 22 of the rules governing archaeological excavations.

Financing

State funding is insufficient. There is now only a small state budget for restoration projects and a small staff to oversee them. The National Institute for Monuments of Culture reduced its restoration staff from 3 000 to 60 in 1990, in a rush towards privatisation. Some former institute staff set up private companies which are among the small number of such companies which bid for work put out for tender by the Ministry of Culture.

The state is using all means to stimulate the private sector, for example tax concessions, VAT exemption for donations, percentage from tourism revenues and preferential interest rates on credit. Unfortunately, a lot of these instruments could not be used in Bulgaria because the state budget is under the strict control of the International Monetary Fund.

Every year, the national institute proposes projects for restoration, conservation and display, according to the available budget. In late 2003, 1 million levas (BGL) was allocated for the restoration of a mediaeval church of national value.

The Ministry of Culture is making efforts to find alternative sources of funding outside the available budget. The non-profit Bulgarian Cultural and Historical Heritage Organisation has been established for project work – they are looking for funding from abroad.

There is a UNESCO project in association with a Japanese trust fund to restore seven houses in Plovdiv, a city of pre-eminent architectural merit and historical importance, whose monuments illustrate all the major phases of Bulgarian history.

The picturesque Russian church in the village of Shipka, near the eponymous pass where the outnumbered Russians and Bulgarians defeated the Ottoman army in 1877, was built as a monument to the Russians and Bulgarians who lost their lives. This has just been restored by a private Russian society. A further project has been proposed for the restoration of the murals in the monumental Alexander Nevsky memorial church, one of the crowning glories of Sofia.

European policies for financing the preservation of cultural heritage have improved exceptionally in the last few years. The EU PHARE programme allocated €7 million for projects relating to cultural tourism in 2003, and the previous year financed a project relating to eco-tourism. The funding of cultural tourism has taken place particularly in areas of high unemployment, financing restoration, conservation, infrastructure and publicity. An eco-tourism strategy project has been finalised and the PHARE eco-tourism project is under way.

The institute was also responsible for the selection of buildings to be restored in the "Beautiful Bulgaria" project, funded in part through the PHARE programme. This is a major initiative, begun two years ago, with work continuing in several regions. Funding is from the EU (€4.5 million), the United Nations Development Programme (€635 000), and eleven Bulgarian municipalities (€725 000). The project is being overseen by the Ministry of Labour and Social Policy, with support from the UN, and is intended to provide employment. In return for winning contracts, private companies must employ 20 people for 6 to 12 months and train them in restoration techniques. This is fine in principle, and the freshly painted facades in the historical city of Veliko Tarnovo, the former capital, look particularly attractive. Professional opinion, however, suggests that there has not been adequate supervision of the trainee workers so they are not being fully trained, which would be difficult anyway in the short length of time available, and the work may prove to be less durable than may be desired. If true, this would underline the importance of ensuring that the authority of the national institute is respected in all projects involving historical buildings and craft skills.

At municipal level, to take one example, the Regional Historical Museum Academician Yordan Ivanov, which has responsibilities in the provinces of Kiustendil, Pernik and Blagoevgrad, has carried out joint archaeological and architectural research projects with university staff and students from Moscow, with the Austrian Academy of Sciences, and with Aristotle University, Thessaloníki. Staff have also participated in international exhibitions and symposia.

The Islamic community has been particularly successful in obtaining financial assistance from overseas for the restoration and building of mosques. Money from Turkish and Arab sources has supplemented local and public authority initiatives and there has also been a United States programme for the restoration of mosques, in collaboration with the American University of Bulgaria.

There is no difference in approach in the monitoring of works between national and international interventions by donors. Proposals are directed through the Ministry of Culture; the National Institute for Monuments of Culture at the appropriate stages then comments, advises, monitors and finally prepares a report on the project which then forms part of the building's documentation.

The 11th General Assembly of the International Council on Monuments and Sites (ICOMOS) was held in Sofia in 1995, with an international symposium on "The Heritage and Social Changes". The proceedings were commemorated in a publication almost as monumental as the subject itself, underlining the long-standing commitment of ICOMOS both to the continuation of its international advisory role and to Bulgaria itself where the organisation has a long-established National Committee which collaborates on a regular basis with the national authorities.

ICOMOS, by definition an international organisation, implements international programmes and projects for financing monuments (the involvement of the Japanese trust fund in Plovdiv came about through the collaboration between the Bulgarian and Japanese national committees of ICOMOS), and for promoting the use of the cultural heritage as a resource, participating for example in the European Heritage Days. It co-operates with international governmental institutions and NGOs.

The World Heritage Committee has also provided technical assistance in addressing the problems associated with preserving two world heritage sites, which were placed on the World Heritage List in 1979 at a "round table" organised in co-operation with the National Institute for Monuments of Culture. These sites are "the Horseman of Madara", a *bas-relief* carved in the rock face above the village of Madara, and the "Ivanovo Rock Monasteries", whose churches, monks' cells and galleries are natural caves cut into the cliff face.

Documentation

The national documentation for historical buildings and archaeological sites is held in the National Institute for Monuments of Culture and in the Archaeological Institute and Archaeological Museum. Documentation is also held in the municipalities but it is not always clear what is being held nationally and what is held locally, and whether it is adequate. The information in the national institute is freely accessible to the public. It comprises text, photographs, maps and drawings in folders. The inventory – the National Archive for Monuments of Culture – comprising individual monuments, ensembles and archaeological sites is held at the national institute. It is compiled in part according to the European Core Data Standard for Archaeological Sites and Monuments but cannot be consulted electronically, although the text of the individual records is computerised. In most cases archaeological documentation in the Archaeological Institute is not publicly available, although it is available to professional colleagues from around the country.

In mapping, a new system is being developed following a new cadastral law. The cadastre is prepared and maintained by the Cadastre Agency within the Ministry of Regional Development and Public Works. It contains data about location, borders, size of properties and the estate rights on them. The property registers are maintained by the regional courts. The cadastral information is in the process of being digitised, together with the identification of property owners. While this goes on, access to information is variable but in principle it is in the public domain. In most cases, archaeological monuments have not been marked on cadastral plans of urban areas.

Training in documentation and information systems and in the employment of European standards will clearly be necessary as the funding for new technology becomes available, but existing staff both nationally and locally are fully qualified in dealing with the documentation as it exists at the moment. If further specialists are needed in particular types of building, they can be enlisted from the university.

The existing documentation is considered sufficient to provide a basis for prioritising activities.

Ethnicity and community

The Constitution of the Republic of Bulgaria provides mechanisms for preventing discrimination and promoting ethnic and religious equality.

Reference has been made above to the role of the religious authorities in the maintenance of monuments. The staff of the National Institute for Monuments of Culture do not perceive any problems in dealing with the various cultural manifestations of the various religious or ethnic communities. The criteria for intervention or prioritisation are not influenced by ethnicity and there are no obstacles to access to the buildings of various ethnic groups, although clearly it is desirable to collaborate with local authorities in the regions. So far as the professional staff are aware, there are no problems recognising the buildings of other communities, not least since members of all communities are involved in the programmes.

The "Bulgarian ethnic model" in the Balkans is now fully established and misunderstandings between the different ethnic groups are unlikely. The Ministry of Culture has a general council on cultural diversity (Section 16 of the Law on Cultural Protection and Development), whose members represent different communities.

The main religious communities are Christian (Eastern Orthodox, Catholic, Protestant), Muslim and Jewish. Steps are taken, however, at a governmental level to ensure proper understanding. There is a parliamentary commission which makes full information available about all ethnicities and within the Ministry of Culture there are staff who are responsible for working on the cultural integration of the Turkish and Roma communities, the relationship between the Bulgarians and the latter being the most subject to misunderstanding. It is of particular importance that educational programmes should be implemented which will increase interest, recognition and awareness of the values of others.

4. Croatia

Historical context

Croatia has a wide-ranging architectural and archaeological heritage, the first vestiges of which date back to prehistoric times. Various cultures, namely Illyrian and Celtic in protohistoric times, Greek and Roman in ancient times, Slav, Croatian, Venetian and Hungarian in the Middle Ages and Ottoman and Austrian in the modern era, have left traces of their presence in this territory.

This cultural wealth affords a miscellany of styles, embracing not only a range of outstanding ancient remains but also many small stone churches and fortresses typical of mediaeval times, traditional farms and rural wooden houses.

Nevertheless, this wealth of architectural complexes and isolated buildings is under threat from dilapidation, many items of property having been abandoned or allowed to fall into ruin. The archaeological sites in particular are endangered by uncontrolled building activities, new roads and the disappearance of excavated items.

Heritage

Croatia has a highly diversified prehistoric and protohistoric heritage, despite the small number of fragments preserved. There are numerous examples of ancient architectural remains dating from Roman imperial times, the most important of which are in Split (Diocletian's Palace) and Pula (amphitheatre and Temple of Jupiter). Mediaeval architecture is also well represented, with a large number of sacred buildings, cathedrals, small stone churches, painted churches, urban nuclei and small fortresses. The Renaissance period is less well represented, but has also left a number of outstanding fortifications, including those at Karlovac, Dubrovnik and Veliki Tabor castle, standing on the foundations of a mediaeval fortification. Many mediaeval churches were transformed during the Baroque renewal period, when a large number of small castles and manor homes were also built.

Croatia's main architectural complexes comprise fortification systems, monastic complexes and Baroque residences complete with gardens.

The main historical centres are Dubrovnik, Torgir and Split, and various historical towns with well-preserved mediaeval or older structures (Porec, Zadar, Sibenik, Korcula, Hvar, and Rab, as well as the small towns in Istria: Motovun, Grožnjan, Pican, Gračišće, Buzet and Hum).

The main traditional settlements are the villages on the Istrian peninsula, on the islands and along the coastal strip, as well as a number of villages boasting well-preserved traditional wooden structures in the Sava basin and at Pokuplje.

The database of the National Inventory of the Cultural Heritage of the Republic of Croatia, run by the Ministry of Culture, comprises 8 395 individual architectural monuments, 6 266 of which are listed buildings, the other 2 129 being merely registered.

The most precarious section of the heritage comprises derelict and inappropriately used historical buildings, as well as urban complexes permanently exposed to incursion from ill-advised new building and urban planning projects. Uncontrolled development is thus threatening the whole cultural landscape, including its traditional and archaeological remains.

Political strategy

Architectural heritage management policies are defined partly by current legislation, despite the many remaining lacunae in this area. The Ministry of Culture has defined a Strategy for the Cultural Development of Croatia in the 21st Century, centring on protection of the cultural heritage. The basic strategic objective is to guarantee the role of the cultural heritage in the economy and in national development and the vital part played by old historical towns in the development of the physical environment.

Under recent amendments to legislation on the protection of cultural heritage, the priority for heritage protection and management is to complete the Register of Cultural Heritage Items of the Republic of Croatia, and simultaneously to establish who owns what in terms of cultural property. This means adding new items to the national heritage inventory.

It is also necessary to devise a methodology for assessing monuments and to enhance the cultural heritage. Where physical protection of cultural property is concerned, incorporating the cultural heritage into everyday life and general economic growth must be a priority, drawing on the concept of sustainable development.

Efforts to protect the cultural heritage should be directed mainly towards its revitalisation, particularly in urban environments, where more investment is needed in the wide-ranging but under-used housing environment in the old parts of Croatian towns and cities.

The cultural heritage should also be used as a prime factor for promoting Croatian tourism, although this should be done in a way that protects the heritage. This calls for close co-operation among urban developers, heritage specialists, economists, tourism experts and other operators.

Popularisation of the cultural heritage by means of educational programmes, exhibitions, European Heritage Days and similar events increases public awareness and can help gradually integrate the cultural heritage into people's everyday lives.

Legislation

The current legislation on historical monuments is as follows:
- the Law on Protection and Preservation of Cultural Property (1999, amended 2003);
- regulations on conditions for excavating sunken cultural items in inland and territorial seas of the Republic of Croatia (1998);
- regulations on identity cards for inspectors responsible for protecting cultural heritage items and on ways and means of recording inspections conducted (1999);
- regulations on the conditions to be fulfilled by natural or legal persons in order to obtain permits for works to protect and preserve cultural heritage items (1999, amended 2000 and 2002);
- regulations on the procedure for issuing permits for carrying out underwater work in sections of inland and territorial seas of the Republic of Croatia protected as cultural items (2000, amended 2003);
- regulations on the register of cultural property in the Republic of Croatia (2001);
- the Law on Renovation of the Threatened Monumental Complex in Dubrovnik (1986, amended in 1989 and 1999);
- the Decree on the Foundation of an Agency for the Restoration of Osijek Fortress (1999).

The Law on the Protection and Preservation of Cultural Property was last amended in September 2003 in the drive to harmonise Croatian law with European legislation. The main amendments concerned the regulations on cultural property franchises and redefined the provisions relating to renting of monuments.

The main European legal texts have been respected in the work on these new laws. Council of Europe conventions, recommendations and resolutions, and the experience of other countries were also taken into account.

Institutions

Responsibility for the overall cultural heritage, regardless of the type, lies with the owners of cultural goods and persons vested with other rights regarding them, as well as other holders of cultural goods. Where the cultural item is neither included in the Register of

Cultural Heritage Items of the Republic of Croatia nor otherwise legally protected, local authority and other self-governing bodies are responsible for protecting it.

The Cultural Heritage Protection Department within the Ministry of Culture is the competent body for performing administrative and expert duties connected with the protection and preservation of cultural goods. The Cultural Heritage Protection Department comprises the central headquarters in Zagreb and eleven conservation offices for the regions, covering the whole Croatian territory apart from the City of Zagreb, which comes under the authority of the Municipal Institute for the Protection and Restoration of Cultural and Natural Monuments. The department is responsible for establishing protection of cultural property, identifying and implementing protective measures, and supervising the implementation of such measures. Supervision of the application of legal regulations in practice is a matter for the Inspectorate Section of the Cultural Heritage Protection Department. This section monitors the status of cultural property and the implementation of measures to protect and conserve them, the utilisation of and trade in cultural items and in particular the performance of conservation, restoration and other similar works on cultural heritage items and their environs, and archaeological excavations and research projects, including underwater excavations and shipwreck recovery.

Information and documentation in the field of heritage protection (development of an information system for the cultural heritage and a national inventory of the Republic of Croatia's cultural property) is carried out by the Cultural Heritage Information and Documentation Service that is separate from the department's organisational set-up for cultural heritage protection.

Moreover, a Croatian Council for Cultural Heritage has been set up to monitor and promote the status of cultural property, comprising experts on the protection and conservation of cultural heritage items.

The Croatian Restoration Institute, which employs 122 craftsmen on a permanent basis, is responsible for the conservation and restoration of the cultural heritage, ranging from the architectural heritage to works of art and crafts.

The museums and archives responsible for cultural heritage protection co-operate with the Cultural Heritage Protection Department in registering and evaluating movable cultural items and archaeological finds.

Universities occasionally co-operate by sending representatives to the Ministry of Culture's committees of experts, and students take part in "summer universities" on conservation and in fieldwork aimed at registering cultural items.

The Ministry of Environmental Protection, Physical Planning and Construction is responsible for the whole area of spatial planning.

Experts from the Cultural Heritage Protection Department are involved in various projects concerning spatial planning and development, for example the National Programme for Agriculture and the Countryside and the Master Plan for Croatian Tourism.

Financing

Different forms of international co-operation have been established, concentrating on monuments and monument complexes included on the UNESCO World Heritage List. Certain problems arising from protection and restoration of cultural items can be solved through international co-operation. For instance, a number of renowned international experts delegated by UNESCO are working on the committee of experts monitoring the renovation work taking place in Dubrovnik.

In connection with rebuilding and protecting the historical centre of Split, which houses Diocletian's Palace, a co-operation agreement has been concluded with a host of stone sculpting experts from Italy, Germany, Scotland and France, while the more important monuments and architectural complexes in this historical centre are being restored under the programme jointly funded by the World Bank in Washington DC.

Co-operation has also been established with the World Monument Fund, which has included the port of Dubrovnik in the World Monuments Watch List of 100 Most Endangered Sites. This list also includes the Osijek fortress historical complex, which has been put forward for inclusion on the World Heritage List.

ECOVAST (The European Council for the Village and Small Town) has launched a project entitled "Both banks of the river Kupa". The international financial institutions are also active in Croatia, having granted loans for conservation work on various cultural monuments.

Furthermore, a number of projects are in hand with other partners in the field of architectural heritage. For instance, the third joint report on historic centres was recently completed by the Project Group on Historic Centres of the Alpe-Adria Working Community, to which the Cultural Heritage Protection Department contributed by publishing a work on "Traditional Heritage in the Republic of Croatia".

The Cultural Heritage Protection Department has also organised two summer workshops for international students, namely the "Mali Brijun" International Summer Workshop on architecture (under the auspices of ICOMOS) and the "Konavle" International Summer Workshop (under the auspices of UNESCO).

In 1999 and 2000 the Cultural Heritage Protection Department took part in the international project on "Cultural Routes in South-East Europe", initiated by ICOMOS Bulgaria as part of the Council of Europe campaign "Europe, a common heritage".

Ever since 2001 Croatia has been a member of the European Heritage Network (HEREIN), which concentrates on the architectural and archaeological heritage.

The Ministry of Culture is also contributing to the international project instigated by the Working Community of Danube Countries, "The Danube Culture Path", which is developing a digital cultural guide to the Danube Region.

The Zagreb Municipal Institute for the Protection and Restoration of Cultural and Natural Monuments co-operates on an ad hoc basis with similar bodies in Vienna and Prague, as well as with the International Association of Metropolitan Towns.

Ruins of mediaeval city Duigrad (Council of Europe)

Documentation

In principle, every institution producing documentation stores its own documents. Each of the 11 regional offices of the Cultural Heritage Protection Department and the Zagreb Central Documentation and Information Service for Cultural Heritage, covering the whole of the Republic of Croatia, archive the documentation that they produce. The largest documentary holdings, such as the picture library, microfilm archives, collections of written sources and map libraries, are stored in the Ministry of Culture, Zagreb, Runjaninova 2. The following also hold documentary collections: the Croatian Restoration Institute, the Art History Institute, the Croatian Architectural Museum, the Zagreb Municipal Institute for the Protection and Restoration of Cultural and Natural Monuments and a number of other similar institutions.

The inadequate state of the property register in the Republic of Croatia makes it very difficult to obtain information on ownership of monuments. It is estimated that only about 30% of land registers are up to date. Obsolete data on property ownership was the main reason for the launch of the review of the existing Register of Cultural Heritage Items of the Republic of Croatia in 2000.

Documentation is accessible to experts, students and the general public. Users can inspect existing documentation and request copies of documents, usually at the normal price for reproductions.

The National Inventory of the Cultural Heritage of the Republic of Croatia comprises all the existing immovable heritage items in the republic. It is in three sections: the architectural heritage, historic complexes and archaeological topography. The main aim of the inventory is to provide an indispensable knowledge base for the work of maintaining and protecting the cultural heritage, but it also serves as a basis for urban and spatial planning and for scientific research in the art history field. Furthermore, the data which it contains can be used by museums, libraries, archives, educational institutions and many other potential users in the culture and cultural heritage sphere. The inventory's data structure is strictly in line with that of the international standards for the documentation of the cultural heritage (the Core Data Index to Historic Buildings and Monuments of the Architectural Heritage and the International Core Data Standard for Archaeological Sites and Monuments). The inventory includes not only the major legally protected monuments but also such cultural property items as are mainly of local importance.

The inventory is available in electronic form, accessible through a database. Electronic research can currently be carried out at the Ministry of Culture, Zagreb. This facility for electronic research is to be extended to all the regional conservation offices and the whole Internet in order to provide a full public service. When all these elements are linked up, a user may ascertain, for example, whether a given historic building is located in a protected urban complex or on an archaeological site.

The inventory is currently being compiled by the Cultural Heritage Protection Department in its regional conservation offices, and by the Cultural Heritage Information and Documentation Service.

Ethnicity and community

Croatia has the following religious communities: Roman Catholic, Orthodox, Evangelical, Islamic and Jewish.

Croats constitute 89.62% of the population. Minorities represent 7.74% (Albanians, Austrians, Bosnians, Bulgarians, Montenegrins, Czechs, Hungarians, Macedonians, Germans, Poles, Romanians, Roma, Ruthenians, Slovaks, Slovenes, Serbs, Italians, Turks, Ukrainians, Vlachs and Jews). Virtually all these ethnic groups have their own communities and historical and educational societies, at both national and international levels.

The Minorities Service is based in Zagreb (Mesnièka 23, 10000 Zagreb). This service is run by the Government of the Republic of Croatia, and has professional responsibilities involving implementation of the policy for the equality of national minorities living in the Republic of Croatia, as well as for the rights of minorities as set out in the constitution and general legislation, and implementation of such rights. It prepares proposals for funding the system for upholding the constitutional rights of members of the national minorities and their associations. It co-operates with the competent ministries and other national administrative bodies and institutions, regional self-governing bodies in the areas where the minorities live and the Council of Europe. It monitors international documents on the rights of national minorities and co-operates with the other international institutions dealing with such rights. It follows co-operation processes underway in national minorities' associations, whose programmes have financial support from the national budget as well as from institutions in the parent countries. The Minorities Service also prepares expert opinions and analyses concerning the introduction of international standards with a view to ensuring the rights of members of national minorities (Decree on the National Minorities Service: *Official Gazette* No. 70/8.3.2001).

Members of national minorities can exercise influence, through their representative bodies in the Croatian parliament, on cultural heritage management policy at legislative level. At the executive level, members of all minorities have the same rights as all other citizens of the Republic of Croatia. Their entitlement to participate in identification, evaluation and prioritisation programmes on protection of the cultural heritage is the same as for any other citizen. Similarly, membership of a specific community is not a criterion for selection of candidates for employment in government departments or other professional institutions.

Croatia is a country with a rich and varied cultural heritage, and this cultural diversification is precisely the result of multiculturalism and the country's multinational structure, which Croatian heritage experts are striving to preserve and improve.

5. Kosovo/UNMIK

Historical context

The land of present day Kosovo, situated in a small territory stretching between west and east Europe, has been called the crossroads of history. It has always been a scene of international exchange of culture, art and architecture.

Its geomorphological position and natural resources reveal the development of life since prehistoric periods, in a time span covering 7 000 years up to the present day. From the activities of the last millennium, Kosovo has inherited traditional, historical environments. These traditions of the past, a social and cultural reflection of various ancient civilisations, can still be seen in the remains of historical cities and sites, dating from the Neolithic and Illyrian Ages to the Early Antique, Middle Ages and beyond.

There are architectural monuments from the Middle Ages, with 14th century churches and monasteries of international significance; there are 16th and 17th century mosques and hammams; *kullas* (Albanian tower houses) and *konaks* (Orthodox residences next to monasteries) from the 18th and 19th centuries; a number of historical bridges; as well as industrial heritage which is only just beginning to be recognised. In summary, this represents an "extraordinary concentration of cultural monuments from prehistoric to modern times" and "attests to the historical continuity of life in Kosovo".

Much of this rich heritage was threatened and destroyed during the recent conflict and its immediate aftermath. In view of this all too recent history, it is understandable that the Kosovan and Serbian authorities are still some way from achieving a harmonisation of views on and strategies for the cultural heritage. There is an absence of awareness among the citizens of both communities that preserving important cultural monuments should be recognised as a common responsibility. There is, moreover, a profound difficulty in enabling the Kosovo Albanian/Serbian dialogue which is fundamental to the creation of a peaceful civil society which respects the rights and responsibilities of all participants.

Nevertheless, over the three-year period during which the Council of Europe has been involved in advising in Kosovo, the situation has improved considerably as the population works towards a better *modus vivendi*. The United Nations Interim Administration Mission in Kosovo/UNMIK, established under Resolution 1244 (1999) of the UN Security Council, is overseeing the transfer of administrative powers to provisional instruments of self-government in all civil areas: the cultural heritage is administered within the Ministry of Culture, Youth and Sport. The UN has a continuing role both in facilitating the drafting of a new law for the cultural heritage and in encouraging the development of a cultural strategy for the heritage. Both of these objectives were identified in the Council of Europe's "Study on the State of the Cultural Heritage in Kosovo" (2001).

Heritage

The archaeological heritage, both movable and immovable, dates from the Neolithic period onwards, with evidence from the Copper, Bronze and Iron Ages, Roman Antiquity and Early and Late Mediaeval periods. There are examples of important sites from all of these periods. It is also believed that the major part of Kosovo's archaeology remains to be discovered.

The architectural heritage may be divided into three principal groups:

- Byzantine/Orthodox monuments, such as the 14th century churches and monasteries at Decan and Gracanica;
- Islamic monuments of the Ottoman period, such as the 15th century Sultan Mehmet II al-Fatih mosque in Pristina and the early 17th century Sinan Pasha mosque at Prizren, with their associated hammams;
- vernacular architecture which may not be so significant individually, but has a collective significance, for example the village of Velika Hoca and the valuable urban vernacular Emin Giku ensemble of residence, guest house and service buildings in Pristina; other important urban ensembles include Qarshia (complexes of shops and craft workshops, with good examples in Gjakove and Peja) and Mahalla (complexes of houses and public buildings); the old cities of Prizren, Mitrovica and Decan contain important monuments of great cultural value, such as the complex of *kullas* in Decan and the mainly Serb historical zones in Pristina and Janjeva are regarded as especially important urban ensembles.

According to registers dating up to 1999, there are 426 fully protected architectural monuments in Kosovo, with a further 600 awaiting a final decision. A new inventory should include about 2 000 buildings. Decisions will then be required on which of these should be fully protected.

The amount of work undertaken on the inventory and the assessments carried out both for the donor conference of August 2003 and by UNESCO suggest that the creation of a costed prioritised intervention list should be achievable.

This rich heritage is endangered. Not only is destruction for ethnic or political reasons still a problem, destruction through illegal building and inappropriate adaptation is also a major current concern, destroying buildings and their environment. There is also the inevitable decay of buildings through ageing, exacerbated by environmental pollution, which is hastened by the lack of protection, preservation and restoration. Limited funding, a shortage of professional staff, the absence of heritage management and the lack of a legal infrastructure all contribute to a climate of decline. It is hoped that the new law will be an agent for opportunity as well as restriction.

Political strategy

Since 1999, Kosovo has been under UN administration. Following the end of the armed conflict in Kosovo, it was evident that there was an urgent need to assign more importance to developing a risk inventory and for immediate, planned preventive measures for damaged historic cultural sites and buildings.

Despite all efforts to safeguard damaged cultural heritage and to integrate it into the process of reconstruction of Kosovo, the process has been very difficult and not very successful. The main problem has been a lack of co-ordination between all actors, including the local administration, communities and NGOs. Other problems have included a lack of specialists, a lack of management experience, the extent of the destruction and insufficient funding. There is also a lack of understanding within the local, national and international institutions.

Since 2000, Kosovo has been visited by many different international actors interested in the cultural heritage situation. A lot of reports and project proposals have been made. Some of them have been realised but others are still outstanding.

Through the efforts of the Council of Europe Directorate of Culture and Cultural and Natural Heritage in co-operation with the Kosovo administration and UNMIK, some very important reports on the situation have been produced. In particular, the aforementioned Council of Europe's "Study on the State of the Cultural Heritage in Kosovo" (2001) provided a starting point for identifying urgent actions to be undertaken. Importantly, this report also provided an analysis of the existing legal situation regarding cultural heritage in Kosovo.

The concept of conserving cultural assets, which was formerly taken to be single buildings and monuments, has changed significantly over the years and it is now being interpreted as a process of revitalisation and integration of the entities which have historical, cultural and architectural values with economic and social benefits for all.

The fundamental role of the heritage as an expression of all the population, in all of its cultural diversity, should be underlined through training, education and popularisation.

Efforts to assign more importance to the conservation of historical environments in Kosovo have also started. The necessity of specific plans for the conservation of the historical environment, the legal and organisational framework for their preparation and the proper implementation of these plans have begun to be accepted during the last four years.

The attendance at a workshop held in Pristina by representatives from the Ministry of Environment and Spatial Planning was a welcome step towards the recognition of the need for "integrated conservation", where the heritage and urban planning departments work in association rather than in opposition or in a state of mutual ignorance or disregard.

The development of a strategy for the cultural heritage and the completion of a new law will improve the situation at a strategic level as well as clarifying the roles and responsibilities of both professionals and owners – those with a direct involvement.

Since one of the concerns in Kosovo is the identification and status of owners of properties, the law could embrace the benefits of ownership of historical buildings, both economic and cultural, as well as advising owners of their responsibilities.

Legislation

Current situation

There is little point in rehearsing the legislative situation in detail: simply because it does not work. Since UNMIK cancelled all laws enacted between 1989 and 1999, due to an absence of full community involvement during that period, the legislation on monuments reverted to the law of 1977, thus removing the Law on Cultural Property of 1994. The law of 1977 is outdated and does not correspond with European best practice.

New draft law

Following the establishment of the new Kosovo Ministry of Culture in early 2002, a Technical Co-operation Programme was established by the Council of Europe, an important part of which relates to legislative and administrative reform through the Council of Europe Legal Support Task Force. An international consultant then started drafting a new law on cultural heritage for Kosovo. Over the next three years, this draft was reviewed by the Council of Europe on several occasions. The draft was also worked on by a large drafting group involving a wide range of Kosovo experts, led by the Ministry of Culture, within the framework for legislative reform recommended by the Council of Europe.

On the recommendation of the Council of Europe, the new law was divided into chapters, including the different heritage sectors (architectural, archaeological and movable heritage), covering issues such as inventory, the criteria for selection for legal protection and the effect of legal protection. The drafting group also worked hard to incorporate the concept of a "cultural historic environment" and the integration of cultural heritage and spatial and urban planning mechanisms.

The drafting group included representatives of many different communities. The text of the law is also designed to bring together all communities within Kosovo to safeguard their heritage equally.

The drafting group finally completed its work on the law early in 2004 and the draft was submitted to the government in mid-August. However, the draft was not considered by the government before its mandate expired at the end of September 2004.

The drafting process recommenced in 2005 and resulted in the approval of a new Law on Cultural Heritage by the Assembly of Kosovo in October 2006. The law, however, is not an end in itself, but the beginning of a process. It is absolutely crucial for the future of Kosovo heritage that the law is accompanied by an implementation strategy supported by appropriate institutions and staff, thus enabling the establishment of a proper conservationist regime.

Institutions

1950-99: the former Yugoslav administration

At the beginning of the 1950s, the former Administration of Kosovo, apparently influenced by trends in Europe regarding cultural heritage preservation, proposed ideas for the protection of single buildings – monuments and archaeological sites – without including the principle of the conservation of the historical environment.

With the aim of preserving and protecting historical buildings and archaeological sites, the Law for the Protection of Monuments, the Institute for the Protection of Monuments and the Museum of Kosovo were created.

However, the positive results of these efforts were very limited, owing to the lack of an effective conservation policy, comprehensive records, inventory, experts, funds and proper management. In addition, during the early phases of the planned urban and industrial development period in Kosovo, very limited ideas and principles regarding conservation of historical environments were implemented. As a result, there was significant decay and demolition of large numbers of valuable cultural historical assets.

Since 1999: Kosovo under UN administration

Since the end of the armed conflict, Kosovo has been under United Nations administration. The new Ministry of Culture, Youth and Sport is responsible for the management of cultural heritage. This management is carried out by the Institute for the Protection of Monuments of Kosovo together with local institutes at Pristina, Prizren, Gjakove and Peja. These have overall responsibility for the protection and restoration of historical buildings and for permitted development within historical areas. This responsibility has not always been appropriately discharged in the past as the reconstructions in the market at Gjakove demonstrate. Two further regional institutes are to be established in Gjilan and Mitrovica. The same structure, together with the Museum of Kosovo, is employed for the archaeological heritage, although this is currently under review.

All of these institutes are centrally funded with occasional additional funding from international donors. It is believed that co-operation between the institutes is now working better than it was some years ago when regulatory responsibilities sometimes fell into the gap between national and local institutes. There is, however, still a weakness in the quality of information exchange between them.

Co-operation outside the aegis of the ministry, with other related ministries, is at an early stage. There was consideration of the built heritage in the Law on Spatial Planning and the involvement of the Ministry of Environment and Spatial Planning in the drafting of the new cultural heritage law bodes well for future collaboration. Similar collaborations with the education and tourism ministries should be encouraged. In day-to-day planning matters, there is the possibility within the Law on Spatial Planning of involving historical building experts as consultants. It is important that the Ministry of Culture takes an active role in this to ensure that such consultations take place and are shown to be constructive.

The institutes do not monitor Orthodox religious buildings, which have been outside their areas of responsibility since 1999. These buildings are managed by the religious communities and by those in the Serb enclaves.

The role of the institutes is under consideration in the course of the development of the cultural strategy, which in turn is related to the new law and associated sub legal acts since it is attempting to prioritise endeavours within the broad cultural heritage. Such prioritising will have a necessary impact on the role and responsibilities of the institutes responsible for managing the cultural heritage.

Staff levels in the institutes are low, they are inadequately trained in project management and the salaries are insufficient. There is a good deal of staff inertia and lack of initiative and there is an absence of supervisory staff to ensure the proper care of monuments. The staff shortages and other difficulties have a political and historical basis, or bias – the Kosovo Albanians were excluded from management responsibilities before 1999, which prevented them from being able to acquire experience and training in this field. The Serbians in their turn have been excluded since 1999, taking with them a great body of knowledge and expertise.

The huge demands in the field cannot be met by the number of experts available, whether they be historians or conservators. The years of isolation of Kosovo and the limited material opportunities have proved discouraging to those who might have taken up careers relating to historical buildings or archaeology. There is also a notable absence of workers trained in traditional craft techniques – this has a negative impact on both restorations and new building.

For documentation purposes, there is a small number of qualified staff capable of taking on work of identification and assessment. However, experience of rapid recording projects in Kosovo suggests that such staff may be greatly assisted by younger, temporary workers, for example students from the Architecture Department of the University of Pristina. The benefits are two-way: students involved in such programmes benefit enormously from the opportunity of learning the techniques of assessment of historical buildings and sites; they also help to raise the spirits of the established staff through their enthusiasm.

During the period 2000-2003, there was productive co-operation between the Institute for the Protection of Monuments of Pristina and the Faculty of Construction and Architecture at the University. This connection was facilitated by the Council of Europe and the former Department of Culture within UNMIK in order to involve students in the inventory programme. There is also an increasing level of co-operation between the local institutes and between the institutes and the Museum of Kosovo on archaeological excavations in Keqekoll and Artane/Novo Berdo.

Prizren - Panoramic view from the fortress (Cultural Heritage without Borders)

Financing

National funding comes largely through the national budget rather than from individuals from whom investments are very rare. The Council of Europe has recommended financial incentives through a sympathetic taxation regime in order to encourage the proper conservation and restoration of private buildings. There are also some investments from religious communities and some work has been done in the Serbian enclaves, funded by the Co-ordination Centre of Serbia and Montenegro and the Republic of Serbia for Kosovo. In individual cases, the institutes of the Ministry of Culture have considerable influence and are able to control and monitor the disbursement of funds, both national and international.

There have been numerous examples of co-operation with international bodies. In addition to the Council of Europe, the Turkish government, through DIANET (Dialogue for Interaction, Advocacy and Networking Capacity Building in Southeast Europe), the University of Ankara and Kfor have also been involved in inventory projects, with some detailed technical appraisal, specifically for buildings from the Ottoman period.

In October 2003, Cultural Heritage Without Borders, with assistance from the institutes and the university, organised a heritage week in Isniq with handicrafts, an ethnographic exhibition, visits to restored *kullas*, folk dancing, traditional games and other similar activities.

The Kosovo International Management Group has carried out damage assessment for the European Commission, evaluating listed and public buildings with costings for repair, issuing the "Kosovo Damage Assessment" on CD-Rom in April 2000. During the same year the German Kfor brigade compiled computerised records of monuments in the Prizren region and Harvard University developed a "Kosovo Cultural Heritage Strategy", which is available as a database. Norwegian Peoples' Aid and organisations from Denmark and the Netherlands have also been involved in initiatives relating to the built heritage.

The donor conference of August 2003 listed 45 monuments in need of restoration and conservation and provided costing, and the UNESCO report was produced following a mission carried out in March 2003. This very substantial document provides a historical description, photographs, condition assessment, recommendations and estimated costs for a significant number of sites: Byzantine/Orthodox architectural monuments – six of "universal significance" and ten of "regional significance"; thirteen Islamic architectural monuments; and nine vernacular architecture sites, including quite substantial ensembles.

The Serbian organisation Mnemosyne, based in Belgrade, has, with Italian financial assistance and the participation of three Italian experts, two of whom were from the Central Institute for Conservation in Rome, also produced a useful book on the cultural and natural heritage of Metohija. The purpose of this exercise was to draw attention to "the alarming condition of heritage in Kosovo and Metohija". In all, 127 cultural monuments were assessed, including some Islamic as well as Byzantine/Orthodox monuments, although the major emphasis of the publication is on the latter. In assessing priorities, this book will be a useful source but it should be seen in conjunction with the UNESCO report since it does not cover the whole of the present territory of Kosovo. It is also not easy to gain an idea of relative values of monuments when so many are of "extraordinary importance". These caveats notwithstanding, this is a significant piece of work, over 400 pages long, with an accompanying CD-Rom.

There have also been projects carried out with international partners on works of restoration. The European Agency for Reconstruction has financed a project for the restoration of five *kullas*, implemented by the Swedish Cultural Heritage Without Borders. Work on mosques in Peja and Gjakove is being carried out respectively by Intersos and by the Packard Foundation (United States). The first two phases in the restoration of the Emin Giku complex in Pristina have been implemented by the European Agency for Reconstruction in partnership with PSF-France and the Museum of Kosovo. Such programmes are now mainly carried out in association with local institutes.

There is a need, however, to create some centralisation of knowledge and authority so that the international agencies and the national and local institutes know what is happening and where the responsibilities lie. Such co-ordination, ideally carried out by the Ministry of Culture, will be very necessary as interventions increase, if confusion is to be avoided, proper priorities established, donors encouraged and works monitored. It has been suggested that donor interventions should be licensed to give a formal structure to their organisation and to clarify responsibility and accountability. There is, however, a fear that such licensing might inhibit investment. The benefits could surely be made apparent to all participants since licensing would confer rights as well as responsibilities.

Documentation

There is still no complete and comprehensive access to all relevant documentation. The return of archives from Belgrade, together with museum objects, is regarded as a priority in cultural heritage management. There are, however, still considerable original archival holdings in Kosovo, as well as copies of documentation relating to historical buildings. It is anticipated that architectural and archaeological documentation will be held respectively in the National Institute for Protection and in the Museum of Kosovo, with copies in the Central Archives of Kosovo. Currently, it is thought that documents go into the archives too quickly, beyond the easy reach of professionals, underlining the fact that access to documentation is not yet seen as a public right.

Although there are experts in archives and in monuments, a central database for cultural heritage documentation is needed, with a trained staff for entering and maintaining records. Until the holdings can be regularised and documented, they will continue to be difficult to access, and there is certainly some way to go before documentation is fully in the public domain.

Documentation on maps is not up to date and land registers are incomplete, a situation which will cause problems in determining ownership rights. However, it should be noted that the UN HABITAT agency was engaged in developing cadastral maps which would certainly assist the process of ownership verification in urban areas at least. The state of completion of this project is not clear but potentially it has a critical part to play in the protection of monuments: some have been destroyed, in fact, because their ownership was not known.

Following the joint Council of Europe and European Commission initiatives in 2000, in which rapid recording projects according to European Core Data Standards were carried out in Pristina, Peja and Prizren, the latter reinforced by a travelling exhibition of photographs, work on identification of historical buildings has continued. Five institutes have been engaged in field work. The results will be checked against existing lists. It is believed that since the data collected in the field includes risk and damage assessment, it ought to be possible to develop a potential priority list as soon as all the material is entered onto the database. It is anticipated that this work will lead to the identification of approximately 2 000 monuments. There is no equivalent programme for archaeology: the institute remains to be reformed, with divisions directed from one central institute: after reorganisation, new programmes of identification will be developed.

It should be noted that the Central Inventory of Immovable Cultural Property, held in Belgrade, is not compiled according to Core Data Standards, having been begun before its introduction. Work on this inventory is said to be continuing despite the difficulties of access to sites.

Ethnicity and community

Kosovo has a diverse society with a number of cultural, religious and ethnic communities. The majority of the population is Albanian, with a variegated culture and mainly Muslim belief. There is also a Serbian community belonging to the Orthodox Christian religion. Other communities include Turks, Bosnians, Roma and Ashkalies. All, in theory, are able to be involved in programmes in the cultural heritage. In practice, however, this is not so straightforward – it is very difficult to engage experts from one community in projects from another, as the UNESCO report has noted. Mnemosyne has noted that Serbian experts are denied access to the enclaves and Kosovo Albanians have noted the impossibility of access to Orthodox monuments. In some particular cases, even officially authorised persons have difficulty in gaining access to certain classes of monument. These are early days on the road to normalisation and the situation, with respect to security and movement, is improving step by step.

The historical divisions between communities have contributed to a reluctance to be considerate of the cultural heritage of others: a reluctance to embrace cultural diversity. This is not for lack of knowledge about what is important to others. It is clear that the cultural heritage targets during and immediately after the recent war were not randomly chosen. Before 1999, some unsuccessful attempts were made to mix ethnic groups in order to improve relations. For specific projects it is obviously desirable to ensure that such a mix is achieved and that a range of people of different ethnicities become involved in the decision-making process: without such a mix, the process itself may be compromised.

Education is perhaps the key to achieving a greater degree of mutual understanding and respect between communities. Although the official institutions and organisations are not yet involved in education in Kosovo, there is an intention within the heritage profession to collaborate with the educational authorities in order to arrange participation in seminars and workshops. This will increase understanding of the fundamental importance of the cultural heritage and, it is hoped, will help to bridge gaps between ethnic groups. Communication of the benefits and challenges of cultural diversity may also be attempted through exhibitions, publications, brochures and the media.

6. Montenegro

Historical context

Montenegro, with an area of 13 812 sq. km, is composed of mountains and high plains in the north, high hills and valleys in the central area and the coast with the steep mountain slopes of Lovcen, Orjen and Rumija. Mountain, continental and Mediterranean climates can all be found in this relatively small area. The combination of the mountain and Mediterranean climates was suitable for the emergence of rare and endemic species of flora and fauna as well as other valuable natural heritage.

Durmitor, rising to 2 522 metres above sea level, is the highest mountain; the Tara River, with its 1 300-metre deep canyon, is the deepest river; and the Skadar Lake, with an area of 391 sq. km, is the biggest lake in Montenegro.

The coast is 293 km long and includes the famous Bay of Kotor, where water is transparent to a depth of 38-56 metres. This area is also famous for having 240 sunny days during the year.

Montenegro is a country of great specific qualities and contrasts, in which traditional values and heritage were always respected and they served as a basis for human life and culture.

There are four national parks in Montenegro: Durmitor, Lovcen, Skadar Lake and Biogradska gora, and two regions are included in the UNESCO World Heritage List (the regions of Kotor and Durmitor).

In 1979, a disastrous earthquake hit Montenegro and destroyed or damaged a huge part of the architectural heritage. Nevertheless, the earthquake gave a strong impetus to research, re-evaluation and renewal of the cultural heritage. To this end, significant material, technical and expert assistance was received from the former Socialist Federal Republic of Yugoslavia and abroad, particularly from UNESCO, enabling restoration of a significant part of the architectural heritage, using new methods and technologies.

Relatively well-preserved conditions and untouched natural environment represent development potential for all types of tourism, which is the main industry in Montenegro.

Heritage

The history of Montenegro is marked by century-long struggles for predominance in this region. Its geographical position at the crossroads of diverse civilisations created the conditions for the emergence of unique cultural and artistic expression, which contains elements of numerous significant cultural movements, resulting in a rich and diverse heritage. In the territory of Montenegro, five civilisation cycles are interwoven – Byzantine, Roman, Islamic, Venetian and Austro-Hungarian – which left significant cultural monuments in their respective historical course.

The main architectural ensembles are urban ensembles and the ancient towns of Kotor, Cetinje, Budva, Ulcinj, Bar and Herceg-Novi. These ensembles contain the largest number of individual cultural monuments. The main archaeological sites are Crvena Stjena (Red Rock) near Niksic, Duklja (the ancient city of Doclea) in Podgorica, Municipium near Pljevlja, and Risinium (Risan).

However, this rich Montenegrin heritage (both movable and immovable) is in imminent danger due to uncontrolled urbanisation, infrastructural and industrial development and lack of an integrated and co-ordinated approach in the protection and planning system. However, the movable property belonging to sacred and secular monuments (paintings, icons, books) is facing an even greater threat.

There is a national inventory, which is incorporated into the Central Registry in the Institute in Cetinje. It essentially contains the basic characteristics of all monuments recorded in the Central Register and also includes ensembles. It is necessary to compare it with European standards and make the relevant adjustments. The inventory is currently being revised but the documentation is not in electronic form (e.g. geographical information systems – GIS) and there is no clear classification of the ensembles protected in the Land Registry.

In Montenegro, there are 357 immovable cultural monuments protected under the law and divided according to structure as follows:

- old towns and urban ensembles (14);
- archaeological sites (42);
- fortifications (18);
- traditional architecture facilities (12);
- profane facilities (76);
- sacral facilities (195).

According to the current law, a monument designated as cultural heritage must incorporate various values – archaeological, artistic, historical, ethnological, architectural, urban, social and technical – that are important for the history and culture of Montenegro.

Depending on their importance, cultural monuments are divided into three categories:

- major cultural monuments (class 1);
- very important cultural monuments (class 2);
- important cultural monuments (class 3).

Monastery of Cetinje (Ministry of Culture and Media of Montenegro)

Political strategy

As far as the built heritage is concerned, the institutions responsible for its protection have short-term plans and programmes. However, there is neither a specific management system nor a strategic document whereby the concept of the national cultural policy could be defined. It was only ten years ago that the Ministry of Culture was established in Montenegro, and it is possibly the main stakeholder in the elaboration of a strategy and action plan for the cultural development of the country.

Defining the cultural policy of Montenegro commenced in 2003 within the framework of the review of national cultural policies undertaken as part of the Council of Europe MOSAIC II project. The following activities have been completed so far within the framework of this project:

- the "National Report on the Cultural Policies of the Republic of Montenegro" (September 2003);
- presentation of the National Report before the Council of Europe Supervision Committee for Culture (March 2004);
- review and report of the Council of Europe Expert Team (May 2004);
- national debate on "Cultural Policy" (June 2004).

The national report on cultural policies clearly shows that existing legal regulations, which are mainly outdated and inapplicable, must be replaced by new regulations that are harmonised with international standards. A national cultural programme must be founded on governmental strategic documents such as the Strategy for Economic Development, the spatial plan, the national programme for university education, financial and fiscal policy or similar.

The report also indicates the need for permanent re-education and further training of professional staff, particularly because of the fact that Montenegro offers no possibility for specific professional education (such as archaeology, ethnology, anthropology, art history, conservation, restoration, etc.). The concept of education in the field of cultural and natural heritage protection has not been sufficiently developed so far at any levels of the educational system, particularly with respect to an integrated approach to this issue.

Priority should be given to the establishment of a new inventory of cultural monuments and the creation of an appropriate database. At the same time, particular attention should be paid to sacred monuments, the victims of a poor conservation policy and an insufficient level of understanding and co-operation between religious organisations and national institutions. One of the main weaknesses is the lack of integrated protection for built heritage, cultural landscapes and natural environment. With regard to the urban planning process and the construction of new buildings, there is a clear lack of synchronisation and co-ordination between the players involved, which is to the detriment of the built heritage.

The Council of Europe team of experts, who visited the Ministry of Culture and cultural institutions of the Republic of Montenegro, reviewed the national report and found that it had been well prepared. Some comments were made concerning the lack of statistical data, insufficient transparency and untimely participation of relevant stakeholders in the cultural field during the drafting of the report.

A national debate on the cultural policy of Montenegro was held in Podgorica on 24 and 25 June 2004, which included representatives of the government and ministries of the Republic of Montenegro, cultural institutions, local management, NGOs and local and Council of Europe experts. The main topics of the debate were issues related to cultural policy and transition of the cultural institutions, as well as culture in general under market economy conditions. Inadequate inter-ministerial co-operation, insufficient allocation of funds for the cultural field and unsatisfactory commitment to development of international co-operation and cultural tourism were highlighted as the main problems.

The protection and presentation of cultural and natural heritage must be seen to be integrated, in accordance with the approach of international organisations, in particular the Council of Europe. In this field, joint activities must be undertaken by various ministries – those responsible for culture, tourism, environmental protection and spatial development – as well as national institutions in the field of culture and local management and NGOs. Cultural and natural heritage must be fully integrated into the planning systems at all levels, which has not been the practice so far. The spatial plan of Montenegro, which is the most important planning document and is currently in the process of being drafted, lacks an adequate basis and structure, starting from relevant basic studies to a spatial protection plan, and it may serve as a drastic example of this. At the moment, Montenegro is hardly in a position to consider establishing elementary links between heritage management and mechanisms for urban and spatial planning, let alone vetoing development plans from the cultural heritage point of view.

Since cultural tourism is one of the priorities of the Montenegrin Government, it is important that tourism respects cultural heritage in a sustainable manner.

Inter-ministerial co-operation has increasingly been a basic means of communication between and within governments. Different ministries, public institutions, civil society and the business sector should work together in order to promote culture and cultural values.

It was noted that the national debate should provide the basis for drafting an adequate platform for achieving a strategic approach to culture and its integration into the scientific, educational, tourism, urban planning and other systems.

Legislation

Current situation

The oldest sources of legislation related to cultural monuments in Montenegro come from the Middle Ages, while the contemporary practice, care and treatment of cultural heritage were launched in the second half of the 19th century.

Legal provisions that constitute the legal framework for the protection of cultural and natural heritage and for the functioning of the cultural institutions in this field were established over the last three decades of the 20th century, while certain activities, such as underwater archaeology, have not been adequately regulated.

Protection of the cultural heritage is currently regulated under the following legal acts:

- the Law on the Protection of Cultural Monuments (1991);
- the Law on Museum Activity (1977, 1989);
- the Law on Library Activity (1977, 1989);
- the Law on Archive Activity (1991, 1994);
- the Law on the Renewal and Revitalisation of Old Towns Affected by the Disastrous Earthquake of 15 April 1979 (1984, 1986);
- the Law on the Restoration of the Monumental Region of Kotor (1991);
- the Law on Monuments, Memorials, Historical Events and Persons (1971, 1972, 1988).

The Law on the Protection of Cultural Monuments (1991) contains definitions of specific aspects, such as the definition of the protection of cultural monuments, definitions of what constitutes a cultural monument, the criteria according to which a monument may be designated as cultural, and a description of ways of assessing monuments, for example according to categories of importance.

Although the basic conditions for protection exist, some examples show that there is a lack of consistency in implementing the law.

New draft laws

The drafting of a set of new laws in the field of cultural heritage is currently underway, such as:

- the Law on Cultural Property;
- the Law on Museums;
- the Law on Libraries;
- the Law on Archives.

The main goal of passing the new laws in this field is to correct shortages of existing legal solutions in each area and to ensure the establishment of a modern system for protection and revitalisation of cultural heritage in accordance with European standards and principles.

It is necessary, therefore, to create prerequisites for overall protection and regeneration of Montenegrin heritage as soon as possible, by introducing adequate provisions for an integrated conservation system, not only in laws related to protection but also in other relevant legal acts.

Institutions

A protection service formally became operative in 1948, when the Institute for Protection of Cultural Monuments and Natural Rarities was established in Cetinje, which has now developed into the Republic Institute for the Protection of Cultural Monuments.

In accordance with the UNESCO Convention concerning the Protection of the World Cultural and Natural Heritage (World Heritage Convention – 1972), after the region of Kotor had been included in the World Heritage List, the Municipal Institute for Protection of Cultural Monuments in Kotor was founded in 1979. In 1992, due to the significant concentration and importance of cultural monuments in the region of Kotor, Tivat and Herceg Novi, this was developed into the Regional Institute for the Protection of Cultural Monuments.

The Centre for Archaeological Research deals with the conservation of archaeological sites and artefacts, while a number of museums both at local and republic level are responsible for the protection of movable cultural property.

The Republic Institute for the Protection of Nature, which was founded in 1961, and the Natural History Museum of Montenegro, founded in 1995 are responsible for the protection of the natural heritage in Montenegro.

The Ministry of Culture and the Media (which includes the three institutes mentioned above) is the highest level agency in the field of protection of cultural and natural heritage in Montenegro. It sets the guidelines, manages and co-ordinates the overall system for the protection of cultural and natural heritage. This responsibility includes the sacred monuments, which make up 60% of the protected heritage.

Institutions for the protection of nature are under the competencies of this ministry, but also within the competencies of the Ministry for Environmental Protection and Spatial Development.

The professional competency of the national institutions is satisfactory. However, there is a lack of people with certain specialised skills in specific fields (architects, archaeologists, art historians).

The official institutes and organisations that play a role in the protection of the historical heritage are involved with various exhibitions and publications, provide the public with definitions of historical buildings and participate indirectly in the educational process.

There are also regular contacts and joint activities with the Institute for the Protection of the Built Heritage and partner organisations, such as museums, universities and archives. This is reflected particularly well in the joint promotion of the cultural heritage through exhibitions, publications and so forth. For many years now, students, structural engineers and, in particular, architects have been able to find temporary employment or work experience in this way.

Co-operation projects with other partners in the field of the built heritage are frequently carried out. The Regional Institute for the Protection of Cultural Monuments is working on cleaning the Kotor Fortress in co-operation with the Employment Bureau and the Kotor local town planning office. Similar projects for the fortresses of Herceg Novi are also about to be launched.

Link with environment, spatial and urban planning

One of the prerequisites for establishing connections and ensuring an integrated approach for protection has been created for the first time, on the basis of changes in the system of the Ministry of Culture and the Media, according to which the Department for Cultural Heritage was replaced by a newly established Sector for Cultural and Natural Heritage.

At the same time, according to this new system at the Regional Institute for Protection of Cultural Monuments, a special organisational unit was established for the first time for the purpose of protecting cultural heritage in Montenegro, and this, besides the architectural heritage, is also responsible for the protection of the cultural landscape and environment, following UNESCO recommendations.

Given the low level of awareness in this field and the beginnings of an integrated institutional approach to conservation, heritage is insufficiently integrated into urban and spatial planning systems, and is considered as a restraining factor rather than a developmental one. Heritage is disregarded or destroyed in practice rather than regenerated. This is particularly the case in so-called "contact zones", in both close and more distant protected areas which surround registered monuments and ensembles. The relationships between heritage and urban planning institutions are established through municipal agencies, which is impractical as these agencies have few skills in the heritage field. In the last few years, instances of failure to respect legal procedures have been recorded in the case of reconstruction work on cultural monuments.

An even more unfavourable situation is in the field of protection and management of the "landscape", even in cases where it is tightly connected with immovable heritage as well as within wider ensembles which are protected, not only under national legislation, but also under international charters and conventions (for example regions included in the UNESCO World Heritage List).

Financing

The renovation of historical buildings is mainly funded from the budget of the Montenegrin Ministry of Culture. The institutions responsible for the protection of the built heritage play a very important role in channelling the funds allocated by the Ministry of Culture in this area. Control of the financial resources is the same for both national and international funding. In certain cases, funding controls are more complex (for instance, the obligation to announce the public funding process on the website). The restoration of a private building is usually funded by the owner of the property.

As far as international partnerships are concerned, mechanisms for discussing, approving and assessing proposed works were established following the 1979 earthquake. These mechanisms take the form of missions organised by the UNESCO consultancy agencies (e.g. International Centre for the Study of the Preservation and Restoration of Cultural Property – ICCROM, ICOMOS) and student camps. After a long break this co-operation is currently being renewed.

Funding by international organisations has recently been used for the implementation of the UNESCO Participation Programme for 2002-2003, which involved the funding of studies and the revitalisation of the Kotor Fortress, and with a project supported by the American Embassy in Serbia and Montenegro to renovate part of the fortress.

There are also several projects in the pipeline, such as the equipping of the architectural workshop and construction unit of the Regional Institute for the Protection of Cultural Monuments, the Cultural Grassroots of Japan project and two partner projects with the UNIADRON organisation and the University of Bologna (education in the conservation and renovation of the Kotor Fortress).

Documentation

The Institute for the Protection of Cultural Monuments and the Centre for Archaeological Research are responsible for documentation.

Virtually all documentation is available for public consultation, but the information is neither indexed nor retrievable electronically. It is generally possible to access planning information and expertise that could influence the prioritisation of buildings and sites. The institutions responsible for the protection of the built heritage possess adequate photographic equipment.

As far as staff trained in documentation is concerned, there are professionals in the national institutions, but there is little expertise at the local level and it could be supplemented by means of a national initiative. There are experts in particular building types who can be called upon to assist. At the same time, representatives of different ethnic communities can be involved in the programme. Structural expertise is available to enable damage and repair costs to be assessed.

Ethnicity and community

Several national communities exist in Montenegro: Bosnian Muslims, Albanians, Croats and Roma. There is a governmental representative for national minorities: the Republic of Montenegro Ministry for the Protection of Minority Rights. Several NGOs operate in the country, their main purpose being the presentation and promotion of the culture and cultural heritage of the Bosnian Muslims. The Croat community also has its own NGOs and cultural associations, which actively co-operate with the state institutions.

7. Romania

Historical context

Romania is the largest Balkan country extending from Hungary and the former Yugoslavia in the west to the Black Sea in the east, from Ukraine and Moldova in the north to Bulgaria in the south. The Danube River runs through Romania and its 2 850 km course passes through nine countries.

Ancient Romania was inhabited by Thracian tribes, the so-called Geto-Dacian people. From the 7th century BC the Greeks established trading colonies along the Black Sea. In the 1st century BC, a Dacian state was established to counter the Roman threat, but ultimately Dacia became a province of the Roman Empire.

Faced with Goth attacks in AD 271, Emperor Aurelian withdrew the Roman legions south of the Danube, but the Romanised Vlach peasants remained in Dacia – hence the formation of the Romanian people. Goths, Huns, Avars, Slavs, Bulgars and Magyars swept across this territory from the 4th to the 10th centuries. Small Romanian state formations emerged, first as *cnezats* (clusters of villages) and later as *voievodats* (princely states) and țari (literally "land"). This led to the formation of the principalities of Moldavia, Wallachia and Transylvania.

Throughout the 14th and 15th centuries, the Romanian principalities of Wallachia and Moldavia offered strong resistance to the northward Ottoman expansion. When the Turks conquered Hungary in the 16th century, Transylvania became a vassal of the Ottoman Empire. After the Ottoman victory in Transylvania, Wallachia and Moldavia also paid tribute to the Turks. In 1600, the three Romanian states were briefly united but this union lasted only one year.

The 18th century marked the start of the Transylvanian Romanians fight for political emancipation – Turkish control persisted in Wallachia and the rest of Moldavia well into the 19th century, but following the national uprising of 1821, native princes were returned to the Wallachian and Moldavian thrones.

The revolution of 1848 in Wallachia, Moldavia and Transylvania was unsuccessful but it gave impetus to a growing national monument that culminated in the creation of the national state of Romania in 1859, with full independence recognised in 1878. The defeat of Austria-Hungary in 1918 paved the way for the formation of modern Romania: at the end of the First World War, the country more than doubled its territory (from 120 000 sq.km to 295 000 sq.km) and its population (from 7.5 to 16 million).

Romania joined Hitler's anti-Soviet war in 1941 but changed sides on 23 August 1944, declaring war on Nazi Germany, thereby salvaging national independence. The Romanian monarchy was abolished in 1947 and the Romanian Peoples' Republic proclaimed. Romania's loyalty to Moscow continued until the late 1950s but after 1960 an independent foreign policy was adopted.

In 1989, the Romanian revolution took place after the collapse of one communist regime after another in Europe. The National Salvation Front (FSN) took immediate control of the country. In May 1990, it won the country's first democratic elections. Romania became a full member of the EU in 2007.

Heritage

Romania has a wealth of monuments from all periods since Neolithic times onwards. In the first half of the third millennium BC, the country formed part of a homogeneous region with Bulgaria, Thrace and Ukraine. This so-called "Black Earth Culture" is distinguished by remarkable painted pottery of high artistic quality in design and shape, which is thought to have oriental affinities with regions as far as Turkistan and China, where similar pottery is found.

This culture came to an abrupt end about 2000 BC with the coming of the Bronze Age, an era of great artistic merit, with some of the finest products of the European Bronze Age in gold and bronze coming from Transylvania. The Romanian Bronze Age continued until the 8th century when devastating invasions from Scythia came from the north-east: Scythian graves may be found in Transylvania and in Wallachia.

Hellenic penetration was marked but never comprehensive, although there is considerable archaeological evidence. There is a plethora of Roman remains. Trajan's Wall can be traced without difficulty between Constanta and the Danube, near Cernavoda. The most impressive of all the Roman monuments is the *Tropaeum Traiani* at Adamclisi. It stands in a wild and desolate region in the rolling steppes between the Danube and Constanta with all of its original sculptured decoration lying in the special local museum.

Post-Roman remains of the time before the Romanians came under the influence of Byzantium are rare, but the great gold treasure of Pietroasa is certainly of Germanic origin.

Byzantine remains are only of moderate importance in Dobogea and Oltenia until the 14th century when the Byzantine church and monastery of Curtea de Argeş was probably built. The frescoes here rank as the finest and oldest Byzantine works of art in the country. A special architectural style grew up after this, particularly in Moldavia, based upon a synthesis between Byzantine and Gothic elements, of a very marked character and great beauty and which flourished mostly in the 15th, 16th and early 17th centuries. The church of the "Three Hierarchs" at Iaşi, founded in 1639, is one of the finest examples of the Romanian Style.

In modern times, Romania presents a panorama of artistic activities in different fields. The National School of Architecture was founded by the architect Ion Mincu, followed by a large number of remarkable architects who tried to combine the local, mediaeval tradition with contemporary tendencies.

After the First World War, the main architectural creations caught up with the European tendencies. The 1980s represent a significant moment for Romanian urbanism, especially in Bucharest, where a large number of buildings were demolished and enormous avenues and megalomaniac buildings were constructed. However, a lot of harmonious churches, houses and other historic buildings remained in Bucharest.

Inventory and protection

The current situation of the protection and preservation of the cultural heritage appears to be characterised by a rather complicated system of organisms and interventions. Concerning cultural heritage categories (types) the Romanian laws distinguish between historical monuments, archaeology and movable heritage. Inventory systems record these three different types of protected items through the Historical Monuments List, the National Archaeological Repertory and the Register of the Listed Movable Heritage. The three standards used are:

- the Core Data Index to Historic Buildings and Monuments of the Architectural Heritage;
- the International Core Data Standard for Archaeological Sites and Monuments;
- the Data Standard for Identifying Cultural Objects – Object ID.

The elaboration of the Historical Monuments List and the Analytic Inventory Files have been standardised under Law No. 422 regarding the protection of the historical monuments and the Decree of the Minister of Culture and Religious Affairs No. 2682 regarding the methodological norm.

The Historical Monuments List was approved through the Minister of Culture and Religious Affairs Order No. 2314/2004 (July 8), and published in the *Official Monitor of Romania*. The Historical Monuments List is the first official list published.

According to current legislation, the structure of the Historical Monuments List has five types of categories:

1. archaeology
2. architecture
3. public forum monuments
4. memorial-funeral monuments
5. ensembles (urban/rural).

These five categories are subdivided into two categories concerning significance:
1. national or international significance
2. regional and local significance.

The monuments, ensembles and sites are categorised according to age, chronology and architectural, artistic, urban, archaeological, memorial and symbolic value.

The list contains 29 435 historical monuments with protected areas: 9 585 archaeological monuments, 17 708 architectural monuments, 678 public forum monuments and 1 464 memorial-funeral monuments.

Out of the 29 435 historical monuments, 6 640 historical monuments are in the first category, having national or international significance.

Out of the 29 435 historical monuments, 25% require urgent intervention for their preservation and consolidation. The necessary budgetary requirements would not even be covered by a government willing to become involved in protection of such cultural patrimony.

The inventory of historical monuments of the World Heritage List is realised in accordance with the provisions of Law No. 564 and Governmental Ordinance No. 47/2000, regarding measures of protection of the historical monuments on the World Heritage List.

The pursuance and elaboration of the Protection and Management Plans of the Historical Monuments inscribed on the World Heritage List have been standardised under Governmental Decision No. 493/2004 (4 January). The most important of the sites, ensembles and historical monuments are inscribed on the World Heritage List. Romania has six items on this list containing 30 objectives.

The inventory is subject to monitoring as follows:
- by the World Heritage Committee of UNESCO, every five years;
- by public and local administration authorities, in two stages:
  - the assessment of the state of conservation, twice yearly;
  - the plan of measures which need to be taken as a conclusion of the assessment report, part of the annual plan for protection and management.

This inventory contains the following items:
- periodic reviews, twice a year, and exceptional reviews, both for the historical monuments and their protection zone, and for the protection area;
- the development of the inventory folder through special files;
- the development of a database and its management;
- the measures plans which establish terms, responsibilities and financial resources to solve any problems.

With regard to the development of the database and its management, the National Institute for Historical Monuments initiated an inventory programme, which contains the following elements:

- a travel programme – to establish the state of conservation of the monuments;
- a communication programme – with the Directorates for Culture, Cults and National Cultural Heritage, the county councils and the public and local administrations, which includes the identification of people responsible and actions accomplished until now;
- a minimal file for the groups of the historical monuments on the World Heritage List;
- a digital database – for data collection;
- studies: pre-feasibility, feasibility, architectural and historical, cultural and tourism – for ensembles and settlements;
- dissemination of the information – symposiums, exhibitions, website, CD and suchlike.

Political strategy

The country is in a state of transition following the passing of communism. Romanians want, however, to make a fresh start and to find the right method of protection in a country which has suffered so many illegal and catastrophic interventions in historical buildings and areas.

Romania has a rich heritage which is greatly in need of enhanced support. The main needs are finance and the training of a new generation of staff to work on the documentation of the cultural heritage and on its restoration. There is a shortage of craft skills as crafts have given way to ordinary building work. A permanent institution for training in conservation is required. Work in the field of historical monuments needs workers who are qualified in the specific technicalities and technologies of restoration and people with experience in traditional crafts.

Education of the wider public in the importance of the heritage is also desirable in order to enlist public support for the common Romanian heritage. Although there are exhibitions and publications, there is no systematic approach to the promotion of the cultural heritage.

The relationships between ministries with overlapping responsibilities are perhaps in need of review, as well as the general heritage management system, which is characterised by its complication and apparent duplication of activities. A strategic management plan would be helpful in determining the way forward.

Legislation

Three different laws from 2001 cover the field of heritage:
- Law No. 422 on Historical Monuments;
- Law No. 378 on the Archaeological Heritage;
- Law No. 564 on the Monuments Inscribed on the World Heritage List.

The three laws are complemented by governmental decisions and ordinances of the Ministry of Culture and religious affairs decrees.

Romania has signed and ratified the international and European conventions but in fact the Romanian legislation does not adopt the exact terms expressed in these conventions. For this reason, Laws Nos. 422 and 378 are undergoing revision, following Council of Europe guidelines.

Law No. 422, regarding the protection of the historical monuments, has the following structure:

- Part I – General dispositions
- Part II – The protection of the historical monuments:
    - Chapter I: Historical monuments
    - Chapter II: Inventory and rating of the historical monuments
    - Chapter III: Interventions on the historical monuments
- Part III – Institutions and speciality bodies with responsibility for protection of historical monuments
    - Chapter I: Institutions
    - Chapter II: Speciality bodies
- Part IV – Responsibilities of the historical monuments owner and of the authorities of public and local administration
    - Chapter I: Obligations and rights of the historical monuments owner
    - Chapter II: Attributions of the authorities of public and local administration
- Part V – Finance of the protection of the historical monuments
- Part VI – Sanctions
- Part VII – Transitory and final.

The term "historic monument" is used for all items protected according to the Granada Convention: monuments, ensembles (groups of buildings) and sites. So, the law allows the possibility of applying historic monument status to entire areas of towns and villages.

These categories are naturally overlapping. That is why the focus is on viewing the monumental architectural heritage in relation to the wider aspects of local and regional distinctiveness as well as national considerations, to the vernacular, to the spirit of regional community and identity and its potential as a living heritage. The law brings Romania closer to a sustainable approach rather than to a museum approach for public observation or for scientific investigation.

Two other laws complete this legislation:
- Law No. 182/2000 for the Protection of the Movable Heritage;
- Law No. 311/2003 for the Organisation of the Museum System.

Work is in progress for laws on the intangible heritage, on the technical heritage and on cultural landscapes in line with the European Landscape Convention, 2000 (ETS No. 176 – Florence Convention) considering the relationship between the man-made heritage and the natural heritage in an integrated development process.

The heritage legislation is currently available in the Romanian language only.

Link with spatial and urban planning

In recent years, a co-operation protocol was established between the Ministry of Culture and Religious Affairs and the Ministry of Transport, Construction and Tourism, concerning the problems regarding urbanism and the protected areas. No solution has so far been found to the problem of illegal building and construction although Law No. 422 includes provisions against illegal construction and illegal demolition.

Institutions

The public authorities engaged in the protection of monuments are:
- the Ministry of Culture and Religious Affairs at central level and through the Directorates of Culture, Religious Affairs and National Cultural Heritage in different counties at decentralised level;
- the National Institute for Historical Monuments;
- the National Office for Historical Monuments;
- national museums;
- different religious cults.

The complexity of legislation influences the administrative structure of the cultural heritage. This complexity and decentralisation in the Ministry of Culture and Religious Affairs can be demonstrated by its structure:

The Ministry of Culture and Religious Affairs is structured as follows:

1. the Directorate of Historical Monuments and Museums;
2. the Directorate of Culture, Religious Affairs and National Cultural Heritage.

Subordinate to the Ministry of Culture and Religious Affairs are:

3. the National Institute of Historical Monuments;
4. the National Office for Historical Monuments.

The scientific organisations with a consultative role in addition to the Ministry of Culture and Religious Affairs are:

5. the National Commission of Historical Monuments;
6. four sub-commissions;
7. eight regional commissions;
8. the National Commission for Archaeology.

A special programme of management for World Heritage Sites is currently being developed: it is hoped that this will help in the protection and management of the heritage overall.

It is obvious that the current personnel – scientific and other – are not sufficient to cover the existing needs for intervention in the cultural heritage as well as to ensure the co-operation of all the above bodies.

There is co-operation between the ministries and the public scientific bodies (universities, museums and institutes of the academy) in research and practical projects, such as the revitalisation of certain villages and towns.

Financing

The state is the main source of finance for all the departments and divisions. Other sources are not excluded, but they need support and stimulation, especially the private sector which would benefit from being given financial and other incentives.

There is no established mechanism for dealing with international partnerships; however, successful intervention has been carried out with the assistance of the World Bank, the World Monuments Fund, a UNESCO/Japanese trust fund and French cities, among others, and there is currently a proposal for assistance with monuments in northern Moldavia in association with an Italo-Romanian association.

Documentation

The multilateral structure of legislation and administration is apparent in the scientific bodies which are involved in the documentation of the heritage. Three different bodies at various levels are involved in the matter:

1. the National Institute for Historical Monuments;
2. the Directorate of Culture, Religious Affairs and National Cultural Heritage;
3. the specialised institutes of the Romanian Academy.

The material is partially accessible to the public, but it is more useful for academic research. An electronic general archive of monuments is not yet available although efforts are being made in this direction.

The inventory is primarily for the purpose of protection but it is also used for academic research by students and for publications and promotion in the media. It mainly follows the Council of Europe Core Data Index to Historic Buildings and Monuments of the Architectural Heritage. It includes ensembles (monumental, territorial and infrastructural) as well as individual buildings or sites.

The existing documentation will enable a first general overview of information on priorities. Although the emphasis will be on major, single monuments, local specialists and co-ordination among the various ethnic groups may help to supplement this information in order to achieve well-balanced results in identifying urgent cases for intervention.

The Great Synagogue (Council of Europe)

Ethnicity and community

Romania has a mixed population of 22.4 million. There are a large number of ethnic and religious groups. The great majority is Romanian (89.47%) but there are also small minorities: Hungarians (7.1%), Roma (Gypsies) (1.8%), Germans (0.5%), Ukrainians (0.3%) and others, in a lesser proportion (under 0.2%). Other nationalities include Croats, Serbs, and Turks, contributing to a truly multi-ethnic society. Romanians consider themselves the direct heirs of ancient Rome. The ethnic diversity is also reflected in the religious mix (and freedom of worship) within Romania: Romanian Orthodox (86%), Roman Catholic (5%), Protestant (3.5%), Uniate (1%), Muslim (0.3%) and Jewish (0.2%).

There is no apparent difficulty in achieving harmonious co-operation between all groups in the maintenance of the cultural heritage. The first criterion for protection is the value of the monument; ethnicity or religious criteria are secondary. In the annual programmes of assessment and protection, a conscious effort is made to ensure proportionate procedures – this is being monitored.

There are no security problems concerning access to the buildings of certain communities but there are restrictions to access to buildings in the care of the state.

8. Serbia

Historical context

Serbia is located in the Balkan Peninsula and extends from the Drina river (the border with Bosnia and Herzegovina) in the west, to Bulgaria and Romania in the east, from Hungary in the north to the Sar Planina Mountains and north-eastern Albania in the south-west, and to the autonomous region of Kosovo-Metohija and "the former Yugoslav Republic of Macedonia" in the south.

Demographically, Serbia is a country with a mixed population (Serbs 66%, Albanians 17%, Hungarians 3.5%, Bosnians 2.5%, etc.).

The cultural history of Serbia is long and complex, starting from the seventh millennium BC with Mesolithic communities of hunters and fishermen and human settlements of later periods. Archaeology has revealed architectural and monumental sculptural evidence from the Lepenski Vir Culture (about 7000 BC). There are remains (clay figurines, vases, etc.) from the Early Neolithic (the Starcevo Culture, about 5500-4500 BC) and the Late Neolithic eras (the Vinca Culture, about 4500-3200 BC).

Following the decline of the Vinca Culture, new populations coming from the east and north-east became established. There is evidence of the Vatin Culture, around 1600 BC, with characteristic artefacts of antler, bone, bronze and gold.

The earliest identifiable inhabitants of Serbia were the Illyrians, followed by the Celts, who arrived in the 4th century BC. The Roman conquest began in the 3rd century, extending under Augustus as far as Singidunum (Belgrade): roads and bridges were constructed and fortifications and imperial palaces built. In AD 395, Theodosius I divided the empire and what is now Serbia passed to the Byzantine Empire.

In 879 Serbia adopted the Christian Orthodox religion. There are numerous preserved churches from the 12th to the 14th century. The 13th century, following the establishment of the Serbian kingdom in 1217, was crucial to the development of Serbian architecture in which an internal Byzantine spatial pattern was married to an external Romanesque form, apparent in many important churches which are distinguished also by the quality of their wall paintings and icons. This period is characterised also by its military architecture and fortifications.

The kingdom lasted until the Ottoman takeover of 1459 which saw the introduction of Islamic culture and the building of important mosques, hammams, stone bridges, covered markets and residential buildings.

The 18th century was a particularly significant period for Serbian art and architecture. Two migrations (1690-1739) of Serbs took place into the regions north of the Sava and

Danube rivers, on the southern border of the Habsburg Monarchy. Caught between two empires (Turkish and Austro-Hungarian) the Serbs developed a national culture full of contradictions. The Serbian people living under Austrian rule experienced rapid development of their middle class and were easily converted to the Catholic faith and the urban architectural Baroque style.

Historicism (Serbian-Byzantine style) followed at the end of the 19th century, then secession and modernism in turn. After the Second World War, the aesthetic of socialist realism flourished in the architectural production of this period. Contemporary architecture is characterised by the influence of post-modernism.

Heritage

The richness, diversity and multicultural nature of Serbian architectural and archaeological heritage may be summarised as follows:

- there are monuments of various ethnic groups (predominantly Serbs, but also Albanians, Hungarians, Croats, Slovaks, Romanians and Bulgarians) as well as various religious and confessional categories (Christians – Orthodox, Catholic or Uniate –, Muslims and Jews);
- there are archaeological sites and ruins from many chronological phases (Neolithic, Roman Antiquity, Mediaeval, and Byzantine/Turkish). The sacral architecture is rich, meaningful and important (Christian churches, mosques, synagogues, etc.);
- there are many kinds of vernacular architecture of different types in various regions;
- there is also valuable urban architecture of the 18th and 20th centuries in Belgrade and such towns as Krusevac, Smederevo and Kragujevac;
- there is a Central Inventory of Immovable Cultural Property, compiled for the purposes of heritage protection and planning as a permanent activity of the Republic Institute for the Protection of Monuments;
- there are about 3 103 single architectural monuments registered in the official archives, although it is thought that the overall number of monuments is 3 800;
- there are also a large number of archaeological sites, architectural ensembles and traditional historical settlements comprising the overall heritage in need of protection and preservation.

Political strategy

The protection and preservation of the cultural heritage in Serbia is in a transitional phase with many of the general problems well-known to many European countries as well as the specific conditions which pertain, some of which are a consequence of recent conflicts.

On the one hand, some risks are connected to the extremely acute economic crisis, which has marked all the activities of the monumental heritage protection service during the past decade. On the other hand, conditions in which protection institutions operate are still unfavourable, and there is a chronic lack of funding for planned activities and adequate protective treatment, including conditions for maintaining and using the protected heritage.

The situation with regard to the protection of archaeological sites of exceptional importance in Serbia has not changed much in recent years. The Roman town of Viminacium and the mediaeval settlement and cemetery in Celarevo are still endangered by nearby industrial plants which exploit mineral deposits (brick clay) precisely from locations where archaeological remains may be found.

Archaeological sites are endangered by treasure-hunters illegally using metal detectors. Although criminal charges may be brought against the offenders, these are still not effective in preventing this lucrative activity. After the bulldozers have passed, whole archaeological layers are irretrievably lost, while ruined buildings and disturbed archaeological layers remain in the wake of prospectors with metal detectors. The protection service is persistent in fighting to protect the rich archaeological heritage, but the prevailing economic conditions render the archaeologists powerless.

In the case of vernacular architecture, the loss of original function and the non-existence of cultural property management mechanisms are identified as very immediate dangers. Modern living conditions lead inevitably to the abandonment of traditional forms of housing, while the preservation of wooden architecture through a chain of open-air museums represents an excellent but unacceptably expensive restoration method. The only financially viable solution would be to devise new uses, which could ensure the survival and maintenance of this form of building.

Historic towns and urban areas are compromised by a lack of appreciation of their worth. Because most of this heritage dates from the 18th to the 20th century, its manifestations are not regarded as sufficiently old to focus the attention of either experts or users. Both these groups find it difficult to accept the idea that buildings which represent their everyday environment actually possess the characteristics of monuments. Though exposed to degradation processes like any other immovable cultural property, this heritage is neglected in comparison to the much older monumental heritage whose much greater age commands greater respect and is fully accepted as a responsibility of the protection service.

It is becoming more and more difficult to protect the endangered urban heritage and the preservation of its authenticity is becoming a prime professional task. Great efforts, however, are being made to find a more adequate conservationist approach to control planning and to achieve greater co-operation between the protection service and urban planning.

Significant efforts are also being made to modernise the legal and administrative systems and to define a well-conceived conservation policy. This would promote long-term conservation strategies and determine the priority of intervention on the basis of the type and degree of risk in which the heritage is found.

Re-establishment of international professional contacts and co-operation with international institutions and organisations in the conservation field is aimed at improving methodology and knowledge in this area. It also creates opportunities for expert consultation on complex professional problems.

*Kalenic, Serbia
(Mr B Šurdić, photographer)*

Legislation

Current situation

The basic legal act in the Serbian legal system related to cultural heritage is the Law on Cultural Property (Goods) adopted in 1994.

The other laws in this field are:

- the Law on the Activities of Public Interest of the Republic of Serbia in the domain of Cultural Affairs *(1992)*, which regulates the system of institutions, responsibilities and budget provisions for various cultural affairs, including protection of the cultural properties;

– the Law on Planning and Building (2001), a controversial legal instrument that is not quite coherent with the 1994 law (particularly with regard to terminology used);

– the Law on the Protection of Environment, which covers the natural heritage.

Only the Granada Convention has been ratified by Serbia and Montenegro (as part of the former Federal Republic of Yugoslavia). The adoption of the Valletta and Florence conventions is still to be undertaken.

The requirements for legislation reform in all fields, including culture and heritage protection, are clear in the period after 5 October 2000 (the breakdown of Milosevic's regime).

The common public will is clearly seen to be a desire for a new democratic society based on the principles of human rights protection, order and peace, as well as a rational organisation of the community.

In this domain, cultural rights, individual as well as collective, have to play a strong role in establishing democracy, peace, social dialogue and general order in the state.

New draft laws

Up to now, there have been three attempts to draft a new law on cultural goods:

Attempt A

Immediately after establishing a new democratic government, the working group drafting the new law on cultural goods was nominated by the Ministry of Culture, responsible for heritage affairs. It followed the form (codex), methodology and general principles of the 1994 law. A draft was finished in September 2001 and presented to the professional community and printed in a daily newspaper as a special appendix. The reaction of the public was that the text was too complicated, too long and primarily oriented to the organisation of institutional work. This is the reason why the authorities decided to try again.

Attempt B

A new working group decided to prepare an umbrella law consisting of general provisions, definition of citizens' rights and obligations, but also to organise administration and research through a set of complementary laws and legal acts. The group, dispersed and unco-ordinated, produced some incoherent texts and gave up, owing to the fall of the first democratic government. A relatively good conception, but only half done, it was completely abandoned by the new government. A part of this set, the "draft law on architectural heritage" was sent to the Legal Support Task Force (LSTF) of the Council of Europe.

Attempt C

The third attempt began in the summer of 2004. The idea was to accept a new law as soon as possible. Originally, some members of the group suggested the preparation of a draft similar to that proposed in case A above. The new text offers some improvements and should be sent to the Legal Support Task Force. It is expected that there will be several revisions and there may be some additional steps to avoid any further loss of time in "trial and error" methodology.

Institutions

The public authorities for the protection and the management of monuments are:

- the Ministry of Culture and Media;
- the Ministry for Religion and Confessions;
- the various religious authorities.

There is a clear lack of co-operation between these authorities as well as between other relevant scientific bodies.

The quality of staff and the available support varies between the different levels and departments of heritage management. There is a lack of knowledge and experience in new technology and a generation gap within the personnel. Young employees would be able to overcome the existing deficiencies in the system given funding and training. Such training would need to embrace the whole spectrum of issues: specialist heritage knowledge, documentation techniques and general management skills.

There are particular deficiencies in professional training opportunities – there is a lack of post-graduate courses in conservation, for example. There are also deficiencies in the educational system which inhibits the possibilities for the wider public to learn about the heritage and then go on to respect and preserve it. Presentations in the media could also have a beneficial educational impact in raising society's awareness of the significance of its past.

Link with spatial and urban planning

There is a lack of real co-operation between those responsible for the heritage and those concerned with developing the needs of the present. There is some discussion between those responsible for planning and heritage but it is at the level of consultation rather than being an institutional and legal collaboration. There is continuing tension between the imperatives of heritage protection and new building. It is hoped that the problem of illegal construction will be addressed in forthcoming legislation.

Financing

The financial contributions of the governmental and local authorities are limited and the chronic lack of funding does not permit adequate conservation treatment of the cultural heritage.

The private sector has not received incentives and so has not been involved in the restoration of monuments. There is now the opportunity for a change of perspective which would encourage partnerships with the private sector.

There is currently a positive co-operation between the protection authorities and international institutions: universities, museums and research institutes. Already underway is the "Atlas" of Traditional Architecture or "The Danube Cultural Route". Other similar programmes show the way forward for the future of the Serbian past.

Documentation

There is a Central Registry of Immovable Cultural Property, compiled for the purposes of heritage protection and planning as a permanent activity of the Republic Institute for the Protection of Monuments. This inventory does not follow exactly the Council of Europe Core Data Standard and is still not retrievable electronically.

Further registries of cultural goods exist in 10 regional institutes (not including Kosovo) and scientific documentation is kept in universities (e.g. Institute of Archaeology).

The registries of movable heritage are under the central institutions (the National Library, the Archive of the Republic of Serbia and the National Museum).

Ethnicity and community

Serbia is a country with a number of different ethnic and religious communities. Most of the inhabitants of the Sumadija region are Serbian Orthodox. In Vojvodina province, Orthodox Serbs form a majority of the inhabitants, but a large Magyar minority lives there, as do many Magyar and southern Slav Roman Catholics and some Magyar and Slovak Protestants. In the Kosovo-Metohija region, the majority of the population is Albanian and Muslim with a minority of Serbs.

The issue of co-operation and mutual policy concerning the protection of the whole cultural heritage is still problematic. Problems will be countered by: *a.* the forthcoming legislation; *b.* education and the development of knowledge about, and mutual respect for, the heritage of all communities; and *c.* supporting and training professionals from the minorities in the work of protection.

9. "The former Yugoslav Republic of Macedonia"

Historical context

"The former Yugoslav Republic of Macedonia" has a rich culture and a complex history.

From the decline of the empire of Alexander the Great until the Second Balkan War of 1913, Macedonia covered parts of what are now Albania, the former Yugoslavia, Bulgaria and Greece. The territory has a rich heritage with substantial evidence of successive occupations by the Romans, the Byzantines and the Turks.

During the 20th century, the repeated divisions of territories culminated in the recognition of Macedonia (presently "the former Yugoslav Republic of Macedonia") as early as 1943 as a separate republic within the Yugoslav federation. With the post-communist break-up of the federation, "the former Yugoslav Republic of Macedonia" has enjoyed independent status since January 1992.

The republic is currently undergoing a period of transition as democratic procedures are refined, the impact of the free market economy is absorbed, new laws are written and new institutional arrangements are established.

Heritage

There are few surviving manifestations of the oldest epoch in Macedonian history, the Palaeolithic, but the Neolithic period is rich in localities and finds, predominantly in areas of strategic importance: river valleys and important roads. There are major examples of settlements which reveal continuous habitation from the Neolithic era through the Hellenistic, Roman and Byzantine periods and onwards to the modern era.

Notable monuments from the Roman period, following their conquest in 168 BC, include the city of Stobi, built in the Hellenistic period but greatly expanded under the Romans, who built a monumental theatre and many palaces with mosaic floors, now in the process of recovery and restoration. In the early Christian period this became an influential religious centre, with the oldest known church dating from the 4th century.

The city of Heraclea has a similarly long history with evidence of Hellenistic and Roman occupation prior to the early Christian period which saw the construction of basilicas with remarkable mosaics and fresco paintings.

Elsewhere, there are preserved churches and monasteries dating from the 9th to the 18th centuries, often with beautiful frescoes, icons and iconostases.

The undisturbed existence of the Ohrid Archiepiscopy, in the south-west of the territory, until 1767, had great importance in the preservation of Christianity in the territories occupied by the Ottoman Empire. During the Byzantine period about 40 churches were built here, including the 11th century Cathedral of St Sophia.

During their five centuries of occupation, the Muslim population created a large number of monumental sacral buildings – mosques, Muslim lodges and mausoleums – mainly in urban areas, together with inns, covered markets and baths. Of the twelve large public hammams constructed between the 15th and 17th centuries in Skopje, two survive: the magnificent late 15th century Daut Pasha Hammam, once the largest Turkish baths in the Balkans, has been the home of the National Art Gallery since 1948.

In addition to individual monuments there are a number of urban and rural ensembles from the 19th and early 20th centuries: there are commercial markets and traditional houses in Bitola (30 streets with 731 stores), Kicevo and Veles, together with a market area in Skopje, substantially reconstructed after the earthquake of 1963. There are also rural ensembles integrated into the landscape of the mountains in such villages as Kicinica (in the west), Krusevo and Malovishta (south-west).

Infrastructural monuments include the Ottoman aqueduct built to serve the needs of the hammams and private baths of Skopje, as well as the stone bridge over the River Vardar in the centre of the capital, dating approximately from the same 15th century period. "The former Yugoslav Republic of Macedonia" had a predominantly agricultural economy until the 20th century when the mining of lead and zinc became economically significant, but there is so far a shortage of expertise in the assessment of industrial monuments.

Some of this heritage was threatened during the conflict in 2001 when many religious monuments were destroyed in the western part of the country. Although the conflict has ended, other threats continue. The abandoned buildings are those which are most at risk. Prior to 1991, this was particularly the case with religious monuments but now that they have been returned to their rightful owners, the situation is much improved. The migration of the population from villages to towns now presents a greater problem. When houses are abandoned, any intervention or conservation by the state protection service inevitably has only short-term effects.

Registration and protection

Currently, the heritage is defined by registration. The Institute for the Protection of the Cultural Monuments of the Republic of Macedonia (National Institute) maintains registers of the immovable and movable heritage and the National Museum of Macedonia maintains inventories of collections.

The new law (December 2003) states (in Article 5.3) that "the cultural heritage shall be protected due to its values, significance and level of endangerment, regardless of time, place and manner of creation or the creator and the ownership or possession, regardless of the character, material or religious, or the type of confession [i.e. faith]".

In practice, there are two categories of protection:
1. registration and identification;
2. legal protection.

In the first category there are between 10 000 and 12 000 identified monuments, including between 4 000 and 5 000 archaeological sites. Of these, only about 10% – around 1 200 – are formally, legally protected: 120 archaeological sites; 182 churches; 228 Islamic monuments (mosques, hammams, inns, bazaars); 220 rural buildings; 379 urban buildings; 47 towers, fortresses and bridges.

To protect the rest in the same formal manner will require extra fieldwork and extra documentation which at the moment cannot be afforded. In order to speed up the process of protection, it is suggested that a facility for temporary protection may be introduced, requiring less documentation, in effect for one to three years depending on the monument, during which time fuller documentation will be carried out; if not, then the monument will be removed from the temporary list.

There is currently no grading of monuments but this will change. It is not yet precisely clear how this will work. Two levels of importance are likely: exceptional national cultural value and local value. The existing lists will then have to be redefined in those terms over a three to five year period. This will involve resurveying the sites and taking the opportunity to carry out risk assessment at the same time.

Political strategy

Within key areas of the new cultural policy in "the former Yugoslav Republic of Macedonia", priority should be given to creating a national strategy for the cultural heritage; to establishing the legal procedures for its integrated protection; and to strengthening the specialist institutions necessary for its sustainable management and utilisation of its values. The integration of the policy of culture in the other policies should enable significant improvement of the state of the cultural heritage in "the former Yugoslav Republic of Macedonia".

The importance of the protection of the built heritage, both monuments and ensembles, is not sufficiently recognised by those responsible for urban and spatial planning.

Education and a greater understanding of the crucial role of heritage in the creation and support of national self-identity must be promoted if this situation is to be reversed. It should also be pointed out, in a developing market economy, that the built heritage is an economically viable contributor to the national treasury: historical buildings perform well both in existing and new functions; and it is crucial also in the encouragement of sustainable cultural tourism. This does not just mean that the monuments themselves should be protected, but consideration should also be given to their environment.

There are, for example, new buildings, both legally permitted and illegally constructed, around the 16th century Ali Pasha mosque in Ohrid which is reported as being enclosed on all sides: "a direct attack on the integrity of the monument …[and] …an obstacle to the real development of the tourism in Ohrid" (B. Shehapi). This is especially unfortunate in one of the major tourist centres within the territory, with historical monuments of both the Orthodox and Islamic religions ornamenting this picturesque historical town overlooking a lake rimmed by mountains.

The importance of tourism was recognised in the international conference "Cultural Heritage Management and its Tourism Exploitation", held in Ohrid in 2000. The conclusions recognised the need for protection, action plans, intersectorial co-operation between all stakeholders, education and an overall strategy for tourism. The improvement of cultural heritage management in such tourist areas as the Ohrid and Prespa regions is seen as being one of the key areas for future intervention.

Other key areas include the restoration of buildings destroyed in the conflict of 2001 in the Tetovo and Kumanovo-Lipkovo regions, the revitalisation of neglected areas in the central and western parts of the state, and of rural sites in the Mavrovo National Park. Also needed in the west are: the revitalisation of urban nuclei, rural sites and fortresses; the repair and improvement of the road system to enable access to sites of cultural significance; and the acceleration of the protection process for archaeological sites in the south-east, which are subject to the attentions of illegal excavators.

In 1996, the National Institute compiled an "SOS" List of 100 Cultural Monuments which require urgent conservation-restoration interventions. This list of significant monuments at risk, of all types, was designed to alert the authorities and the public to the problem of maintaining an endangered cultural heritage. The latest proposal, to put the "best" 100 monuments into the care of the new National Conservation Centre, acting on behalf of the Ministry of Culture, represents a similar strategy. It has the benefit of focusing attention and public interest on a finite number of buildings and sites, at the risk of downgrading the rest. The experts remain committed to the principle of informing the public about its shared heritage and engaging their enthusiasm and support. They see the use of the electronic and print media as fundamental to this programme of public information.

Legislation

Current situation and new law

The Law on Protection of Cultural Monuments dates from 1973, supplemented and influenced by the provisions of some 50 other regulations of different kinds, among which are the laws on crime, spatial and urban planning, and investment project development.

A new Law on Protection of Cultural Heritage in "the former Yugoslav Republic of Macedonia" was adopted on 19 March 2004, entering into force as of 1 January 2005 (after enacting 18 subsidiary, small, regulatory laws). Starting from this date, the existing law (which has been effective since 1973) ceased to apply.

The Law on Protection of Cultural Heritage establishes a necessary legal framework for realisation of the constitutional concept of protection of goods with cultural and historical significance. Instead of the existing system for the protection of cultural monuments, the new law creates an integrated system for the protection of cultural heritage. This approach will enable a sustainable development of the cultural heritage and its integration into society.

The objectives of the Law on Protection of Cultural Heritage are:

- the precise definition of the responsibilities in the system of protection of the cultural heritage, emphasising the place and role of the state and its authorities and institutions;
- active participation of the cultural heritage in the contemporary development of "the former Yugoslav Republic of Macedonia", and creation of conditions for its effective protection and its use in the scientific framework;
- the application of contemporary scientific and expert views for establishing, developing and promoting the national systems for the protection of the cultural heritage;
- ensuring the compatibility of the national system for the protection of cultural heritage with the international and regional systems of the same kind;
- establishing a connection between the protection of cultural heritage and the concrete economic, social, cultural, historical and other conditions and processes in "the former Yugoslav Republic of Macedonia".

In order to reach these goals, the new law provides support for significant reforms in the area of cultural heritage. The new law is in compliance with international law and protection standards, and it addresses the previous gaps concerning some standard legislative institutes for heritage.

According to the new law, the objects for protection are all material (immovable and movable) and intangible goods which have, for the first time, been introduced into the legal system.

The new law should provide a way to overcome the problem of illegal activities carried out by organised groups or individuals – both foreign and domestic. For example, common illegal activities include the theft of icons from churches, illegal excavations of archaeological sites, and the damaging and destruction of parts of the cultural heritage.

The new law is very long and detailed. It should be noted that it is going to be crucial for its implementation to produce guidance notes, both for professional practitioners and for the greater understanding of the public. These will be necessary not only for purposes of definition and interpretation, but also in order to explain the responsibilities of the various institutes which will be implementing the law, ostensibly on behalf of the public.

Link with spatial planning and development

There is currently no co-operation between heritage experts and urban and spatial planners. The occasional public debates concerning urban and spatial plans provide the only forum in which the heritage experts might express their opinions. This schism between two disciplines which ought to have a symbiotic relationship appears to stem from the implementation of the laws.

Within the Law on Investment Project Development, the protection of the heritage is treated in only one article, which requires that the investor provides technical documentation (carried out by the responsible institute) only for those buildings which are legally protected.

Within the Law on Spatial and Urban Planning, no obligation beyond notification of proposals is laid upon the planning institutes to collaborate with those responsible for cultural heritage. In addition to the problems posed by approved planning which may be insensitive to the needs of the heritage, there is also the growing problem of illegal construction, particularly in urban areas.

The new management structure which will follow the implementation of the new law is expected to eliminate some of the pertaining heritage planning difficulties.

Until 1999, if owners wished to carry out works on protected monuments they needed the permission of the relevant institute. In 1999, this power was removed and given to the Ministry of Urban Planning and Construction, which could receive advice from the institutes but was not obliged to follow it. This strategy was adopted in order to encourage investment by removing what was seen as an impediment: permission for works could be granted within 10 to 15 days irrespective of the implications for cultural heritage.

The new law will return powers of decision to the Ministry of Culture and will also enable the ministry to comment on urban planning proposals. It will also provide many control mechanisms for the protection of the cultural heritage in all phases of spatial planning as well as during building and other activities which impact on the appearance of the space.

Institutions

Current situation

The current management structure has three divisions which are under the overall administration of the Ministry of Culture, all financed from the national budget:

- the Institute for the Protection of the Cultural Monuments of the Republic of Macedonia (established 1949);
- the Institute for the Protection of the Cultural Monuments of the City of Skopje;
- the five local Institutes for the Protection of the Cultural Monuments and Museums in Strumica, Stip, Ohrid, Bitola and Prilep (the local institutes were established over a 15-year period following the 1963 earthquake).

These national and local institutes are responsible for both the built and the archaeological immovable heritage, including the sacral cultural heritage. The local institutes are responsible also for museums, although this will change with the new law.

The National Institute has responsibility for 70% of the territory, with the local institutes having responsibility for the remaining 30%. By the provision of the Law for Culture of 1998, all local institutes were given the same status as the National Institute even though they have less responsibility and fewer staff. Before 1991, the local institutes were under the control of the municipalities; now there is greater centralisation but the National Institute has no control over the local institutes: it offers professional advice but they report directly to the Ministry of Culture.

The National Institute is responsible for all aspects of heritage management: identification, documentation, valorisation, protection, preparing projects, research, conservation, restoration, presentation, publication and international co-operation. Its staff includes specialists in architecture, archaeology and art history as well as conservators and legal and economic experts. The national/local relationship is currently in a state of flux.

The institutes' protection staff do not have a formal role in heritage education although individual experts may participate in particular programmes, for example with the Faculty of Architecture at the State University. The principal means of informing and popularising is through publication, particularly through the annual magazine *Cultural Heritage*, and through monographic publications.

The National Institute co-operates on a regular basis with other branches of government, particularly with the Ministry of Economy (on tourism) and the Ministry of Environment and Physical Planning (on the protection of natural heritage), ensuring joint participation, for instance in seminars and conferences. The institute also has strong relationships with the Museum of Macedonia and with the State University of St Cyril and St Methodius (the creators of the Cyrillic alphabet in the 9th century, whose disciples taught at a monastery in Ohrid). The institute collaborates with the museum on excavations, archaeological research and conservation. There is also close co-operation on conserving and exhibiting icons.

The collaboration with the university is within the Faculty of Architecture (urban planning and conservation) and the Faculty of Philosophy (History of Art and Archaeology). There is productive collaboration on research, preparation of documentation and publishing.

Institutional reforms

The new law will divide the responsibilities of the current National Institute into two parts:

- one half will become a National Conservation Centre, responsible for protecting the cultural heritage, controlling conservation, keeping records of protected monuments and advising the local institutes (which will continue to be conservation centres). The new centre will take direct responsibility for the 100 or so outstanding national monuments, which in effect puts the government in charge of the "best" monuments, leaving the rest to the local institutes;
- the other will become an arm of the Ministry of Culture, responsible for administration related to the protection and management of database inventories of protected monuments.

Museums will take responsibility for the movable heritage.

Henceforward there will be a distinction between the roles of museums (research and presentation), the institutes (conservation and restoration) and the ministry (administration and legal matters).

In effect, this shuffling of the pack will increase the authority and control of the centre, reducing the authority of the local institutes and enabling national valorisation and local practical conservation. Local institutes will thus become institutes for conservation rather than institutes for protection.

This centralising strategy is being adopted in order to ensure that the government becomes more aware of its responsibilities for heritage. But, it carries the obvious risk, inherent within "cherry-picking", of emphasising the importance of some to the detriment of the majority, which may, as a result, be neglected and may perhaps be less attractive to donors.

The service overall will be in need of expansion since there are currently only about 200 employed workers in the field, the majority being in the National Institute (96), the Bitola Institute (39) and the City of Skopje Institute (27). Although the local institutes are understaffed, the National Institute has an obligation to provide them with professional assistance.

However, even at national level there are insufficient numbers of trained staff in all of the heritage branches: there is a particular shortage of industrial and landscape experts. There is also a shortage of specialist conservators. There are, for example, only about 20 trained conservators of wall paintings, icons and wood carving. Since these are areas of especially high artistic quality in "the former Yugoslav Republic of Macedonia", this shortage of trained staff is particularly problematic: priority should be given to establishing appropriate training programmes.

Currently, the optional courses in the Faculty of Fine Arts in the State University do not provide the numbers necessary to fulfil requirements and there is no governmental institution with a responsibility for maintaining craft skills. The students do, however, profit from the opportunity to participate in conservation work carried out at the conservation laboratory of the Institute for Protection.

Financing

The Constitution of "the former Yugoslav Republic of Macedonia" provides public support for culture by obliging the state to provide incentives, support and development of art and culture. The State Budget – through the Ministry of Culture – provides direct financial support for the cultural heritage of national interest. But since independence, state funding for cultural heritage has fallen dramatically. Previously, funds were secured through taxation and the budgets of local communities. Protection received 35% of the overall funds allocated to culture. This proportion fell to 13.21% in 1994 and 1995, and fell further, to 12.79%, in 1996.

Public support for culture is also provided through some indirect measures taken by the state, such as some tax and customs benefits for culture, acceptable credit rates as an incentive for investments in cultural heritage and property tax relief.

The Law on Value Added Tax, for example, provides that turnover from cultural institutions and other bodies that perform cultural activities, by issue of the Ministry of Culture, is exempt from VAT. The owner can be compensated in the event of damage to property if he or she is obliged to open the property at certain times for the benefit of the public.

The Law on Income Tax provides that donations and grants for cultural purposes have a tax relief of up to 3% of the whole income if they are invested in public cultural institutions financed by the state budget.

According to the Law on Protection of Cultural Heritage, there is a possibility for establishing funds and foundations in the area of culture. Cultural institutions can also use financial support from other sources, such as gifts, inheritance, sponsorships or donations. In the formal sense, there is a legislative basis for tax incentives to encourage private support, for example sponsorship for culture.

Financial investments for protection from other sources, such as sponsorship, donation or publishing, are insignificant and incidental, although the monuments in the ownership of the religious communities (the Macedonian Orthodox Church and the Islamic Community of Macedonia) tend to fare better in this respect. Reality shows that foreign donations are more present than local foundations in the area of culture.

There is no single established mechanism for proposing or approving collaborations with international bodies. The National Institute oversees and monitors international funding partnerships on behalf of the Ministry of Culture, employing delegated authority. There is also within government a central body responsible for co-ordinating and registering all foreign investment and interventions.

There are continuing projects which have been developed by the Institute for Protection in association with the European Centre of Byzantine and Post-Byzantine Monuments (Thessaloníki) on the research and documentation of relevant monuments. There are also two internationally funded projects which have been established in response to damage to churches, incurred in the conflict in 2001: the European Agency for Reconstruction is financing the reconstruction of the 19th century church at the monastery of Lesok, near Tetovo; the Dutch government is financing the conservation of the building and the wall-painting of the 14th century church of Matejce, near Kumanovo.

The National Institute has participated in co-operative partnerships with a number of academic and conservation establishments, including the Getty Conservation Institute, the University of York, the Polish Institute and the Moscow Institute of Restoration.

Documentation

The national and local institutes all maintain architectural and archaeological documentation, with separate registers for the movable and immovable heritage. There are municipal and central registers, but there is no official list of monuments, since the current law did not provide for such a compilation. The new law proposes a categorisation of all types of cultural monument. The current records include references to non-monumental structures which are within the immediate surroundings of protected entities.

The National Institute currently maintains records on the cultural monuments of all the territories which are not covered by local institutes. It also holds copies of the registers of all the registered cultural monuments which are the responsibility of the local institutes, so that a central list can be held in the Documentation Centre of the National Institute. The institute does not hold complete duplicate sets of all the detailed documentation which is held in the local institutes. In the new system there will be a national register and a central registry of files, with local files being maintained by the local institutes. There is, so far, no standardised national approach to documentation – this is being developed by the National Institute.

The registers cover all types of immovable heritage, with the exception of landscapes and the industrial heritage which have not been dealt with in this way so far. The process of inventory has been a continuing activity since the establishment of the institutional system in 1949 (although some of the local institutes were not set up until the 1970s). The experts involved in the work include art historians, architects, archaeologists, historians and ethnologists. Although the documentation is not completely digitised, some of the photographic and graphic material is available electronically. Funding for the digitising of text records has not so far been accomplished. Such a programme would need to include a staff training component.

The Museum of Macedonia, which carries out most of the excavations, keeps the appropriate archaeological documentation. Local museums also hold documentation concerning the sites and finds within their areas of responsibility. At the university, the Faculty of Architecture maintains documentation on the architectural heritage and the Institute of Art History and Archaeology also holds material gathered for its scientific and research projects. Lastly, the State Archive of "the former Yugoslav Republic of Macedonia" also has architectural and archaeological documentation.

The property ownership information on maps is inconsistent, with data imprecisely noted. There are particular problems with the properties of religious communities. These were expropriated from the communities in the 1950s and were partly restituted in 1991. With respect to the buildings in the immediate surroundings of protected religious monuments, the relations between the government and the owners are still not defined. This has an impact on ownership assessment, compounded by the frequent incompatibility between old and new property records and cadastral reports.

Almost all of this documentation is accessible to the public. As a result, it is often used for information by the media and for publication and educational programmes, as well as providing the basis for further scientific research.

The church of Panteleimon, village of Nerezi, near Skopje (National Conservation Center)

Ethnicity and community

"The former Yugoslav Republic of Macedonia" is a multi-ethnic country. Together with the population of Macedonians, there are Albanians, Armenians (Vlachs), Serbs, Turks, Roma and others. The constitution guarantees equality to all. There is, therefore, no official religion in the republic although the Christian Orthodox community is larger than the Muslim community. Representatives of these bodies (Macedonian Orthodox Church and Islamic Community of Macedonia) are not directly engaged in the assessment of monuments, since the process is led by experts from the institutions, but they often help the process by offering their own assessments and by reporting on buildings at risk. This information can then be checked and evaluated by experts, but it should be noted that there are insufficient numbers of trained staff in the institutes who are knowledgeable about all aspects of cultural heritage. There is, for example, a particular lack of Albanian professional expertise in the field of cultural heritage. This is a historical problem, which remains to be addressed, of encouraging further education in this subject. There is no impediment, in principle, to involving the authorities of all ethnicities and communities in this programme. It should be noted that relations on an official level between the institutes and the Orthodox and Islamic community authorities are harmonious, co-operative and productive.

Before the conflict of 2001, there were no security problems in researching the architectural heritage of all communities. Following a period of insecurity, including the destruction of cultural monuments, it appears now that cases of continuing instability are rare and where they exist the problems are being addressed.

10. Comparative summary

At this stage of the study, and with a view to further activities related to the Regional Programme for Cultural and Natural Heritage in South-East Europe (see Part 4 of this publication), a number of conclusions can already be drawn. Further operational conclusions arising from this study are identified in Part 3 of this publication.

These interim conclusions are based on comparative analysis of the nine partner countries' policies. They focus on the five types of action which the Council of Europe sees as holding the key to improving their heritage policies:
- reforming laws
- strengthening institutions
- encouraging civil society participation
- increasing financial resources
- devising and implementing sustainable political strategies.

Reforming laws

The cultural heritage policies of the regional programme's nine partner countries are currently in a transitional phase.

In the early 1990s, the fall of communism and the conflicts in the former Yugoslavia generally had the effect of creating a legal vacuum, disrupting institutions, reducing financial resources, and so making heritage policy ineffective, and indeed chaotic, in certain countries/regions, such as Kosovo/UNMIK and Bosnia and Herzegovina.

Since then, the authorities have set about adapting their policies to match the new European context, both economic (free market) and social (democracy, rule of law).

In legislative terms, this mainly involves bringing existing laws into line with European (e.g. the Council of Europe's European Cultural Convention, and Granada, Valletta and Florence conventions) and international (e.g. UNESCO's World Heritage Convention and Convention for the Safeguarding of the Intangible Cultural Heritage) practices and standards, although some partner countries have not yet ratified all of these conventions.

An unprecedented legal reform programme has thus been under way for the last ten years or so. In terms of progress made, countries fall into three categories:

Countries which have completed most of their legal reforms

Croatia: the Law on Protection and Preservation of Cultural Property (1999, amended in 2003) is implemented in accordance with several decrees.

Romania: Law No. 422 on Historic Monuments (2001), Law No. 378 on the Archaeological Heritage (2001), Law No. 564 on Monuments Inscribed on the World Heritage List (2001) and Law No. 182 on Protection of the Movable Heritage (2000) are in use. Romania is currently working on the intangible heritage, the technical heritage and landscape.

Countries whose new laws have still to be implemented

Albania: the Law on the Protection of Movable and Immovable Cultural Assets (1994) remained in force until the new Law on Cultural Heritage (No. 9048), passed by Parliament in April 2003, was fully implemented.

"The former Yugoslav Republic of Macedonia": the Law on the Protection of Cultural Monuments" (1973) was in force until the end of 2004 with the new Law on Protection of Cultural Heritage in "the former Yugoslav Republic of Macedonia" entering into force on 1 January 2005.

Kosovo/UNMIK: since the rescinding by UNMIK of the laws passed between 1989 and 1999 (including the Law on Cultural Property, 1994), the Law on the Protection of Cultural Monuments (1977) still applied, but could not be enforced. A Law on the Cultural Heritage was approved by the Assembly of Kosovo in 2006, but awaits the approval of sub-legal acts before it can be implemented.

Countries whose legislative reforms are still in progress

Bosnia and Herzegovina: at national level, the Dayton Peace Agreement established a Commission to Preserve National Monuments; at the level of the three entities (Federation of Bosnia and Herzegovina, Republika Srpska and the District of Brčko) there are some dozen laws on heritage. A draft law on the protection and conservation of cultural monuments in Bosnia and Herzegovina will be applicable at national level (if approved) and is currently available and being examined.

Bulgaria: the Law on Cultural Monuments and Museums (1969, amended between 1989 and 2004) is still in force. A new law for monuments of culture is currently being drafted.

The Republic of Montenegro: the Law on the Protection of Cultural Monuments (1991) is still in force. A new draft law on cultural property has been developed.

The Republic of Serbia: the Law on Cultural Property (Goods) (1994) is still in force. Three draft laws have been formulated since 2001 and the last of these was being examined at the end of 2004.

It should be noted that the Legislative Support Task Force (LSTF) of the Council of Europe's Technical Co-operation and Field Action Unit provided guidance on the countries' draft legislation.

Strengthening institutions

Cultural and natural heritage is mainly the responsibility of the ministries of culture in the partner countries. The exception is Bosnia and Herzegovina, where the Dayton Peace Agreement established a Commission to Preserve National Monuments for the period 2001 to 2006. Some ministries are assisted by specialised agencies (e.g. commissions in Romania and an expert council in Croatia).

The "natural" heritage is the responsibility of the Ministry of Environment and Regional Planning in the Republic of Montenegro and "the former Yugoslav Republic of Macedonia", and of the Academy of Sciences in Albania, which is also responsible for archaeology.

In Serbia, Romania, Kosovo/UNMIK, Albania and Bulgaria, the Ministry of Religious Affairs and/or the religious authorities manage/co-manage "religious heritage", on the same basis as the other places of worship which belong to them.

Finally, some powers which are more concerned with "execution" are delegated by national ministries to regional/local authorities (Romania, Kosovo/UNMIK, "the former Yugoslav Republic of Macedonia", Croatia, Bosnia and Herzegovina).

The division of powers between the various national, regional and local institutions reflects these countries' characteristic complexity. In Romania, for instance, responsibility for heritage is shared by no fewer than eight authorities.

This institutional complexity often results in a lack of co-operation between the various authorities responsible for heritage (Kosovo/UNMIK, the Republic of Serbia), or between these and other authorities concerned, such as those responsible for the environment, regional planning and urban planning (Kosovo/UNMIK, the Republic of Serbia, the Republic of Montenegro). In other countries (Bulgaria, the Republic of Montenegro), the problem is more a lack of co-operation between national and regional/local authorities. There is nothing fated about this, however, as the effective co-operation noted in Romania, Croatia and Albania makes clear.

Some countries (Montenegro, Romania, Albania) seem satisfied with their heritage teams, while others (Kosovo/UNMIK, "the former Yugoslav Republic of Macedonia", Bulgaria, Albania, Serbia) admit that they "lack knowledge and experience" in certain areas, for example the new technologies, data bank management, technical documentation, heritage assessment and management – and also the restoration trades, with direct effects on the quality of restoration. These latter countries feel that priority should go to training more young people and improving the skills of existing officials and restorers. International exchange programmes are seen as a valuable source of mutual enrichment (e.g. the training recently provided for Albanian icon restorers at the Museum of Byzantine Culture in Thessaloníki).

Most countries also complain that they lack personnel, particularly in certain specialised areas (Albania, Romania, Montenegro, Kosovo/UNMIK, "the former Yugoslav Republic of Macedonia" and Bulgaria).

In this connection, some countries have still to decide whether specialised restorers should remain in the public sector or be "privatised" (as they usually are in western Europe), although this is a key factor in institutional reform. Another problem is that salaries are lower in the public sector than in the private sector – which tends to discourage young people and specialists from joining the public service.

It should be noted, however, that the partner countries do not state clearly that they mean to carry out institutional reforms (which would include regionalising powers). The one exception is "the former Yugoslav Republic of Macedonia", which is planning reform following the new heritage law coming into force in 2005.

Encouraging civil society participation

So far, civil society involvement in heritage policy is not developed, visible or organised in these countries, and so they say very little about it.

The fact is that civil servants are no longer, as they were under the communists, the only ones concerned by heritage. The new private owners, either native or foreign, now have a major role to play in preserving it. As managers and guardians of their protected property, they are vital auxiliaries, and not the authorities' opponents.

Private firms, too, have a heritage role. As owners or developers of protected property, they can fund operations on a scale which few governments can match. In the restoration field, they are – and will be even more so in the future – a major source of specialised manpower with vital skills.

Close co-operation or partnership with private owners and firms is, therefore, one major solution to the chronic lack of staff and public funding, a complaint raised by all the countries concerned.

None the less, these countries are aware that such partnerships demand a fairly radical change of behaviour on the part of the authorities (policy makers and civil servants). A genuine communication and information strategy is needed for the partners to co-operate in a spirit of mutual confidence in the long term, since the property market essentially does not produce results in the short term.

In fact, most of these countries intend to devise means of (written, spoken, televisual) communication between the authorities and various target groups. For example, countries (Bosnia and Herzegovina, Bulgaria, Kosovo/UNMIK, the Republic of Serbia) which sometimes have trouble with the religious authorities – either because they fail to seek advice or permission before starting work, or because they do not make heritage a spending priority – are anxious to lay the foundations of fruitful dialogue and co-operation with them.

Similarly, several countries (e.g. the Republic of Serbia and "the former Yugoslav Republic of Macedonia") complain that defects in the educational system (and particularly the media) make it hard to mount large-scale information and consciousness-raising campaigns to encourage the public, and especially young people, to protect and respect the heritage. Civil society needs to grasp the importance of the role played by heritage in the living environment, so that it organises itself to defend heritage and heritage values.

Increasing financial resources

Heritage conservation in the partner countries is funded from state budgets allocated (annually) to the ministries of culture, which supervise use of these funds to maintain and restore the heritage. In Bosnia and Herzegovina, however, heritage is funded only from regional government budgets.

Unfortunately, public funds are used on public property only, and private owners have to cover all their own requirements.

In some countries (e.g. "the former Yugoslav Republic of Macedonia" and Bulgaria), public funding has been heavily cut in recent years, since heritage has not been a government priority. Both these countries provide indirect funding in the form of tax incentives for private owners or donors (reduced VAT, tax rebates, preferential interest rates, reduced inheritance tax, donations and sponsorships deductible from income tax, etc.). In Bulgaria, these incentives have not operated in practice, due to the state budget being controlled by the International Monetary Fund.

In the case of the religious heritage, religious communities sometimes fund upkeep and restoration themselves (Bosnia and Herzegovina, Kosovo/UNMIK, the Orthodox Church in "the former Yugoslav Republic of Macedonia" and Albania).

Unlike western European countries, most of these countries often dodge the heavy cost of funding and managing their heritage by granting "concessions" to private operators. Unfortunately, the conditions negotiated are not always ideal.

These various approaches to public and private funding at national level are supplemented by partnerships with European and international organisations: foundations, associations, foreign embassies and governments, universities, banks, the Council of Europe, the EU and UNESCO, among others. Funding from these sources often exceeds national funding (Kosovo/UNMIK, "the former Yugoslav Republic of Macedonia" and Bosnia and Herzegovina, where, in the Republika Srpska, inadequate public funding has been partly offset by funding from religious and foreign sources).

The many examples of foreign funding cited by these countries show how dynamic the funding agencies are, but also illustrate the need to co-ordinate funding on the basis of clear policies and priority actions.

At present, the ministries of culture in the various countries are responsible for monitoring and co-ordinating funds from foreign sources, both governmental and private. In "the former Yugoslav Republic of Macedonia", a government authority registers and co-ordinates all foreign investments and projects, while the Ministry of Culture monitors investments in culture. Kosovo/UNMIK, where foreign involvement is running at a particularly high level, is thinking of setting up a co-ordinating and supervisory body to "license" foreign donors. In the Republic of Montenegro, the Ministry of Culture is assisted by UNESCO agencies, which assess foreign projects. Innovative approaches to finding funds from abroad are also being devised – for example, in Bulgaria, where a non-profit making association has been founded for that purpose.

Devising and implementing sustainable political strategies

Two countries already have cultural heritage strategies: Albania ("Guide to the Cultural Policies of the Albanian State", 2000) and Croatia ("Strategy for the Cultural Development of Croatia in the 21st century").

The "Bulgarian Cultural Policy 1990-1995", however, no longer matches the present situation in Bulgaria and needs to be reviewed and co-ordinated with the country's regional development plans.

The Republic of Montenegro has already completed the first stage of its strategy for cultural heritage management by producing the "National Report on the Cultural Policies of the Republic of Montenegro" in September 2003 and organising a national debate on cultural policy in June 2004.

The other partner countries have no strategies as yet, but clearly feel the need for them. They have already pin-pointed some of the challenges in certain recent documents, such as the "Report on Legislative Reform in the Field of Cultural Heritage".

Conclusions

Examination of these documents shows that the problems and challenges identified by the various countries are astonishingly similar – which makes it unnecessary to discuss each country separately. The challenges can be grouped under three main headings:

1. getting the public and the authorities to recognise the importance of the role played by heritage in society, and making them more aware of their responsibility to preserve it, and particularly:

    – getting them to recognise the economic role of heritage, bearing in mind the part which tourism and the culture industries can play in modernising countries and boosting their economic development;

    – getting them to recognise the social role of heritage, since better heritage conservation is directly linked to better living conditions for the whole community;

- getting them to recognise the environmental role of heritage, since the rehabilitation of urban and rural complexes opens the way to harmonious development of the physical and cultural environment;

2. improving the resources necessary for any policy for integrated and sustainable management of the cultural environment by:
   - reforming laws to bring them into line with the current transition to a market economy, participation-based democracy and the rule of law, while respecting and building on the characteristic assets of cultural heritage;
   - improving institutions: increasing the number and skills of personnel, increasing financial and technical resources, ensuring better co-operation between specialised institutes and with other ministries concerned with heritage, and developing international co-operation with the help of training, exchange and expert assistance programmes;
   - increasing public funding for heritage maintenance and restoration, and finding further funds from home and foreign sources, particularly via co-operation and partnership schemes;
   - devising and implementing clear heritage strategies, backed by policy makers, dovetailed with other national strategies (sectoral and global), and meeting the needs of professionals and the public;
   - informing the public and raising their awareness via educational programmes, exhibitions, publications and the media, and by giving them maximum access to heritage;

3. finding solutions to the problems of these transition countries, which are currently adjusting to the new economic and social context in Europe, for example by:
   - preventing and rectifying illegal building projects, inadequate rebuilding, lack of maintenance and all other sources of heritage damage, by promoting dialogue with developers and introducing a genuine policy for integrated conservation and sustainable development;
   - finalising/up-dating inventories and documentation on cultural heritage (whose condition has changed more in the former Yugoslav countries than in others), using a digital information system to provide reliable data on heritage already protected or requiring protection;
   - drawing up a priority list of "outstanding and endangered heritage" which requires urgent action and on which current resources (particularly foreign funding) should be concentrated;
   - solving certain problems linked to these countries' communist past, such as restitution of property confiscated or taken abroad, review of concessions, new forms of co-operation with private owners and investors, new public consultation procedures.

Part 2

Eight themes and corresponding debates

Theme 1 – Purpose of law, harmonisation of terms, categorisation of protected items and the link to inventories/registers

1. The purpose of law

Since its foundation, the Council of Europe has developed a rigorous philosophy of democracy based on the protection of human rights. This includes the participation of citizens in community life; respect for the rights of others; the right to own property; freedom of association; the right to pluralist information; freedom of the press and so forth. These issues are embodied in the European Convention on Human Rights and have been confirmed by the subsequent findings of the European Court of Human Rights in Strasbourg. Moreover, the right to heritage necessarily forms one element of the whole entity. Furthermore, the need for unity and the recognition of diversity in the protection of cultural heritage was specified in the Final Declaration of the Fourth Conference of European Ministers responsible for the Cultural Heritage:

> "Knowledge of the cultural heritage should be propagated at local, regional, national and international levels and must emphasise both the elements which reflect Europe's unity and the diversity of its cultural identities. A thorough understanding of the values inherent in heritage is conducive to appreciation of diversity, tolerance and ability to surpass mere differences. The now established concept of a common cultural heritage should lead individuals and communities to acknowledge shared responsibility for protecting it regardless of its physical location or current political context."

In the context of developing legislation for the protection of cultural heritage, it should be recognised that there are two distinct and separate objectives for managing this process within a democratic society. First, legislation is required to regulate the actions of private citizens (to safeguard the cultural heritage for the enjoyment of society as a whole in the wider public interest) whilst at the same time recognising the right to own property as a fundamental issue of human rights. Secondly, legislation is required for the purpose of delegating power to specific authorities and for establishing appropriate public institutions (including for the protection and management of the cultural heritage). The provisions that regulate the behaviour of citizens should not be mixed with provisions that regulate the public bureaucracy. In relation to these objectives, the legislation should be clearly defined and easily understood by all citizens.

When considering drafts for the reform of legislation, the members of the Legislative Support Task Force have frequently come across a major problem in that the texts submitted for consideration are often long and complicated, and without a logical framework relating to particular heritage disciplines. Moreover, they frequently mix the two objectives for legislation within one law. This makes it very difficult for members of the public to understand the procedures that may affect them. For example, two draft laws recently considered have extended to over 70 and 90 pages and are repetitive in their detail. Furthermore, articles concerning the designation of protected assets, for sanctions, control, supervision and suchlike are considered together for all heritage disciplines, rather than in their separate disciplines. The owner of an architectural monument needs to be able to find the procedures that will affect him/her easily in a clear sequence rather than having to pick out the provisions from different areas of the law. For us to find it difficult to read and understand the draft is one thing, but for the ordinary citizen this legal complexity is potentially a major problem. Another consideration is the intangible heritage – should this be in the law and who will be subject to its regulation? Or is it a matter for public policy and education?

2. The harmonisation of terms and the simplicity of language

One of the key aspects of the Council of Europe conventions is that they identify the types of procedures that should be included in laws on the cultural heritage. Although they do not attempt to set out actual legal procedures, they indicate in clear terms what type of issues should be included. This is a lesson that should be followed through to the development of actual laws.

Evidence also shows that most countries that have signed and ratified the conventions do not adopt the exact terms expressed in the conventions – the point being that so long as the adopted approach is logical, straightforward and in line with the conventions, this should not give rise to any problems.

2.1. Movable heritage

The *movable heritage* necessarily involves a number of different categories and different conventions and directives considering issues relating to cultural property. The Council of Europe's European Convention on Offences relating to Cultural Property (ETS No. 119, Delphi Convention, 1985) is an important legal document in this respect despite the fact that it has not come into force.

Appendix II to the Delphi Convention usefully enumerates a detailed list of 28 categories of cultural property, for which it suggests protection should be mandatory. This list covers a wide range of matters, for example products of archaeological exploration, statuary art and sculpture, paintings, works of applied art, tapestries and furniture, old books, cinematographic film and various types of rare collections. Article 2.3 of the convention further suggests that states may declare any other property presenting an "artistic, historical, archaeological, scientific or other cultural interest" as being protected cultural property whether it is in public or private ownership.

In this respect an identified list and interest factors (providing the basis for the criteria for selection of movable objects) are coherent. Whether a law should identify all the items covered in this appendix is another matter. It may be sufficient to provide a general definition of the movable heritage rather than identify every type of item, which can be specified by other regulations. This approach should also be considered in relation to the immovable heritage.

2.2. Immovable heritage

It has been the tradition of some eastern European countries to recognise the immovable heritage in total rather than the separate themes of the *architectural* and the *archaeological* heritage. However, the Council of Europe's conventions differentiate between these two heritage sectors, each having different particular procedures that are applicable. Moreover, this is necessary as the architectural heritage is a living heritage, which has an impact on everyday life, whereas the archaeological heritage is more concerned with retracing the history of mankind.

We also now have to consider the relationship between the man-made heritage and the natural heritage and the idea of cultural landscapes within the concept of the immovable heritage, which is now considered through the European Landscape Convention of 2000.

2.3. Architectural heritage

The architectural heritage is considered through the Convention for the Protection of the Architectural Heritage of Europe (ETS No. 121, Granada Convention, 1985).

Formulated in 1985, this convention sought to expand the concept of the architectural heritage from individual architectural monuments such as religious buildings, castles and monumental public buildings to a wider concept, encompassing groups of historical buildings in historical towns and the vernacular architecture, private houses, industrial structures and engineering works, as well as to sites and areas. Moreover, it was recognised in 1985 that in most countries ever-wider categories of buildings and the built environment were being considered to merit protection and that an integrated form of conservation had become an important ingredient in the improvement of quality of life. Twenty years on, this idea has developed through the principles of sustainable development. But in many eastern European countries the notion of utilising this heritage as a *living heritage* is only just starting to be considered.

The Granada Convention defines the component parts of the architectural heritage according to three categories:

– monuments;
– groups of buildings;
– sites.

These three classifications for the component parts of this heritage were chosen in line with definitions used in the 1972 World Heritage Convention and in the Council of Europe Resolution (76) 28 of the Committee of Ministers concerning the adaptation of laws and regulations to the requirements of integrated conservation of the architectural heritage. The convention does not, however, make a prescriptive requirement for the use of these terms nor does it say that all signatory countries should harmonise the component terms for protection of assets of the architectural heritage.

The explanatory note to the convention also indicates that the categories may naturally overlap – monuments, for instance, may be found within groups or sites, and landscape areas and historical gardens may fall within these categories. In fact it was recognised in 1985 that the trend was for enlargement of the concept of heritage.

Moreover, whilst the Granada Convention confines the idea of "groups of buildings" to those of a "homogeneous" character, groupings are now considered for wider qualities such as the picturesque quality caused by heterogeneous and accidental groupings.

Perhaps the most significant development is in relation to the idea of "sites", which the convention explains as meaning "areas" where the mark of humans has been left and which are partially built on.

The focus has now definitely moved from the monumental architectural heritage to the wider aspects of local and regional distinctiveness as well as national considerations, of vernacular, of the spirit of community and human identity in areas and its potential as a living heritage. The explanatory notes to the convention indicate that "… the best hope for the future of the heritage lies in it being used. Whilst the conservation of properties costs money, it is also a source of revenue and job creation …". Hence the more global and integrated approach to areas which can be considered for their economic and social potential on equal terms with their heritage value (a sustainable approach rather than as a museum for public observation or for scientific investigation). Many deprived areas in many countries have an identity rooted in their heritage. If we can engage the community of these areas by helping to them to recognise their inheritance it may be possible to turn them into thriving places where people connect with their surroundings and utilise the built environment of the past.

However, returning to one of the original aspects of this theme, the purpose of the law, we have to bear in mind the need for simplicity and for the law to be understandable to the citizens that will be affected by it. Hence, there is a need not to overcomplicate the terms used for categories. Thus, whilst it is not necessary to follow exactly the terms of the convention it is useful to have a similarly straightforward approach whereby the ideas of a broader heritage are reflected. In fact, very few countries that have signed the convention have adopted the terms "monuments, groups of buildings and sites" (the exception being the Walloon Region of Belgium), but the terms adopted reflect these broad categories.

The term "monument" is frequently used for single items (some countries adopt the idea of a "cultural monument" or a "historic monument") or similar simple terms are used. For example, the United Kingdom and Denmark use the term "listed buildings" and the Republic of Ireland "protected structures".

A wider use of terms can be found covering groups of buildings and sites and this is a reflection of the need to cover wider categories of heritage through integrated mechanisms. These include *secteur sauvegardé* and ZPPAUPs (zones of architectural, urban and landscape interest) (France), "conservation zones" and "sites" (Czech Republic), "monument ensembles" (Thüringia, Germany), the Survey of Architectural Values in the Environment (SAVE) system (Denmark), "urban parks including ensembles and complexes" (Georgia), "architectural conservation areas" (Ireland), and "conservation areas" (United Kingdom). Historical sites that form a townscape unity, or form groups of immovable objects, can be specifically designated in Spain and the Netherlands respectively. Buildings can be listed for "group value" in the United Kingdom, "sets" of objects can be declared in the Czech Republic, whereas an *à la carte* approach in Belgium allows different approaches depending on the merits of the case. In France, the law allows the possibility of applying historical monument status to entire areas of cities, towns and villages.

These approaches are consistent with the convention. However, in recent drafts of proposed new laws being developed in South-East Europe a variety of terms can be found covering the same matter.

For example, in a recent draft from Kosovo the following were mentioned:

- "*construction ensembles*: as construction groups, defined or related, which according to their architecture, integrity and inclusion with the landscape, represent special cultural values, from a historic, artistic and scientific point of view" (Article 3.2);

- "*ensemble of buildings*: means separated and related groups, which according to their architectonic importance, homogeneity or their position in the landscape, have special historic, artistic and scientific values" (Article 6.5);

- "*cultural-historic entirety*: is considered as a building with its environment, a settlement, a quarter or part of quarter, an ensemble, a complex or region that is treated or protected as cultural heritage" (Article 6.20);

- "*groups of buildings*: are one of several ensembles, related and defined by their compact architectonic" (Article 7.3);

- "*sites and spatial comprehensiveness*: are topographic zones, created by the human hand, or works created by the human hand or nature which distinguished compact features from the architectonic, historic, scientific, social, technical or industrial viewpoint of view" (Article 7.4);

- "*quarters in urban and rural zones*: are quarters defined as urban or rural, with distinguished architectonic characteristics within a compact, compositional and setting structure" (Article 7.6);
- "*historic cities*: are historic spaces formed by the symbiosis or material proofs, created by the human hand in combination with nature, with a multi-layer structure, a legible chronologic stratigraphy and in harmony, where every object is an integral part of the urban context" (Article 7.7);
- the term "architectural heritage" also includes "an urban-architectonic ensemble that is functional" (Article 6.29).

This is repetitive and very confusing not just to ordinary members of the public (who have to abide by the law) but also for heritage officials and other officials such as those working for planning authorities who may have to include such mechanisms in land use and development plans if there is to be an integrated system.

It is, therefore, preferable to use terms for the protection of assets that are straightforward and easy to understand such as those used in the convention (monuments, groups of buildings and sites). In the recent draft law developed by Serbia on architectural heritage these exact definitions were used – but also reference was made to archaeological sites (by definition) and cultural scenery and reservations (without definition). Otherwise, similar definitions to those used in the convention could be adopted.

2.4. Archaeological heritage

Distinguishing the *archaeological heritage* from the architectural heritage, the European Convention on the Protection of the Archaeological Heritage (revised) (ETS No. 143, Valletta Convention, 1992) deals with this heritage discipline. This convention does not, however, prescribe interest factors nor does it define details in relation to specific categories or components as in the Granada Convention. The convention simply states that the definition of the archaeological heritage covers "all remains and objects and any other traces of mankind from past epochs". This means that any evidence, of whatever nature, that can help to provide understanding of the past of humankind and its relationship to the natural environment is important. This is qualified by the process of gaining such information within the limits of a particular state. In this respect, the explanatory notes indicate that the first action should be to conduct a survey and then there are various non-destructive techniques and sampling processes available before proceeding with the decision to excavate. In other words, excavation should be regarded as the last resort, not the normal method.

The Valletta Convention does suggest protection for:
- monuments
- areas (where the extent of a site or monument is unknown).

The convention also mentions that protection could be through a third type of designation, that of:

- archaeological reserves.

These should be areas of land subject to restrictions where the non-renewable archaeological resource should be managed carefully as a last resort in the future and where the most desired option is to leave the remains *in situ*, that is, undisturbed. Future archaeological investigation should preferably be by new non-intrusive methods and excavations should only be permitted when they are absolutely necessary.

The convention further defines the archaeological heritage as including:

> "structures, constructions, groups of buildings, developed sites, movable objects, monuments of other kinds as well as their context, whether situated on land, water or under water" (Article 1.3).

However, these are just examples of the types of assets that are included within the archaeological heritage and it is stressed that this is not an exhaustive list, but illustrative only. It is therefore not necessary to attempt to define these particular items in the law.

Thus, with the archaeological heritage it is also useful to maintain a simplicity of terminology in law for the definition of protection of items.

2.5. Cultural landscapes

The European Landscape Convention (ETS No. 176, Florence Convention, 2000) has brought a new philosophy on landscape protection. For the purpose of the convention, this is defined as "actions to conserve and maintain the significant or characteristic features of a landscape, justified by its heritage value derived from its natural configuration and/or from human activity", that is, not just based on biological, geological, landscape/aesthetic values but linking with the immovable heritage – both the architectural and archaeological heritage.

It is appropriate for the law to consider the designation of such sites and there are already many examples elsewhere of dual site status, but it is important not to duplicate. Cultural landscapes (where the effects of man and nature are revealed) should be differentiated from purely natural areas and a law on cultural heritage should not seek to designate purely natural areas. Moreover, the concept of landscape covers natural, rural, urban, and peri-urban areas and inland water or marine areas.

The landscape convention has not yet resulted in detailed recommendations on designation and management, but a key issue here is the development of integrated processes.

3. Interest factors/selection criteria

3.1. Archaeological heritage

Concerning the archaeological heritage, the Valletta Convention identifies that each state should determine interest factors and criteria in the light of circumstances and the types of sites that may be encountered. This implies a need for qualitative criteria for selection (interest factors) to be established and, as with the definition of protected items, it is important to limit the detail actually contained in the law. To some extent this will depend on whether all items of the archaeological heritage are automatically protected (the tradition in many southern European countries). Otherwise, qualitative criteria could relate to such issues as rarity, diversity, fragility, group value, documentary evidence and categorisation of periods.

3.2. Architectural heritage

For the architectural heritage it will be necessary to identify criteria for selection as the whole of the built environment does not merit protection. The convention identifies that this should be according to the qualitative criteria of "conspicuous historical, archaeological, artistic, scientific, social or technical interest" (one or more), but something similar could equally be adopted. It must be reiterated that it is important to limit the details in the law.

By comparison the United Kingdom uses the following terms and criteria for the architectural heritage:

- listed buildings: buildings of special architectural or historical interest that are deemed worthy of preservation;
- groups of buildings: groups of listed buildings of special architectural or historical interest;
- conservation areas: areas of special architectural or historic interest.

In fact, the detailed meaning of what these definitions include is not expressed in law (where a simplified definition is used) but in policy documents and instruments – so that the public is not confused by detailed explanations. So, the simpler consideration of interest factors of "special architectural or historic interest" for selecting items for protection (two in total), is much shorter than the "conspicuous historical, archaeological, artistic, scientific, social or technical interest" (six in total), but in fact more detailed information can be obtained in policy and other documents that are available to the public should they wish to have access to them.

As with the component parts of the heritage, the qualitative criteria for selection does not need to be the same as those expressed in the convention so long as they are in harmony with them, that is, in the spirit of terms used in the convention. Certainly, many signatory countries to the Granada Convention use a variety of different interest factors: for example, "landscape" (Walloon, Belgium), "revolutionary" (Czech Republic), "architectural" (Denmark, Malta and United Kingdom), "aesthetic" (Georgia and France), "palaeontological" (Spain), "ethnological" (France, Italy and Spain), "spiritual" and "religious" (in Georgia and Ireland respectively), "urban design" and "folk-lore" (Thüringia, Germany). Social interest may also be represented by "public interest", "events" or "persons of note in history" and "military significance", while environmental and economic considerations may also be used. The key issue is that most countries limit the criteria to a maximum of four or five within the law and detailed explanation of these are provided outside of the law.

3.3. Examples from South-East Europe

In general terms, in the drafts recently developed by South-East European countries there is a tendency to have a very extensive reference to interest factors/criteria for selection, which is both confusing and provides too much detail. For example, a recent draft law for Kosovo makes reference to "high cultural, historical, architectural, archaeological, artistic, pictorial, scupturesque, ethnological, anthropological, technical, environmental, topological, educational and traditional values" (14 in total), when discussing the scope of the cultural heritage. It further considered other values in other parts of the draft, including aesthetic, urbane, industrial, social, and scientific (making a total of 19 values). A draft developed by "the former Yugoslav Republic of Macedonia" included 11 interest factors and the draft developed by Montenegro had a similar number and repeats reference to interest factors in several places.

The approach adopted in Bosnia and Herzegovina must be commended, as a regulation entitled "Criteria for the Designation of Property as National Monuments" was published in 2002 and precedes the process of drafting a new state law. This new law will be able to refer to this regulation, which is divided into two parts concerning:

1. A subject of legal protection (*a*. portable cultural property; *b*. immovable cultural property such as: i. historic buildings and monuments; ii. groups of buildings; and iii. sites – including archaeological sites and cultural landscapes);

2. Values (time frame, historic value, artistic and aesthetic value, evidential value, symbolic value, townscape/landscape value, authenticity, uniqueness/rarity and integrity).

These criteria are in the form of a clear list of different items that may be subject to legal protection and a checklist of issues relating to each of the values, which the Commission to Preserve National Monuments uses to make decisions on items to be designated. This is transparent. This also enables a swift procedure for the designation of the items by the commission (which meets every two months for six days to make collective decisions).

3.4. Cultural landscapes

Concerning cultural landscapes, the convention identifies that "landscape quality objectives" should be established, stating clearly the special features and qualities of protected landscapes, which have resulted from identification and evaluation surveys. Further guidance is awaited on the approach to selection in this context.

4. Categories and levels of protection and the use of inventory standards and selection methods

4.1. Protection by category or type

The use of different categories (types) of protection must be differentiated from different levels (significance/importance) of protection.

Concerning cultural heritage "categories" (types) the recent draft law of the Republic of Montenegro, for example, defines the concept of cultural property in two pages of detailed text (Articles 2 and 3). This is repetitive as the draft also considers cultural property in relation to the immovable, movable and non-material heritage in a further two pages (Articles 18 to 20), which should be sufficient for the law. However, the draft then considers nine "types" of cultural property by characteristics (archaeological, historical, architectonic, artistic, construction, ethnological, old and rare books, film materials and technical) (Articles 21 to 30) in a further two pages. This information on types is more a matter for recording through inventory systems and criteria for selection (which can be separated from the law to reduce the excess of detail).

4.2. Inventory systems

Inventory systems can record the different types of protected items and other core data information. In this respect the Council of Europe's *Guidance on inventory and documentation of the cultural heritage* presents three internationally agreed standards for the documentation of the cultural heritage (in relation to the architectural, archaeological and movable heritage respectively) and additional information on the recording of ensembles. These three standards are:

- the Core Data Index to Historic Buildings and Monuments of the Architectural Heritage;
- the International Core Data Standard for Archaeological Sites and Monuments;
- the core data standard for identifying cultural objects – the Object ID.

For example, the Core Data Index (architectural heritage) provides for the recording of "functional types" and under this heading further sub-divides this information to be recorded so that a building category (such as agricultural) and type (such as a barn) can be recorded.

4.3. Selection: scientific investigation or rapid survey

In fact, the explanatory notes to the Granada Convention differentiate between scientific inventories and simplified documentation/rapid surveys. The purpose of the latter is to provide information on items not yet protected or included in an inventory but which are threatened by development schemes or by proposals for their demolition or serious alteration for the purpose of assessing properties. One of the concerns of the Legislative Support Task Force in assessing draft legislation is that the process of identifying properties for protection often involves in-depth scientific investigation (the "Academy of Sciences" approach) leading to a lengthy assessment period. This involves extensive effort and time (and may be a drain on already limited financial resources) and where properties are under threat there is a danger that property is damaged or destroyed before protection is legally instituted. The purpose of the criteria for selection/interest factors is to determine whether something complies with one or more of the criteria so that it can be chosen for protection, which should be undertaken by a simplified and swift survey procedure. The approach adopted in Bosnia and Herzegovina is, therefore, a useful example to follow.

Moreover, one of the roles of the Commission for the Preservation of National Monuments in Bosnia and Herzegovina is to consider the endangered heritage. Registers of heritage assets at risk (whether protected or not) can similarly be considered by a rapid survey. A swift selection system could also be linked to an assessment of risk so that priority action can then be directed where it is most needed. This may be more preferential than having different levels (importance/significance) of protection (see below).

4.4. Levels of protection

Concerning "levels of protection", the recent draft Serbian law identifies three levels of significance (national, regional and local). These are used to identify not only the level of importance of assets but also the degree to which interventions should be permitted. Similarly, the recent Montenegrin draft makes reference to three levels of property (extreme importance, great importance and important) but what results from these different categorisations is not so clear. In Bosnia and Herzegovina, the recent outline for a draft law suggests that "national" level monuments will be designated by the state (and come under state rules), but "local" designations will be applied by entity or district authorities (possibly under separate provisions).

Different approaches are adopted in European countries regarding the need for one single category or other levels of protection. This is more likely to occur in relation to the architectural heritage, but in South-East Europe there is a tendency to have different levels for all aspects of the cultural heritage.

The argument for having more than one level of protection would seem to be tied to the question of economics and not just "importance". A higher level may warrant priority support (largely due to the limited funds available to support conservation action), whereas countries that have chosen one level have decided not to discriminate on the basis that all monuments should be equally eligible or for other reasons. For instance, Denmark formerly had both A and B levels of listed buildings but due to a reassessment of the selection criteria (which recognised the importance of industrial buildings for example), the distinction was removed. The argument against having different levels of protection is that there is a danger of prioritising action in support of assets at the highest level while other heritage assets may not be properly considered and this may result in detriment to some assets. Priority action may be better designed in relation to the endangered heritage in a general sense.

In relation to the architectural heritage in particular, it may be possible to use other avenues for protecting/preserving locally important buildings through local planning and development objectives. In France, rules incorporated into the ZPPAUP as an annex to the *Plan d'occupation des sols* and in *secteurs sauvegardés* ensure an integrated process, which is further assisted by spatial development schemes that include measures to safeguard the unprotected heritage. However, this will require a fully integrated system of management and it will take some time before this can be implemented in most South-East European countries.

5. Conclusions

The first key conclusion to this theme is that a law on the cultural heritage should be to regulate the actions of citizens in relation to the cultural heritage in the wider public interest and not to delegate responsibilities to competent authorities concerning the management of the cultural heritage (which can be achieved by separate regulation).

In this respect it is important to be succinct and to use clear terminology that is understandable to the ordinary citizen (and particularly to private owners of heritage assets). This then emphasises the need for the law to be designed in a way that is logical and understandable, without repetition and excessive detail.

The various conventions (and their explanatory notes) made under the auspices of the Council of Europe provide a useful starting point in defining the component parts of the cultural heritage in different heritage disciplines. Such definitions do not need to be the same as the convention, so long as they are in the spirit of the terms used in the conventions. However, the separation of heritage disciplines (vertically) and distinguishing the aspects of the immovable heritage will help the ordinary citizen and owners of protected assets to understand the legal procedures that are relevant to their interests.

The categorisation of types within different heritage disciplines, as well as the interest factors and criteria for selection need only be defined in brief terms, leaving the detail to other regulations that will have more relevance to heritage officials.

6. The Serbian case

The basic legal act in the Serbian legal system related to cultural heritage is the Law on Cultural Property (Goods), 1994.

The other laws familiar to this object includes the Law on Realisation of the General Interest of the Republic of Serbia in the Field of Cultural Affairs (1992), which regulates the system of institutions, responsibilities and budget provisions for various cultural affairs, including the protection of cultural properties.

Then there is the Law on Planning and Building (2001). This law considers the issue of integrated protection and urban planning. However, it is a controversial law as it is not quite coherent with the 1994 law. This is due to the fact that it uses different types of terminology concerning the levels of protection and categorisation. In this respect, it is rather strange that the authorities did not respect the existence of the established terminology.

There is also a Law on the Protection of Environment, which deals with a range of natural heritage issues, and the Law on Sremski Karlovci, which is a special law concerning one historical town.

Considering this theme, the Serbian point of interest is in relation to the 1994 Law on Cultural Property (Goods). But to some extent, as it is necessary with regard to this topic, it is important to consider the other mentioned Acts, as well as some proposals for the reform of the 1994 law.

The idea of making reforms commenced after the fall of the Milosevic regime. Amongst the public there has been a will for reform.

Three attempts have been made to draft a new law on heritage: Attempt A (2001); Attempt B (2003); and Attempt C (A1) (2004).

The third draft was prepared by the same specialists that were involved in developing the first draft – and therefore it is a continuation of this effort.

In this process it is recognised that heritage should be a resource for sustainability. Moreover, there is a need to crush the elitist view of the heritage. Laws should be clear and transparent.

6.1. Purpose of law

Using as a starting point Article 72 of the Constitution of the Republic of Serbia 1991 ("The Republic of Serbia shall regulate: …System in the field of … culture and protection of cultural goods …") it is possible to investigate the purpose of the 1994 law. This article clearly defines the responsibility of the state, as well as the need for further legislative regulations.

An immediate consequence of Article 72 of the constitution is found in Article 1 of the 1994 law, which states that:

> "By this Law, the system of the protection and use of cultural properties has been established as the conditions for the performance of the protection of cultural properties."

Reading this article we can hardly speak about "protection of human rights" and consequently, "rights to heritage", as an inherent human right and an aim of this law. The 1994 law is focused on the "protection of the properties" and establishing the institutional system in support of this task.

Fortunately, in the 1994 law there are provisions concerning rights, obligations and limitations, for example, related to the owners and users of properties (truly, it is relatively difficult to deal with the idea of property without the idea of owners) but this is not specifically related to this theme of discussion.

Taking into account attempts A, B and C (A1) the sub-topic of the purpose of law of this theme can be developed in considering the battle for a new title for the law: Attempt A insists on the term Law on Cultural Properties – because it was in the tradition of Serbian legislation; Attempt B requires the use of the term "heritage".

At first sight this dichotomy could be merely considered as scholastic but some discussion about this dichotomy could provide, at least, a new fruitful discussion. "Property or heritage?" It is a similar dilemma to "to be or not to be?" but it is more traumatic than Hamlet's dilemma.

Wittgenstein said in *Tractatus* that a language disguises a thought, but in this case it can reveal some political as well as philosophical approaches to the problem of heritage.

Simply, this terminological dispute traces two different approaches. The idea of "cultural property" (or in Serbian, more appropriately translated as a "good") is connected with ownership, as well as some features of the objects defined as "cultural". It is more or less understood as a matter of excellence, something separated and distinguished. On the other hand, it is a "good" – meaning a resource of some benefit.

The idea of "heritage" is connected with continuum, something that was inherited and that has to be kept for future generations. In this sense, "heritage" is closely connected with the concept of a resource of identity, and with sustainability as well. The development of attempt B was widely inspired by the work on the draft of the new Council of Europe Framework Convention on the Value of Cultural Heritage for Society (CETS No. 199), as well as the resolutions from the Fourth European Conference of Ministers responsible for the Cultural Heritage (Helsinki, 1996).

The intentions and aims of political decision making and the consideration of the philosophy of profession (or federation of professions) within the same time period require a choice to be made.

At the same battlefield, the supporters of the 1994 law are in favour of a codex (or "umbrella law") while the supporters of attempt B have tried to separate the law concerning heritage from the sets of laws about archiving, museums, conservation laboratories and other heritage services.

This choice is, in fact, in the choice of approach and a matter of decision, and *eo ipso*, the purpose of law.

6.2. Standardisation of terms

In order to understand the Serbian case, it is important to note that Serbia had not signed any Council of Europe or UNESCO conventions since 1986 until September 2007 when the Valletta and Florence Conventions were signed.

The spirit of the Granada Convention is partially incorporated in the 1994 Law on Cultural Property (Goods). The law identifies three sorts of properties: immovable, movable and spiritual (intangible) properties, but actually operates in relation to immovable and movable items. More specifically these are categorised as follows:

Immovable property

- monuments of culture;
- spatial, cultural and historical entity (equivalent to group of buildings, urban and rural area, historical town);
- archaeological site;
- momentous area (memorial).

Movable property

- museum objects (art-historical objects);
- archive materials;
- film archive;
- old and rare books.

Intangible property (proposed in Attempt A)

- language;
- folk heritage;
- traditions and old crafts.

At first sight, it is obvious that the terminology used (and proposed) is not in harmony with the conventions and international standards. This kind of problem could be easily solved if the conventions are adopted and implemented, as well as relevant recommendations (such as the Council of Europe Recommendation No. R (95) 3 from the Committee of Ministers to member states on co-ordinating documentation methods and systems related to historic buildings and monuments of the architectural heritage).

It is true that the convention does not make a prescriptive requirement for harmonisation of terminology, but it gives an opportunity to do this. Hence, the problem of harmonisation of terminology in a future Serbian law will be deeply connected with a process of acceptance of the conventions and careful implementation of the international recommendations and standards.

The extraordinary problem for the future is likely to be in relation to the introduction and implementation of the concept of "cultural landscapes" (due to the present organisation of the heritage protection system and the separate and direct responsibilities of the Service for the Protection of the Environment).

It is reasonable to expect that the harmonisation of terms, although necessary for informing and including Serbian heritage policy in the international professional community (Article 17 of the Granada Convention), will meet some resistance from professionals. However, the willingness for change in everyday practice clearly demonstrates there is a desire for reform.

6.3. Categorisation and links to inventories/registers

According to the 1994 law, the inventory of the immovable heritage has been structured as follows:

- the Central Registry – under the responsibility of the Republic Institute for the Protection of Monuments of Culture (core database);
- registries of cultural goods, under the responsibility of the regional institutes (at present 10, not including Kosovo).

The registries are organised for every sort of immovable asset. There are, of course, some similarities with the standards established by the Core Data Index to Historical Buildings and Monuments of the Architectural Heritage, the International Core Data Standard for Archaeological Sites and Monuments and the data standard for identifying cultural objects – Object ID, but obviously the rule book on registries is very different to these standards.

The registries of movable heritage are under the central institutions (the National Library, Archive of the Republic of Serbia and the National Museum).

Categorisation: three levels of protection

There are three levels of protection: outstanding importance; great importance; and important. Attempt B to draft a new law did consider the idea of "national, regional and local levels" of protection.

Relating to the issue of budget support, categories 1 and 2 could be defined as being at the national level and under direct patronage of the republic, while category 3 would come under local responsibility. There is no obligation for a register of the "heritage at risk", and no methodology for a priority intervention list.

Attempt A1 establishes the possibility for the minister to announce the priority list every year, according to the special rule book. It is a good idea, and necessary, but an insufficient and unsatisfactory one. The protection methodology relating to the issues of vulnerability, risk and sustainability of heritage is not a usual and accepted practice.

The remnants of an elitist approach are evident in the concept of categorisation. A struggle against elitism is mostly a revolutionary activity and, therefore, it must be founded upon best practice, promotion and persuasion.

The activities tied in with Component B of the Regional Programme for Cultural and Natural Heritage in South-East Europe (Integrated Rehabilitation Project Plan) are of vital importance for the success of Component A (Institutional Capacity Building Plan). Namely, the results of the harmonisation of practices could provide a change of rules. The approach oriented towards implementing best practice results can offer more opportunities for reforms and fend off possible and expected threats.

Contemporary technology will change the world, perhaps more rapidly. At the same time, it provides new possibilities for information exchange. Without standards and a common thesaurus, we should lose ourselves in the Tower of Babel. But the bitter truth of globalisation is that the Tower of Babel is much larger than we imagined.

6.4. Conclusions

The process of developing a new law on cultural heritage in Serbia is still in progress. Decisions must be made on the way forward. At present, relevant conventions and recommendations are not acknowledged although this situation may change. This would help to harmonise the terms that are recognised in European standards.

Presently, all attempts to reform the law have chosen to consider different levels of protection. A priority intervention list has been considered in one draft but not in another. The registration system is similar to the European standards, but slightly different.

At the heart of the reform process and the continuing debate on a new law, it is still to be clarified whether the law will be an umbrella law covering different disciplines or whether it will centre on the cultural heritage itself. Moreover, there are different opinions on the way forward – some are more open to change and endorse the heritage within a framework of sustainable development, whilst others have a more traditional and elitist approach to control. Undoubtedly, there is a need for greater transparency and recognition of the right to heritage.

7. Summary of questions and views

The following issues of debate and responses were raised in relation to the presentation of papers on Theme 1:

Issue 1 – With respect to the definition of terminology, it must be recognised that some definitions have different meanings, even in a dictionary. It is, therefore, sometimes necessary to define more broadly or specifically what we have in mind to avoid double meanings, misunderstandings and misinterpretations. Regarding the length of a legal text, the issue should not be whether the draft is short or long, but whether it is adequate in covering all necessary issues. Our countries have gone through many troubles and are in transition – it is no wonder that we do not understand concepts uniformly and there are different meanings and interpretations of almost anything.

Response

It is recognised that society is changing quite dramatically in the countries undergoing transition. Moreover, it is important to think differently in terms of how members of the public will have to address the rules and regulations that will affect them resulting from new laws. In previous times the state system controlled everything and the power was from there. But now a democratic process has begun. The public, therefore, has the right to understand the laws that will affect them. It is agreed that the point is not whether a law is long or short, it should be adequate. Having said this, some of the details that can be found in the draft laws presented to the Council of Europe could be taken out and placed in policy documents to explain things to people, for example, or through secondary legislation or other regulations. It is important to try not to over-complicate a law with details. If a draft law is confusing when read by a member of the Council of Europe's task force then it is more than likely it will be confusing to ordinary members of the public.

The key point is to create a system through law that is understandable to the general public. A law on cultural heritage will have to highlight which institutions somebody will have to send an application to and other regulations that will affect them. They do not need the detailed information on how the authorities are internally regulated mixed in with the regulations that directly affect the public. It is, therefore, important to separate the provisions of law that *a.* regulate the actions of citizens and *b.* regulate the delegation of powers to specific institutions.

Issue 2 – In order to change the experience of the countries represented here we should consider the issues of categorisation and importance (levels of protection).

In the former Yugoslav federation, categorisation concerns the level of importance of the heritage: first, second or third category, or outstanding national importance and local/regional interest. The other term that is very problematic, which we are considering in a subsidiary law about the methodology of terms, is "valorisation" which can have different meanings in different countries. In our country it is to have a methodology of valorisation – information concerning the identification of significance of monuments. On the other hand, the European standards suggest the idea of "identification" instead of valorisation. If we say valorisation, what is an inventory? Is a museum inventory only for identification of information about an object or objects, for example size or number. So, there are many difficulties when considering these terms.

There are also different terms for types of monuments – because the type of monuments could not only be architectural or archaeological, but also movable or immovable. There are different levels of interpretation.

It is important to explore these terms further to find the differences between them. It should not be necessary to have a unified system and only one term on which we agree. It is, however, necessary to have a system of terms that are useful for officials involved with protection. A methodology is the first step to know what you are doing, what is your subject of work. It would be useful to exchange our experience on this matter.

Response

The conventions and recommendations provide a guide to the sort of terms to be used but, as has already been mentioned in the theme presentation, there is not a prescriptive need to adhere exactly to the terms used in the conventions or similar documents. They do, nevertheless, provide a useful guide which could be used when drafting new laws. Moreover, this would allow the possibility to review the terms used in the context of a wider heritage and the integrated form of conservation/protection.

In some countries an inventory can have a legal status in terms of identifying what is actually protected. In other words, the inventory is the registered list of protected items. In other situations, the inventory is used only as a documentation system from which items are then chosen for designation.

The key issue is to reconsider the practices of the last 50 years and to reconsider the use of terms within a new legal system that serves not just to "control" but also to "manage".

One of the legal task force's concerns is that there is a tendency to define everything in detail. There must be an in-depth investigation – for instance a scientific investigation or restoration. The situation has changed because property is not owned by the state anymore (or is awaiting a process of restitution to private owners). A democratic society should be open to a broad ownership, a broad tenancy. We have to think of heritage not as a museum that we protect but as something that we manage, that we live and work in. The sustainable approach is saying, for example with a historical building, if it is vacant, if it is in disrepair, then we need to take care of the causes. We need to have it occupied, used and maintained, and for it to earn its keep. Then there is money coming in to allow for its preservation. We allow it to be used to meet current needs but also protect it for future generations. We are managing the process rather than having a museum for protection. A different approach is necessary.

For example, in terms of identifying heritage assets to be designated as protected items the tradition in South-East Europe has been to complete a very detailed examination before decisions are made. In the meantime a lot of the heritage becomes "at risk" due to the requirement to undertake a detailed scientific valorisation, as there is insufficient time and resources to undertake a detailed assessment of all properties. Many assets that could be designated remain unprotected because it has not yet been ascertained whether they have certain recognisable values.

So, new approaches are being suggested for establishing whether property has recognisable values. A rapid survey approach rather than a scientific assessment can be determined very quickly and thus those items can be brought within the sphere of the law. Therefore a proper management strategy can be developed for their use, rehabilitation, conservation and so forth. This sort of approach has been developed through the "criteria for selection" adopted in 2002 in Bosnia and Herzegovina.

The very detailed approach often leads to a restoration approach rather than a conservation approach. Many of the draft laws from South-East European countries have indicated the need to restore "the original building, the original monument". But what is original? All historical assets change over time. Many have been re-used and changed over time, and the additions in themselves may add value. Is it really possible to go back to the original? Scientific analysis may assist this process but there is always a danger that it becomes a conjectural process. Should we not think more in terms of conserving "as found" and rehabilitation, and think of it not as a protection activity but as a management process?

The use of defined selection criteria should speed up the process of designating assets as protected assets. After this stage, it should be possible to make a further analysis in terms of identifying what features should be safeguarded or what could be changed, for instance, to allow new use.

Issue 3 – The example of the regulations defining the selection criteria of protected assets from Bosnia and Herzegovina has been cited as a good example. It should be further explained that these criteria, in relation to the immovable heritage, highlight both "monuments" and "buildings". These can be differentiated. For "monuments" there is a link with "memory"; for "buildings" the association is with the "living heritage". But this raises a question in relation to a church or another religious building – is it a monument or part of the living heritage (or both). Concerning the issue of levels of protection or significance – should this relate to "national" importance or significance or other criteria?

Response

The answer to this question should lie with the criteria for selection, for example in the Granada Convention of "conspicuous historical, archaeological, artistic, scientific, social or technical interest", rather than nationalistic ideology. The Council of Europe has identified the "common heritage" and the need to recognise the heritage of all people in all its diversity.

Theme 2 – Integrated conservation systems

1. The basic principle: integrated conservation

The purpose of this first part of the paper is to define the concept of integrated conservation and outline its practical implications for heritage policy in order that all the participants agree on the values and principles involved.

1.1. Definition of the concept of integrated conservation

The "integrated conservation" of the cultural and natural heritage is one of the major principles of the heritage policies advocated by the Council of Europe.

The expression "integrated conservation" first appeared in 1975 in the European Charter of the Architectural Heritage, adopted and promulgated at the end of European Architectural Year. It refers to two essential objectives: conservation and integration.

Conservation of heritage is understood in the broad sense through:
- protective mechanisms;
- measures for the physical conservation of constituent elements;
- enhancement processes.

Integration of this heritage into the actual social environment is through:
- urban restoration and revitalisation programmes;
- regional and local development programmes;
- co-operation with town and regional planning players.

In other words, the integrated conservation of cultural heritage monuments and sites includes a "whole range of measures aimed at ensuring the perpetuation of that heritage, its maintenance as part of an appropriate environment, whether man-made or natural, its utilisation and its adaptation to the needs of society".

This definition appears in Council of Europe Resolution (76) 28 of the Committee of Ministers concerning the adaptation of laws and regulations to the requirements of integrated conservation of architectural heritage, which should be read because it deals precisely with the concept that concerns us here.

1.2. Practical implications of integrated conservation

Implementation of the principle of integrated conservation in heritage policies means adopting new approaches to the types of heritage to be dealt with, as well as policies and management methods.

1.3. Types of heritage to be given priority

The great novelty of the principle of integrated conservation, compared with earlier policies, is that it gives priority to the restoration of "groups of buildings" and "areas", that is, groups of urban buildings and old neighbourhoods or historical centres or rural buildings (traditional villages), as decisive elements in the quality of people's environment. This particular attention to groups of buildings (rather than just to isolated monuments) is one of the key messages of this debate since they are at present generally under-recognised – or even ignored – in the heritage policies of the countries of South-East Europe.

When the exceptional quality of "individual monuments" requires that they be conserved, this should be done within the existing context (or neighbouring environment), as it is important to preserve the original atmosphere. This new, integrated approach is implemented by defining "protection zones" where the activities and interventions effected on buildings and the surrounding public spaces are subject to stricter controls than the rest of the territory.

Furthermore, according to the Valletta Convention (1992), the archaeological heritage should also be covered by integrated conservation policies. In view of the increasing impact of major construction work on the archaeological heritage, the convention requires states to take steps to protect and conserve buried archaeological sites (or sites of archaeological interest), including "preventative" archaeological excavations prior to the implementation of development programmes.

This new, integrated approach to the conservation of monuments, groups of buildings and areas and archaeological sites is also reflected in the conservation of movable heritage which is an integral part of immovable assets (being regarded as immovable because of its purpose) and in some cases considerably increases their cultural value (see Council of Europe Recommendation No. R (98) 4 on measures to promote the integrated conservation of historic complexes composed of immovable and movable property, adopted by the Committee of Ministers on 17 March 1998).

1.4. Policies and heritage management methods

The principle of integrated conservation requires a new, integrated approach to the heritage in terms of policies and management methods. It gives priority to a conservation policy (or "active management") of the cultural heritage, rather than focusing on protection. Such heritage management requires a comprehensive approach to the complex problems connected with maintenance, restoration and enhancement of the various constituents of cultural heritage, and groups of buildings and areas in particular.

Integrated conservation, therefore, requires a truly integrated management method which seeks a comprehensive approach to situations and the mechanisms that produce them. In this context, urban revitalisation and restoration programmes are highly recommended in so far as they require a multitude of competencies generating economic development and reinforcing social cohesion and the cultural identity of the populations concerned (in this connection, see Theme 5).

In order to intervene adequately, management mechanisms need to be put in place to enable co-operation and co-ordination at every stage of the decision-making process between all those involved in the heritage, town and regional planning fields.

Integrated heritage conservation is now becoming one of the fundamental constituents of town and regional planning, while the legal instruments in this field (strategies, plans, regulations and permits) are now bolstering heritage conservation policies.

2. Problems at legislative, institutional and political levels

Although it has existed for 30 years, the principle of integrated conservation is still relevant. However, it is difficult to transpose and apply, in particular to the countries of South-East Europe.

2.1. At the legislative level

Generally speaking, the principle of integrated conservation barely exists in cultural heritage legislation. Legislation usually contains two or three sections referring to town planning (the granting of urban planning permits and plans), but they are imprecise and do not refer to implementing orders that might specify how they are to be applied. In other cases, implementing orders are provided for in law but have not yet been drafted or adopted, making the legal provisions ineffective.

2.2. At the institutional level

In most of the countries of South-East Europe the minister responsible for cultural heritage and the minister responsible for urban and spatial planning are two different people. This is not a problem in itself but, none the less, it requires that there are co-ordination mechanisms between the different institutions if genuine integrated conservation policies are to be successfully implemented. Unfortunately, such (formally defined) mechanisms are generally lacking.

2.3. At the political level

This legal and institutional void is often the result of a lack of political will to adopt strategies and action programmes inspired by the basic principles of integrated conservation. Therefore, prior to the implementation of legal and institutional reforms, it is essential to inform and raise the awareness of politicians to the value of integrated conservation. Indeed, the content of such reforms is to a great extent dependent on the decision to apply the principle of integrated conservation.

3. Proposals and examples of good practice

Taking this observation as a starting-point, the third part of the paper will put forward various ways of including the principles of integrated conservation in legislation and institutions. Successful examples of good practice in western Europe will be presented here as illustrations.

3.1. State the intention to apply integrated conservation from the outset

It is important to state at the beginning of any law that the intention is to apply the principles of integrated conservation. This may be done in different places: in the explanatory memorandum, the preamble, the introduction to the law or the definitions (generally contained in the first part).

It is also useful to mention that this will be included in the strategic documents and action plans decided upon by the authorities responsible for the heritage in order to strengthen the effect of the statement of intent and the consistency of policy and legislation.

3.2. Mapping all protected properties

It is useful to include in the legal provisions on the protection of cultural property the mapping of the delimitation of protected properties and any related protection zones.

The mapping may be done at the different stages of the protection procedure: when owners are informed of the intention to protect their property, during the inquiry prior to the decision to protect and, above all, when the protection order is officially published.

Mapping is especially useful as a supplement to the publication of the "register of protected properties" as it is far clearer and more easily understandable than the interminable lists of addresses and parcels of land typical of such registers. This is particularly true when it comes to locating or visualising protected architectural groupings, sites and areas which do not lend themselves to land registry delimitations or police addresses.

The flexibility of "geographic information systems" (GIS) allows the presentation of maps to vary according to need: according to degree of protection, types of property, targeted areas or, again, the uses foreseen with respect to town and regional planning.

For example, a specific map showing archaeological sites will enable the authority responsible for granting planning permission to identify the presence of a site and order "preventive" digs prior to the work mentioned in the planning application (see also section 3.4).

3.3. Involvement in drafting land use plans

"Land use plans" play a part in protecting the heritage in that they control to what use it may be put. Such plans lay down the legally permitted use of all the buildings, green spaces and roads in a given territory. They include a map and regulations specific to each category of allocation shown on the map. Thus, they supplement heritage protection orders, which seldom set out the legally permitted uses of protected properties.

Whether they are general (covering a town or region) or particular (covering a neighbourhood or street), such plans therefore make it possible to protect the heritage by avoiding uses or allocations which would be detrimental to it.

For example, the land use plan could prevent an old neighbourhood consisting of small houses being transformed into an administrative area requiring large office capacity, a natural site being divided into plots, car parks being built or roads widened in the middle of a historical centre, for example.

Another advantage of such plans is that they enable the immediate protection of property that as yet enjoys no legal protection as part of the cultural heritage, and this is currently the situation of many groups of buildings and natural sites.

In Brussels (Belgium), for example, the inclusion of groups of buildings of architectural importance in the regional land use plan has enabled a whole series of very interesting monuments to be safeguarded that were not yet legally protected. The buildings have been saved from destruction through a special system of permits and planning controls concerning work planned within these groups. They have also been able to benefit from advantageous financial subsidies granted to their owners, in particular within the framework of urban renewal and housing policies.

It is, therefore, useful for heritage officials to be involved in the drafting (or revision) of land use plans in order to ensure that the uses allowed under them are compatible with safeguarding the heritage.

3.4. Involvement in the drafting of urban planning regulations

In addition to the land use plans drawn up within the framework of regional planning policies, "urban planning regulations" favour heritage conservation by legally determining building/renovation regulations (building line, size, materials, shapes, colours, etc.). In some countries they also regulate advertising hoardings, signposting, street lighting and tree felling.

Like land use plans, urban planning regulations apply either to the whole of the national or regional territory or to particular areas (a town, village or old neighbourhood).

It is, therefore, useful for heritage officials to take part in the drafting or revision of urban planning regulations in order to ensure that heritage considerations are taken into account and will, therefore, be respected in work requiring urban planning permits (splitting up into parcels, building, demolition).

When such regulations concern areas where important historical groups of buildings, sites or areas of archaeological interest are located, it is legitimate for heritage officials to guide the drafting process since what the issue concerns is heritage more than urban planning.

For example, in Belgium a partnership was established in the 1970s between Wallonia's urban planning and cultural heritage departments and the History of Art Faculty of the University of Louvain to draw up planning regulations for the region's historic town centres. These atlases of historic town centres consist of maps (see section 3.2) identifying the monuments and groups of buildings to be protected in different areas and their related urban planning regulation provisions. The maps and provisions are supplemented by documents explaining the objectives (overall strategy), as well as the heritage and planning characteristics of the buildings mentioned.

The success of these has led to the production of atlases of old rural centres and the buried archaeological sites in the region so that the regional heritage as a whole is now protected by planning instruments.

Similar principles have been applied in Brussels through regional urban planning regulations, in France through the ZPPAUP protected areas, in Denmark through the SAVE system and in Spain through special plans.

3.5. Involvement in the issuing of urban planning/heritage permits

Another urban planning legal tool that the defenders of the heritage can use is "urban planning permits" (permits to build, split into parcels or demolish). They allow permission to be granted (or refused) to undertake work on legally protected buildings and sites, located in a protection zone of a listed property or in an area of archaeological importance, on the basis of compliance (or non-compliance) with the urban planning regulations mentioned above.

It is, therefore, important for laws (and the related implementing orders) on cultural heritage to define as clearly as possible the respective roles of the partners involved (ministry/ies of urban planning and heritage), as well as the procedures for issuing such permits.

A series of questions should be answered according to the specific contexts of each country, for example: within what time limit must the two authorities responsible give their opinion? Is the opinion of the authorities responsible for the heritage binding or advisory? Where the opinions differ, does the more restrictive one prevail? Is it possible to have a single permit, rather than separate urban planning and heritage permits?

This last question is particularly important since single permits have many advantages in terms of time and human resources, organising controls and penalising owners who contravene the regulations. Ireland, the Netherlands and the Wallonia Region (Belgium) have therefore opted for a "single permit" and the United Kingdom has recently decided to follow this approach.

For example, in Wallonia, after it was found that a great many owners had "cheated" in order to obtain a permit and that it was difficult to co-ordinate the provisions for heritage with those for urban and spatial planning, the authorities responsible decided to merge the requirements on these three subjects into a single code. The new Walloon Regional and Town Planning and Heritage Code (CWATUP), adopted in 1991, is divided into four parts, one dealing with aspects specific to the immovable cultural heritage (definition, identification, listing and protection of the heritage, including archaeological sites), the others containing provisions specific to the heritage within their respective subjects (spatial plans, urban planning regulations and permits, penalties).

4. Conclusions

i. Integrated conservation results above all from a clear political choice since it has many legislative, institutional, operational and technical implications which cannot be left to chance or improvisation.

ii. It should concentrate its resources on architectural groupings, both urban and rural, protected areas around monuments and sites and areas of archaeological importance (buried heritage).

iii. It should favour active integrated management of this heritage, rather than a policy focusing on prior studies, lists and legal protection, in order to guarantee its sustainable conservation and improve the population's environment.

iv. It is only possible if it is backed up by town and regional planning policies. Legislation on immovable cultural heritage cannot on its own meet the challenge of the broader notion of heritage implied by integrated conservation. A historic neighbourhood cannot be conserved in the same way as a single monument.

v. It requires institutional reforms that lay down co-operation mechanisms to co-ordinate the various authorities responsible (heritage, town and regional planning) at the different levels of power concerned, local authorities perhaps taking responsibility for certain aspects of implementation and checks on the ground.

vi. Cultural heritage legislation should explicitly mention integrated conservation and establish direct links with the legal instruments of town and regional planning, setting out the minimum procedures to be followed and defining the respective roles of the institutional partners. This should result in a single code or a single permit system.

5. The Montenegrin case

The natural environment and relatively well-preserved conditions within the Republic of Montenegro represent a potential for development of all types of tourism, which is the country's main industry. However, the value, quality and survival of the Montenegrin cultural and natural heritage is being put at risk by uncontrolled urbanisation, infrastructure and industrial development and by the lack of an integrated and co-ordinated approach in the protection and planning system.

Montenegro is at the centre of a region that has a history of long struggles for predominance. It is positioned at the crossroads of diverse civilisations, which has created the conditions for the emergence of a unique cultural and artistic character, containing elements of numerous significant cultural movements and resulting in a significant, rich and diverse heritage. Four civilisation cycles are interwoven – Byzantine, Roman, Islamic and Venetian – which have left significant cultural monuments in their respective historical course.

In Montenegro there are 357 immovable cultural monuments protected under the law, and these are grouped into three categories, and divided in structure as follows:

- old towns and urban ensembles   14 facilities
- archaeological sites   42 facilities
- fortifications   18 facilities
- traditional architecture facilities 12 facilities
- profane facilities   76 facilities
- sacral facilities   195 facilities

5.1. Problems and shortcomings

Notwithstanding the number and importance of cultural monuments and other forms of cultural and natural heritage, there are numerous disadvantages and shortages in this field. There is an insufficient awareness of the importance of this heritage, which causes huge problems, primarily at a community level, that is, a lack of care while using these facilities and inappropriate use, which causes minor, and sometimes major, damage to natural resources and the movable and immovable heritage. Insufficient financial resources have led to a lack of valid documentation and specialist training development and reduced scientific and research work. Due to the insufficient number and inadequate qualifications of the staff working in the protection institutions, as well as in the scientific institutions, numerous activities required may not be undertaken in a timely and professional manner. The opening of the Cultural Faculty in Cetinje following the 1979 earthquake led to the creation of a new resource – professional conservation and protection staff – until its closure eight years ago. However, the economic crisis and other difficulties that directly or indirectly have affected Montenegro over the last 15 years meant that some of the professional staff lost their jobs.

Certain initiatives have been launched recently aimed at gaining knowledge and experience in order to recognise the values and potential of cultural and natural heritage, particularly through examples and assistance provided by international organisations. In the field of conservation, the revitalisation of sacral facilities, performed by all religious communities in this region, has been a trend lately. But due to an insufficient level of understanding and co-operation between the religious organisations and national institutions, these activities have been performed without the adequate participation of experts and institutions from Montenegro.

The current situation relating to the protection of the cultural and natural heritage in Montenegro is given below, including the very delicate issue of urban and spatial planning, from the aspect of national policy, legal regulations and institutional protection system.

5.2. National policy

Montenegro has no strategic document as yet, whereby the concept of the national cultural policy could be defined. It was only 10 years ago that the Ministry of Culture was established in Montenegro, possibly the main stakeholder in the elaboration of a strategy and action plan for the cultural development of the country.

The defining of new cultural policies for Montenegro began in 2003 within the framework of review of national cultural policies carried out as part of the Council of Europe MOSAIC II project. The following activities have been completed so far within the framework of this project:

- the "National Report on the Cultural Policies of the Republic of Montenegro (September 2003);
- the presentation of the National Report before the Council of Europe Supervision Committee for Culture (March 2004);
- the review and report of the Council of Europe Expert Team (May 2004);
- the national debate on "Cultural Policy" (June 2004).

The national report on cultural policies identified existing legal regulations, mainly outdated and inapplicable, which must be replaced by new regulations that are in harmony with international standards. A national cultural programme must be founded on governmental strategic documents, such as a strategy for economic development, a spatial plan, a national programme for university education or a financial and fiscal policy. The report also indicates the need for permanent re-education and further training of professional staff, particularly as Montenegro offers no possibility for specific professional education for archaeologists, ethnologists, anthropologists, art historians, conservators and restorers, for example. The concept of education in the field of cultural and natural heritage protection has not been sufficiently developed so far at any level of the educational system, particularly with respect to an integrated approach to this issue.

In 2004 a national debate discussed issues relating to cultural policy, the transition of the cultural institutions and culture in general under market economy conditions. Inadequate inter-ministerial co-operation, insufficient allocation of funds for the cultural field, unsatisfactory commitment to development of international co-operation and to cultural tourism were indicated as the main problems.

The protection and presentation of cultural and natural heritage should be considered in an integrated manner, according to the approach advocated by international organisations in this field. Joint activities must be undertaken by various ministries, primarily by those responsible for culture, tourism, environmental protection and spatial development, as well as national institutions in the field of culture, local management and NGOs.

Cultural and natural heritage must be fully integrated into the planning systems at all levels, which has not been the practice so far. The Spatial Plan of the Republic of Montenegro, which is the highest level of planning document, and currently in the process of elaboration, lacks an adequate basis, in particular regarding relevant basic studies for spatial protection mechanisms.

Taking the aforementioned into account, at this time we can hardly talk of the establishment of elementary links between heritage management and mechanisms for urban and spatial planning, and much less about putting a veto on development plans from the cultural heritage point of view. Since cultural tourism is one of the priorities of the Montenegrin Government, it is important that tourism respects cultural heritage as a resource in terms of sustainable development.

Inter-ministerial co-operation has increasingly been a means of communication between and within the government. Different ministries, public institutions, civil society and business sector should work together in order to promote culture and cultural values as an integrated process.

The national debate has considered the need for drafting a new strategic approach for culture and its integration into the scientific, educational, tourism, urban planning and other systems.

5.3. Legislation

The first legislation related to cultural monuments in Montenegro comes from the Middle Ages, while the contemporary practice, care and treatment of the cultural heritage were launched in the second half of the 19th century. The legal framework for performing activities relating to the protection of cultural and natural heritage and for the functioning of the cultural institutions in this field was established over the last three decades of the 20th century, although certain activities (such as underwater archaeology) have not been adequately regulated.

Protection of the cultural heritage is currently regulated under the following legal acts:
- the Law on Protection of Cultural Monuments (1991);
- the Law on Museum Activity (1977, 1989);
- the Law on Library Activity (1977, 1989);
- the Law on Archive Activity (1991, 1994);
- the Law on Renewal and Revitalisation of Old Towns Affected by the Disastrous Earthquake of April 15, 1979 (1984, 1986);
- the Law on Restoration of Monumental Region of Kotor (1991);
- the Law on Monuments, Memorials, Historical Events and Persons (1971, 1972, 1988);
- the Regulations on keeping the Register of Protected Cultural Monuments (1992);
- the Regulations on conditions and manner in which the archaeological research and cultural monuments' excavation may be performed (1992).

The drafting of a set of new laws in the field of cultural heritage is currently in process. The main goal of passing the new legal regulations in this field is to correct shortages of the existing legal solutions in each segment and to ensure establishment of a modern system for protection and revitalisation of the cultural heritage in accordance with European standards and principles and, in particular, to develop integrated mechanisms.

5.4. The institutional protection system and the development of integrated mechanisms

The protection service formally began to be operative in 1948, when the Institute for Protection of Cultural Monuments and Natural Rarities was established in Cetinje, which developed into the Republic Institute for Protection of Cultural Monuments.

In accordance with the World Heritage Convention (1972), after the region of Kotor had been included in the World Heritage List in 1979, the Municipal Institute for Protection of Cultural Monuments of Kotor was founded, which, in 1992, due to the significant concentration and importance of cultural monuments in the region of Kotor, Tivat and Herceg Novi, was developed into the Regional Institute for Protection of Cultural Monuments. Other institutes and museums have been established for the protection of the natural heritage (1961 and 1995) and a Centre for Archaeological Research deals with conservation of archaeological sites and artefacts. There are also a number of museums, both at local and republic level, which are responsible for the protection of movable cultural property.

The Ministry of Culture and the Media is the highest level of authority in the field of heritage protection. It is responsible for establishing guidelines, as well as managing and co-ordinating the overall system for protection of cultural and natural heritage. Institutions for the protection of nature come under the authority of this ministry and also of the Ministry for Environmental Protection and Spatial Development.

Work has already commenced for establishing connections and ensuring an integrated approach for protection by the Ministry of Culture and the Media. In this respect, the Department for Cultural Heritage was replaced by the newly established Sector for Cultural and Natural Heritage. At the same time, according to a new systematisation of the Regional Institute for Protection of Cultural Monuments, a special organisational unit was established for the first time for the protection of cultural heritage in Montenegro, which, besides the architectural heritage, is responsible for protection of the cultural landscape and environment, following UNESCO recommendations.

There is a low level of awareness of integrated systems for the cultural heritage particularly in relation to integrated urban and spatial planning systems. Heritage is disregarded or destroyed in practice rather than regenerated. This is particularly the case in the so-called contact zones, close to or relatively distant from protected areas which surround registered facilities and ensembles.

A more difficult situation is in the field of protection and management of the landscape. This is even in the case where landscape is tightly connected with the immovable heritage as well as within wider ensembles which are protected, not only under the national legislation but also under international charters and conventions (for example regions included in the UNESCO World Heritage List).

5.5. Conclusions

It is necessary to create prerequisites for the overall protection and regeneration of the Montenegrin heritage as soon as possible by introducing adequate provisions for the development of integrated conservation systems not only in laws related to protection, but also in other relevant legal acts. To this end, the experience of the Council of Europe is indispensable, as well as relevant conventions, recommendations, expert reports, seminars and suchlike.

6. Summary of questions and views

The following issues of debate and responses were raised in relation to the presentation of papers on Theme 2:

Issue 1 – How do we deal with the issue of natural and cultural heritage areas without collision?

Response

In Belgium, and more particularly in the Walloon Region, there is a "single code" known as the Walloon Regional and Town Planning and Heritage Code (Code Wallon de l'Aménagement du territoire, de l'Urbanisme et du Patrimoine, CWATUP). This code brings together all the legislative provisions affecting regional and town planning and heritage, including the archaeological heritage. It also links in directly with environmental legislation, especially on nature reserves. This means that the laws were drafted from the outset to form a coherent whole. There are, therefore, no contradictions between the aims and provisions in any of these fields, for example between archaeological aims and environmental objectives.

However, despite all this, it is sometimes necessary to resolve a dilemma (for example either to enhance an archaeological reserve by cutting down the trees that have grown up there, or to protect and conserve the trees, which may be of botanic interest). In such cases, there is a discussion. All parties sit around a table in an attempt to find a compromise that will satisfy all as far as possible. In Belgium, the attempt is always made to settle problems and conflicts of interest through discussion, before resorting to legislation or the courts. In most cases, matters can be resolved as long as everyone settles for less than 100%, so that a reasonable, acceptable and peaceable solution can be reached.

If, on the other hand, a solution cannot be reached through discussion, very strict legal provisions are invoked. To go back to the example given above, if the trees which have grown on the archaeological site are absolutely outstanding (being the only examples in the country), the decision will be taken that protecting the trees is more important than enhancing the archaeological site, as long as the latter is not really exceptional in itself. It is therefore the provision that has greater force or is backed by greater arguments that will take precedence over the other. Where representatives of heritage and planning come together around the table, for example, it is usually the heritage view that is adopted because it is the more demanding, since a project may be acceptable from a planning standpoint but unacceptable from a heritage perspective.

Naturally, where people are not satisfied with the decision, there is legal provision for them to refer the matter for review by a tribunal. Sometimes, therefore, decisions which have been taken by the political authorities are reviewed by the courts.

There are thus three levels of decision making:
- discussion aimed at finding an amicable agreement;
- application of whichever legislation has the greater force;
- appeal tribunals and/or the courts.

Issue 2 – In Bosnia and Herzegovina there is a desire to introduce "cultural heritage impact assessments" before giving a permit. Do we need a system of impact assessments and are there any examples?

Response

In the United Kingdom development proposals are considered in relation to whether the proposal fits in with the policy defined in an approved development plan, but other "material considerations" must be taken into account. The desire to "preserve" a listed building, for example, is one such example. Moreover, there is presumption in favour of the preservation of protected and other features of the "historic environment" when assessing development proposals.

Issue 3 – Terminology on integrated conservation is confusing. Is it integrated conservation, integrated protection or integrated preservation?

Response

Analysis of the legislative provisions of various South-East European countries reveals that where the Council of Europe speaks of "conservation", these documents talk about "protection". This is a problem: sometimes the same word is used to mean different concepts, and vice versa. According to the Council of Europe Recommendation (76) 28, "integrated protection" is one of the aspects of "integrated conservation" because integrated conservation includes protection in the sense of legal protection/ listing, which protects a building from any form of destruction or alteration.

Issue 4 – What is the extent of maps/plans utilised for issues such as tourism, archaeology or heritage?

Response

The maps described in Theme 2 in relation to Belgium (Wallonia) have a regulatory function. Their main aim is to provide the general population with information about the heritage situation of their property (owners wishing to know whether their property is protected or not, architectural practices in charge of projects, planning officials who have to issue permits for building, demolition, division into plots, etc.). Since they take the form of databases, specific information can be put together when necessary. The relevant items can be extracted from the maps, using different scales (a district, a town or a whole region), according to requirements and the enquiries to be conducted.

The maps are also used to back up regulatory provisions since it is not always possible to define geographical areas solely in words (using police numbers or Land Registry references). In cases of dispute, it is the map which takes precedence over the text of the order. That is why a map is always published in the Belgian *Moniteur* (Official

Gazette) at the same time as the listing order; to define the exact address of the monument or site.

While these maps are not designed to make information available on tourist sites, with a little creativity other uses for these maps could easily be envisaged (research, tourism, etc.).

Issue 5 – There are some older areas in parts of Brussels where there is a problem with social issues and immigrant communities. Is this very difficult to manage in an integrated programme?

Response 1

Until 1991, Brussels had no way of protecting its heritage since this responsibility lay, in principle, with the other two regions (Wallonia and Flanders). Between the 1950s and 1991, the pressure to build from property developers was, therefore, immense since they were completely free to work as they wished. They would, for example, buy up whole areas of old housing to put up new buildings instead, which was obviously far more profitable than restoring the old houses.

Since 1991, when Brussels became an entirely separate region, it has had its own ministry and legislation, although it is very hard to reverse the balance of history and to change habits. Since then, the political authorities have been trying to limit the degeneration of older areas, which are also poor and house a large number of marginalised and even illegal immigrants.

In order to achieve a genuine heritage conservation policy, despite the major financial interests at work in Brussels, a very strict system of sanctions has had to be introduced:

- planning sanctions: buildings illegally constructed or renovated (without a permit) may be pulled down;
- financial sanctions: deterrent fines for property developers;
- criminal sanctions: possibility of imprisonment for offenders.

To make this system of sanctions work, officials from the Ministry of Planning and Brussels Heritage are responsible for on-site "control". The officials, therefore, spend their time on the streets checking whether illegal building work is being carried out (unauthorised demolition, construction or restoration) and investigating reported offences.

Response 2

In England two funding programmes for heritage-led regeneration for historic areas have been operated recently. These are the Townscape Heritage Initiative and Heritage Economic Regeneration Schemes. Both of these programmes have provided subsidy (grant aid) assistance for conservation, restoration and rehabilitation in areas of heritage importance (usually covering defined "conservation areas") that are suffering from economic and social problems. Therefore, they concentrate on areas of deprivation. This is a sustainable approach using the heritage to support economic and social regeneration in problem areas.

Issue 6 – Returning to the issue of maps and the issues of agricultural land being restored to private ownership, owners are not always aware of heritage assets such as archaeological remains in or under the land. Is there a system of archaeological maps or how is the information given to the new owners so that they are aware of the heritage that is situated in such locations? Are archaeological maps important for supervising bodies? Furthermore, the majority of towns do not have approved plans and maps – and, therefore, the question is raised as to whether violations of the heritage constitute breaches of the law.

Response 1

Where there is no threat to the heritage, there is plenty of time to carry out in-depth investigations, with thorough mapping of the existing heritage, before legal protection is introduced or conservation work is undertaken. But where there is no time because the heritage is under threat, emergency measures have to be taken, given that it takes ten years to draw up a scientific listing, during which time the heritage will have disappeared and the listing will have been a waste of effort.

These emergency measures must allow rapid identification of the property under threat (rather than in-depth, scientific investigation) and the emergency protection required, so that planning permits (for demolition or renovation) can be barred. Once the property is protected and a stop is put to any work, damage is prevented in the short term, and the situation is stabilised.

It is, therefore, wise not to launch any major scientific investigations that will take years to publish, but to keep to lists of addresses and identification photos which will enable you to protect the heritage temporarily for a few years, until you have time to carry out a more thorough study. Also, devote time and human resources to applying sanctions, making inspections on the ground and checking that no-one is doing illegal work.

To that end, "two-stage" legislation might be introduced:

- short-term emergency legislation for the next five years to stop the haemorrhaging, change mentalities, reorganise institutions and revise the law so that it reinforces the political authorities;
- more thorough legislation aimed at long-term integrated heritage conservation.

This is what was done in Brussels in order to call a rapid halt to the destruction of the heritage by property developers. In the 1991 legislation, for example, a measure was introduced to provide automatic temporary protection for monuments dating from before 1931, until a complete register could be drawn up (within 4 years) of the properties to be definitively protected. A simple list of addresses and brief descriptions enabled sites to be protected temporarily.

In 1994, an atlas was also made of the underground archaeology in Brussels, with a brief set of rules forbidding the carrying out of works in the archaeological areas listed without prior permission from the Monuments, Sites and Excavations Service. This temporarily stabilised the situation until the general context could improve.

Each country, therefore, needs to assess the degree or urgency facing its heritage and the need to take temporary emergency steps ahead of long-term measures.

Response 2

In the United Kingdom "areas of perceived archaeological importance" may be defined in development plans. Before any development can take place in such locations then the developer may have to undertake (and pay for) an archaeological impact assessment, and, if necessary, a detailed archaeological investigation may be required. This is usually organised by conditions attached to any planning permission. There is the British Developers' and Archaeologists' Code of Practice for working on such sites. Under this, developers may enter into voluntary agreements (contracts) for archaeologists to enter a site for a period of time. This code of practice was the basis for the development of a Council of Europe Code of Good Practice ("Archaeology and the urban project") which highlights the working relationships that need to be created between developers, archaeologists and planners.

Furthermore, with respect to the threatened heritage (i.e. protected sites), two types of survey are carried out: "monuments at risk" (for archaeological sites) and "listed buildings at risk". These are recorded in registers so that preventative or other action can be determined.

In other respects, English Heritage is constantly involved in research projects. For example, since 1992 English Heritage commenced work assessing the archaeology of historical towns through "intensive urban assessments" (IUA) and "extensive urban assessments" (EUA).

Intensive assessments have been undertaken for over 35 major historical centres where the survival of archaeology remains good but is under intense development pressure. English Heritage has provided grant aid to the relevant local authority to undertake the assessments. Extensive assessments are being undertaken in other towns on a county-by-county basis, led by county archaeological services in conjunction with local authorities. Both types of assessment comprise three stages.

- *Setting up a database*: this includes the compilation of information from archaeological records and other sources (such as historic maps, documentary sources, topographical drawings and museum collections). A key feature of the database is the use of geographical information systems (GIS) based on large scale digital Ordnance Survey maps. The results from this part of the assessment are provided to the county "Sites and Monument Record" or in an Urban Archaeological Database. The information can also be integrated into local authority GIS and planning information systems.

- *Assessment stage*: this stage results in a report that assesses and maps the archaeological and historical character of each town. The assessment is period-based in a plan form that divides the information into a series of discrete topological components (such as market place, monastic precinct, burgage plot, etc.). English Heritage intends to publish the IUA reports, while the EUA reports are to be disseminated via the Internet.

- *Strategy stage*: this stage is based on the assessment report and is to be used to develop future management policies. The definition of the archaeological importance of each town will be used to guide strategic planning decisions and development control. In fact, some local planning authorities have used the information to develop supplementary planning guidance.

This meets current requirements to assess the historic environment more fully, as a whole, and is relevant to the new focus on sustainable spatial and regional planning policy.

It should also be noted that the Survey of Architectural Values in the Environment was developed in Denmark as a means of integrating the heritage into other mechanisms (following ratification of the Granada Convention). Each survey is carried out and then published as a *Heritage Atlas*, which can inform planning policies.

Theme 3 – Institutional reform: a new role for private owners and enterprises and their professional advisers

1. Introduction – democratic principles: participation and consultation

This theme builds on the issues developed in Themes 1 and 2 concerning the purpose of the law and integrated systems.

Any law concerning cultural heritage must be based on democratic principles and the protection of human rights including the participation of citizens in community life; respect for the rights of others and the right to own property. The principle of non-discrimination should apply to the identification and protection of heritage assets, maintenance and restoration action, assistance to all categories of owners (whether public or private individuals, groups or associations, civil or religious), appropriate training for those working in the heritage sector and awareness-raising. All citizens should have equal rights of access to documentary sources and relevant information concerning the heritage and all types of heritage should be equally respected.

The Fifth European Conference of Ministers responsible for the Cultural Heritage (Portorož, 2001) resolved, amongst other issues, that individuals and communities have a fundamental right to their future through their heritage including "a right to enjoy their heritage". The European ministers called upon national, regional and local authorities to promote integrated conservation of the cultural heritage in a manner that would respect the contribution of past and present communities, their cultures and patterns of use, "including by allowing proper participation in consultation and decision-making processes affecting the heritage". They also adopted a Declaration on the role of voluntary organisations in the field of cultural heritage, which requested public authorities to take account of the importance of such organisations in building and consolidating societies, with particular reference to their role in education and in monitoring heritage protection policies in the interests of democracy.

What is the relevance of these issues to the management of the architectural and archaeological heritage?

As we have considered under the first theme (purpose of law, etc.), the provisions that regulate the behaviour of citizens should not be mixed with provisions that regulate the public bureaucracy. It must be reiterated that the administrative framework for the management of cultural heritage should be defined in separate provisions, the exception being in the case of specific duties where public or private concerns are involved, such as the control of activities, consents, supervision or enforcement, which should be mentioned in a law on cultural heritage.

2. Reform and new roles for heritage institutions

2.1. The old structure of institutions

Having had discussions with various ministries and institutions in different eastern European countries it has become clear that there is a need to reform the authorities and institutions that manage the cultural heritage as a matter of public bureaucracy. Many institutions operate under legal provisions that are dated (for instance, the framework of national and regional institutions for the "protection" of the cultural heritage in Kosovo and "the former Yugoslav Republic of Macedonia" have been derived from laws from as long ago as the 1970s or before).

Under the former political regimes the role of institutions was organised by the state on behalf of the state. The emphasis was on scientific investigation and state institutions undertaking conservation and restoration work (and even reconstruction work), which would be more relevant for property held in public ownership. This type of framework is not appropriate in the new democracies of today particularly as one of the most significant changes that has happened has been the restitution of property interests into private hands (an ongoing process in some countries).

It is in this context that the institutions' role will need to be radically reviewed. Moreover, in small territories such as Kosovo and "the former Yugoslav Republic of Macedonia" it is hard to justify the continued existence of the present structure of institutions (with many regional institutions). It is no longer relevant for official services to continue to maintain their monopoly regarding certain activities (such as major restoration projects), as the private sector should incur responsibilities in this area. Whilst this may be a source of pride, heritage preservation should not be an elitist activity for public officials as specialists – it has to have relevance to the wider public and to recognise the rights of private owners. There is a need to accept the idea that the private sector has a role to play in heritage preservation and, in particular, that qualified or experienced private enterprises/companies or consultants/professional advisers could undertake necessary works while the institutions set the conditions and act as supervisors. Inevitably, this may result in a new emphasis for official roles particularly if integrated management systems are to be created.

2.2. Other problems facing institutions

There are also other problems concerning institutions in that in many countries there has been a reduction in experienced staff in recent years and, therefore, a need to recruit and train new staff. However, reduced budgets make this difficult. There is also a fear of change and concerns about employment security as a result of change. This often leads to inertia and a failure to grasp the need to change.

A review of the Kosovo network of Institutions for the Protection of Monuments and job assessments of employees (carried out by a member of a Swedish NGO on behalf of UNMIK/Ministry of Culture in 2001-2002) came to a similar conclusion. This review found that the different institutions (national and regional):

- developed independently from the 1950s and later decades (mainly the 1970s) and had not significantly changed in approach;
- had a traditional expertise-oriented approach (conservation/restoration, etc.);
- had a split and disproportionate staff (some having over twenty years experience and others with very little – often with the experienced staff representing one or two fields of expertise and newly employed staff representing other areas);
- lacked modern administrative and other guidelines;
- were isolated – with little sharing of experiences between the regional institutes and the national institute and also with the ministry, as well as having poor physical conditions (offices, infrastructure, etc.);
- lacked any form of real co-operation with municipal authorities.

Moreover, there was a general view amongst staff that the legally protected heritage was entirely an interest for the public sector and there was very little understanding of procedures whereby qualified companies or consultants could undertake actual work (with the institutions setting the conditions and acting as supervisors).

2.3. The need for new roles

This situation is not singular to Kosovo – the situation is similar for most of the South-East European countries. There is a clear need for reform and training in new approaches. In this respect, new organisational structures for the management of cultural heritage issues should aim to concentrate on a number of key activities:

i. to develop policies for the heritage sector;
ii. to carry out research (to increase knowledge of the cultural heritage);
iii. to develop and maintain inventories, archives and databases for the cultural heritage;
iv. to inform the public and provide education on matters concerning the cultural heritage (including exhibitions, publications and policy/guidance documents on particular issues);
v. to maintain and assist in developing traditional craft techniques;
vi. to administer financial funds to support heritage preservation activities;
vii. to provide advice concerning proposals that may require official consent;
viii. to supervise conservation and restoration work and works of alteration according to granted consents;
ix. to monitor unauthorised activity and implement enforcement action and sanction proceedings.

For certain types of activities these could be managed centrally (points i-vi) (or in larger countries, regionally) whilst other activities may need to be managed at a local level and integrated with other activities (points vii-ix). Indeed there is a degree of recognition for these changes. For example, in recent discussions with officials in the Republic of Montenegro it was acknowledged that there is a need for a system of local inspection and control – possibly linked with local (municipal) authorities – and a need for management plans for protected areas within such localities.

In Bulgaria, it has been noted that the National Institute of Cultural Monuments, which deals principally with the architectural heritage, previously had over a 1 000 staff spread throughout the regions, but today there are only 60 or so employees making it very difficult to manage matters at local levels. In fact, the Council of Europe's review of trends in European cultural policies (from 2003) reported that, paradoxically, the state had acquired greater control and that there was an absence of clear rules of interaction between central and municipal governments. Furthermore, it has been noted that damage has occurred to some important heritage areas due to some municipal authorities granting consents for new development. This emphasises the need for integration between land use planning and heritage management not just through the land-use/development plan systems, but also through the administration and new roles for officials.

Increasingly as the societies of the South-East European countries open up, there will be more pressure on the heritage from tourists and development/investment activity – emphasising the need for a new type of local heritage inspector/supervisor/controller:

- to liaise with both planning officials and with applicants who may apply for consents for new development/construction in areas of architectural or archaeological importance;
- in relation to the alteration or rehabilitation of protected architectural structures;
- to ensure the works that have received consent are carried out according to the terms of the consent;
- to supervise conservation and restoration work (e.g. work carried out by an owner, with the assistance of a subsidy, through an employed enterprise or by an NGO);
- to take coercive action where obligations are not carried out (to keep in good repair, prevent damage, etc.);
- to take enforcement action against unauthorised or otherwise illegal works.

2.4. Proposals for new institutional structures and roles

In Bosnia and Herzegovina there is a proposal for the regional entity planning ministries to receive applications and issue consents concerning proposed works for protected heritage assets (of national importance), but that the proposals are considered by the State Commission to Preserve National Monuments which will define the measures. The entities will, therefore, require specialised staff who understand both the heritage and the planning/development control functions.

Moreover, the role of the commission is proposed to be much wider, covering the designation of protected heritage assets and a wide range of measures concerning the evaluation of projects (conservation, restoration, rehabilitation, etc., for which consents will be required). This will include consideration of tenders, supervision of contractors, and managing and prioritising financial budgets for assistance. This will also require localised supervision in some form.

In addition, it has been proposed that the State Ministry of Civil Affairs will have a limited inspectorate (for the "control of law"), or, presumably, to check on unauthorised or illegal activity and to take coercive, enforcement and sanction measures. This also implies the need for representation at local level and co-ordination with the entities and the commission.

This example, as yet to be worked out, shows that action has been initiated to consider a new institutional regime to be integrated with other public functions and envisages a system of supervision of private enterprises, rather than conservation/restoration work being carried out by public institutions. This opening-up process will be challenging and difficult as there are bound to be some concerns about the relative experience of private enterprises undertaking conservation/restoration work and whether the works are being carried out in accordance with the terms of consent. Yet, this is the approach generally adopted in western Europe.

It may, therefore, be useful to consider how the process of management and control undertaken by public bodies operates in other countries and how work undertaken by private enterprises is supervised.

3. Public and private sector roles in management and control within western Europe

In most western European countries, there is a different approach to the supervision of works on the immovable heritage. This is largely due to the fact that a significant amount of property is held in private ownership.

There is also a need to balance the desire for protecting the heritage in the wider public interest with the need to use land and property for economic and social purposes.

Public authorities and institutions largely play a supervisory role, allowing the private sector (owners and their advisers) to conduct works once approval has been given for a scheme of works (by consents/permits). This can be explained by reference to the example of England and other countries.

3.1. The approach in England: national and local government responsibilities, consent regimes and the integrated process

In England, two government departments (equivalent to ministries) deal with the immovable heritage:

- the Department of Culture, Media and Sport has responsibility for designating "listed buildings" (architecture) and "scheduled ancient monuments" (archaeology), for law and policy on coercive, enforcement and sanction measures in general and for the consents/control of works to protected archaeological sites only;
- the Department of Communities and Local Government is the government department that handles policy and law with land use planning and development control within which the immovable heritage is fully integrated.

Both departments are advised by an independent state agency: the Historic Buildings and Monuments Commission for England (English Heritage) – which has a statutory role defined by legislation to be the legal adviser to the government. English Heritage has a similar role to that proposed for the commission in Bosnia and Herzegovina as it makes recommendations on the designation of items to be protected and also carries out research on all aspects of the historic environment. It also supervises works on the most important protected items, operating a system of grant aid and, in limited circumstances, taking enforcement action.

However, in practice the majority of consents for work in relation to protected immovable heritage are dealt with by local planning authorities (generally municipal or borough local governments) such as:

- the approval of building regulations (technical safety and health issues concerning the construction of new buildings and the change of use of existing buildings including listed buildings);
- the approval of planning permission for new construction (development) and the change of permitted use of buildings (NB: planning permission for the change of use of listed buildings may be required in addition to listed building consent; planning permission may also concern development on sites of known or perceived archaeological importance – but any works affecting a scheduled ancient monument will require specific consent at the national level);
- the approval of listed building consent for works that may affect the character of listed buildings (the opinion of English Heritage may be required in relation to some schemes involving the most important buildings and where finanical assistance is requested through an application for grant aid).

Local planning authorities also have a legal responsibility to designate conservation areas (of which there are over 9 000 in England) and to develop policies for the preservation and enhancement of such areas. This reflects the idea that the historic environment is a living environment. Thus, local authorities also deal with:

– the approval of conservation area consent for the demolition of any unlisted building located in a conservation area.

Moreover, the legislation concerning listed buildings and conservation areas is in the sphere of town and country planning legislation under the remit of local planning authorities. While the legislation on ancient monuments and archaeological sites is not under the direct responsibility of planning authorities, there is a link created with the planning system by national policies. In practice, this means that the immovable heritage is integrated into the planning system: the preservation of listed buildings and archaeological sites, as well as the preservation and enhancement of conservation areas, are key issues in development plan policies.

The interface between the roles of the public and private sector can be explained in relation to the architectural heritage and the archaeological heritage.

3.2. The architectural heritage: local officials in an integrated system

In England, most of the work for assessing applications for consents is dealt with by special officials employed by the local planning authority.

If a developer/investor or owner of a listed building or a site within a conservation area wishes to apply for consent for an alteration/rehabilitation scheme or for new development that may affect such designated assets, an application is submitted to the local planning authority. Before consent is granted, proposed projects are usually considered by a specialist "conservation officers", who can advise the applicant concerned whether the proposed scheme is likely to be approved (or other conditions that may be required in order to be approved). There are over 300 local planning authorities in England and most of these employ at least one conservation officer. There are some medium-sized cities that have a "team" of conservation officers or related experts. If consent is granted, the conservation officer will have responsibility to ensure that the works are carried out in a proper manner and according to the terms of the consent.

Conservation Officers can be professionally qualified as town planners, architects, building surveyors or archaeologists and usually have a specialist qualification in conservation. Since 1998, Conservation Officers have been supported by their own specialist professional body (the Institute of Historic Building Conservation, which now has 2 000 members). Most new employment positions for Conservation Officers usually require the applicant for the position to be a member of this professional body or to have considerable experience in relevant work.

The Conservation Officer is a key person in the integrated system and, in fact, has a variety of tasks to complete, including to:

- undertake character appraisals of conservation areas and advise on conservation policies in development plans (so that heritage assets are properly considered);
- undertake surveys of historical buildings at risk (through vacancy and disrepair);
- provide advice to applicants for consents concerning projects on listed buildings and in conservation areas and make recommendations as to whether a project should be approved;
- supervise the work in relation to such applications and to ensure that it is carried out according to the consent;
- advise the decision makers on the need to implement coercive action such as:
  - requirements for emergency repairs or other legal repairing obligations under the law including the possibility of compulsory purchase if requirements are not met; and
  - enforcement action to stop unauthorised work, including any requirements for reinstatement where changes have been made illegally backed up by penal provisions (fines and the possibility of imprisonment) (NB: enforcement officials may be separately employed to commence proceedings where unauthorised activity takes place);
- supervise (with officers from English Heritage) any conservation or restoration work that has been given financial assistance.

Moreover, the Conservation Officer may be a key person in heritage regeneration/rehabilitation strategies (which use the heritage as a basis for improving depressed areas), liasing with English Heritage and property owners, developers and investors.

The owner of a listed building (architectural monument) must have the right to use the property, but within the terms of the law. The emphasis in England is to keep buildings in use as this generally means that they will be maintained and preserved for future generations. Properties that are at risk (through disrepair, vacancy or partial occupation) are now the subject of priority action. This may include the rehabilitation of a property for a new use (particularly where the original use is now redundant and the building is obsolete). In such circumstances, a change of use may require alteration to accommodate a new use, which may also require that some changes to the fabric should be allowed. The degree of permitted intervention will depend on the relative importance of the building and its flexibility to change; it will also depend on the extent to which the interest factors/values of the protected asset will be affected. This requires the expert official to have the professional skill to determine whether the scheme proposed is acceptable (and it is at this point that detailed assessment of the protected asset may be necessary). It will also require that the owner's professional advisers and contracting company have the relevant skills and experience. This is also the case with purely conservation or restoration schemes.

3.3. The architectural heritage: public and private sector supervision of works

For work conducted on architectural monuments practice differs amongst European countries. In some cases it is necessary to have a specialist qualification for both enterprises and their supervisors (in rehabilitation and conservation/restoration work). However, qualification requirements are not always applied to enterprises and experience in the field may be sufficient, bearing in mind that the works will be overseen through an official authorisation (consent) system and through official supervision/inspection during the course of the works.

3.4. The architectural heritage: owners and professional advisers

One of the difficulties of relying on owners to safeguard the heritage is whether they will actually carry out necessary works and whether they will undertake them in a proper manner. Certainly, the provision of incentives (technical guidance and financial assistance) can assist this process. Furthermore, to assist owners of historical buildings to be proactive in looking after their property, the Monumentenwacht organisations operating in the Netherlands and Belgium provide a yearly check-up of their building at subsidised rates. Owners receive a technical report, which highlights priorities for maintenance (or restoration), and these reports can be accepted as technical proof when an application for a financial subsidy is made. In Denmark, an association of owners of historical houses (Bygnings Frednings Foreningen) has negotiated a tax relief for maintenance costs based on an "annual decay" scheme relating to all aspects of the building fabric as a way of encouraging action.

In other respects, the approach in western Europe is for historical building owners to employ special advisers to supervise works (whether rehabilitation or conservation). In England, the Royal Institute of British Architects and the Royal Institution of Chartered Surveyors provide accreditation systems in conservation work for architects and building surveyors respectively. Moreover, it is now a requirement to use such accredited professional advisers where work is supported by grant-aid (financial subsidies) from English Heritage. Such grant-aid is given on the condition that the work must satisfy the officially imposed standards and the money must be returned if the property is sold within five years.

In France, l'Ordre des architects controls the activities of architects. There is no specific organisation to regulate architects working in the heritage field, but a number of them have gathered in associations to provide a framework of assistance, promotion and expertise (such as the Association des architects du patrimoine). In Italy there is no requirement for architects to be specifically qualified in conservation/restoration work, but some schools of architecture specialise in this type of training – the general approach is for the *Soprintendenze* to supervise this work.

The key issue for professional advisers is that they have the requisite knowledge gained through qualifications or experience, but it is not usual for cultural heritage laws to specify such requirements. It is the control system (supervision by officials and the possibility of imposing correction measures through the law) that provides the necessary safeguards for regulating owners and their professional advisers.

3.5. The architectural heritage: contracting organisations, traditional building crafts, training and standards

In England, the general approach is that conservation officers may advise someone who is seeking approval for work on suitable companies that have the necessary skills, experience and a good track-record for work on listed buildings. However, no particular firm is recommended, as the basis for contracts is a free market approach based on competitive tendering (allowing the owner/investor to choose a contractor based on cost and skills). The owner's professional adviser may also be able to recommend a suitable contractor who specialises in conservation and restoration work.

Some companies specialise in historical building work and are listed in an annually published *Building Conservation Directory* and some are loosely associated under a Historic Buildings Contractors Group. Moreover, the positive attitude of authorities encouraging owners to take action on their historical buildings has resulted in a greater number of companies specialising in this field in the last ten years. For example, English Heritage financially supports a body known as the Conference on Training in Architectural Conservation (COTAC). This umbrella organisation has given support to the revival of specialist craft trades and for the production of traditional materials (such as traditional timber materials and lime-based mortars) that had been in decline due to modern building techniques.

Other support is given by voluntary and other heritage organisations. For example, the Society for the Protection of Ancient Buildings (established by William Morris in 1877) also runs special training courses for historical building owners, contractors, craftsmen and professional advisers. The British Standard Institution (an independent national body responsible for preparing national standards to improve the quality of products and services) issued a standard entitled "The principles of the conservation of historic buildings" in 1998 as a guide for "building owners, managers, archaeologists, architects, surveyors, contractors, conservators and local authority building control officers" to provide information relevant to developing conservation policies, strategies and procedures.

English Heritage previously had its own group of craftsmen and specialists to work on historical buildings in public ownership (based in different regions). But this was disbanded in the mid-1990s, with most of the regional groups being privatised, and they now compete with other companies in the market for work on historic buildings.

This sort of approach is mirrored in other countries. In Denmark, the Raadvad Centre established in 1987 provides specialist training in traditional crafts and in Belgium the Walloon Heritage Institute has a similar role. In the Netherlands, the National Contact Monuments founded in 1972 provides a platform for over 300 private organisations involved in conservation and restoration work. In France, since 1994, QUALIBAT (a professional certification organisation) has used a classification system involving 11 quality approval standards expressly linked to heritage conservation and restoration activities for historical and other older buildings so that the small number of building companies who specialise in this type of work have a form of regulation. Furthermore, the Groupement national des entreprises de restauration des monuments historiques is a national association of restoration firms involving over 150 companies. Moreover, in many countries non-governmental organisations are active in conducting and promoting conservation, restoration and rehabilitation work such as the Architectural Heritage Fund (supporting over 200 non-profit-making "building preservation trusts") in the United Kingdom, the Deutsche Stiftung Denkmalschutz (a German foundation for historical monuments) and the Fondation Roi Baudouin in Belgium.

3.6. The archaeological heritage

While the archaeological heritage presents different issues and ways of working compared to the architectural heritage, the opening up of work to non-public sector archaeologists may also be relevant. Certainly, the archaeological profession is differently organised in different countries within Europe. In some countries, only the state or official institutions may undertake archaeological excavations, while in other countries they can be undertaken by universities, museums, consultants or quasi-public archaeological organisations. The main issue to clarify with legislation and licence procedures is that excavations are only carried out by skilled archaeologists and that records are made available to professionals and researchers.

The situation where archaeologists independent of official institutions are perhaps most likely to be involved is where proposals for new development/construction may have an impact on the archaeological heritage. The approach to archaeological investigation in such circumstances may depend, first, on whether the whole of the archaeological heritage is given a total and automatic protection (the tradition in southern Europe) where control of activity is more likely to remain in the public sphere or, secondly, whether the law is used to protect particular heritage assets with others safeguarded by development plan mechanisms (such as identifying areas of perceived archaeological importance which may require certain other safeguards).

Whichever is the situation, the Valletta Convention (1992) on the archaeological heritage stresses the need for integrated mechanisms between heritage conservation and territorial planning. Moreover, the presence of archaeology will never preclude the need for new roads, infrastructure and other construction developments. Where archaeological interests may be affected in these circumstances there is a need for preventative archaeology.

In this case the general principle to follow is "the disturber pays". In other words, the developer must follow regulations allowing and paying for archaeological investigation before approval for development can take place. But such processes should not be unduly restrictive.

In Denmark, archaeological remains found during construction works have to be reported, resulting in local museum-based archaeologists being given one year to excavate remains. In practice, most archaeological investigations are carried out as part of the design phase of construction work because archaeological evaluations are part of the planning process.

In England, strict rules are required concerning investigation of protected archaeological sites before consent for "disturbing works" is given. But in sites of perceived archaeological importance (mapped in development plans) pre-application discussions (i.e. before consent is given) may lead to an archaeological investigation. In fact, the established policy indicates that a developer may wish to commission an "independent archaeological assessment". This implies that an archaeological consultant is employed (not a public official). Moreover, whilst English Heritage archaeological officers undertake general research, local planning authorities (at county level or now more frequently at local government level) have an archaeologist to advise when development is proposed in areas of potential archaeological importance. These officials can provide a list of archaeological consultants for developers to chose and employ. Such archaeologists, as with professionals advising owners of architectural monuments, have a professional association through the Institute of Field Archaeologists.

Moreover, if an initial evaluation (using non-destructive techniques) suggests that a more detailed investigation is required, the developer may have to agree (via conditions attached to consent for development) to more extensive evaluation including excavation before the development can proceed, or to redesign the proposed works. For this purpose, a form of model agreement (and contract) based on the British Developers and Archaeologists Code of Practice can be used, whereby investigations may be agreed for a period of time at the cost of the developer. Again, in such circumstances, professionally recognised archaeologists can be employed (i.e. independent archaeologists).

In fact, the code of practice was used as the basis of the Council of Europe's European Code of Good Practice entitled "Archaeology and the urban project", which sets out guidelines for close co-operation between public authorities, planners, architects, developers and archaeologists. This further recommends the need for the publication and deposit of discovered artefacts and records.

So, as with the architectural heritage, the key issue for developers is that they must use skilled professional advisers – the role of the public sector archaeologists may be to supervise. This does not prevent the general work of public sector archaeologists in the field of archaeological research.

4. Conclusions

One of the main objects of reforming cultural heritage laws is to define provisions that regulate citizens' actions (including owners of heritage property and developers). In a democratic society, there must be a right to own property and for citizens to use that property. Where such property is of heritage value then there is the need to regulate that use in the wider public interest. The aim should be to create a living rather than a museum heritage.

In turn, this emphasises a new role for official institutions in inspection and supervision, notwithstanding the need to constantly update heritage research, to promote understanding of the heritage (including education, training and guidance).

The idea that legally protected heritage is the sole remit of the public sector is outdated and elitist in an open society. The experience from elsewhere shows that owners and their advisers and contracting organisations can undertake conservation and other work to safeguard the heritage and rehabilitate it for continued use in society. Where public institutions are to retain a role in this work there must also be a real possibility for private organisations to compete in the open market.

It is also important to decentralise some official functions to local levels so that there is an integrated process of management. This also emphasises a new role for advice, information and supervision concerning immovable heritage within the broader framework of territorial planning and for economic and social development.

For this type of approach to develop, it will require an acceptance of the role of private owners and their professional advisers. In turn, they have a responsibility to present and carry out their projects in a satisfactory manner. This means there is a need for professionalism, which can be attained through specialist training, experience and accreditation. Public institutions have an important role in fostering this approach.

Furthermore, non-governmental and non-profit-making organisations have a role to play in education and also in conservation work.

In order to ensure that the private sector can play a satisfactory role in this process, there is a need for proper regulation and supervision but balanced with positive incentives (grant aid, tax relief, technical assistance, etc., which is considered in Theme 4).

The reform process will take time, but it is necessary to start as soon as possible. There are many practical, financial and psychological hurdles to cross. Moreover, the greatest barrier is the resistance to change based on fear and insecurity.

5. The case of Bosnia and Herzegovina

The word "reform" is one of the most commonly heard words in Bosnia and Herzegovina these days. Everything is being reformed and brought up to date, from the state and entities' institutions to the education and tax system, the military and the police. The purpose of reform is to introduce new, functioning structures, compatible with those of Europe, so that Bosnia and Herzegovina may become a member of the EU.

5.1. Legislative reform for the cultural heritage

Legislation governing the cultural heritage of Bosnia and Herzegovina is no exception. It must be in line with directives from the Council of Europe, as well as with the general state of the cultural heritage of Bosnia and Herzegovina which, despite considerable advances in its preservation, renovation and rehabilitation over the past few years, is still far from satisfactory. The Commission to Preserve National Monuments of Bosnia and Herzegovina (established according to Annex 8 of the Dayton Peace Agreement) has set in motion the procedure to enact a new state-level law for the preservation of cultural heritage. For the Bosnia and Herzegovina cultural heritage, this is second in importance only to the establishment of the commission itself in the post-war period.

To this end, a working group has been set up, consisting of representatives of both entities (the Federation of Bosnia and Herzegovina and Republika Srpska), the District of Brčko, the Bosnia and Herzegovina Ministry of Civil Affairs, the Bosnia and Herzegovina Council of Ministers, and the commission itself. The working group has drafted an initial version of the law, on which anyone who is interested both in Bosnia and Herzegovina and abroad may make suggestions, so that it may be worked on and improved before the final bill is debated in Parliament. In this regard, we expect the full support of every international institution involved in the implementation of the Dayton Peace Agreement, including the Council of Europe.

One of the factors supporting this belief is the current state of legislation governing the cultural heritage of Bosnia and Herzegovina, which can broadly be described as in a state of "legislative hyperinflation", but almost total ineffectiveness, as is vividly evident by the rapid deterioration affecting cultural monuments of the highest world value. No more should be needed to illustrate this than the fact that since 1993, 19 different laws and decisions governing heritage protection in Bosnia and Herzegovina have been adopted at the entity and cantonal level, but throughout that time there has not been a single legally binding provision at any government level for funds allocated for the purpose.

A second feature of the current heritage protection legislation is the absence of a legislation hierarchy, or in other words a hierarchy of responsibility accruing to various levels of government. The interests of the entities and cantons on the one hand, and of the state on the other, are often in conflict, and the absence of political will acts as a brake on any constructive effort to overcome this state of "legislative anarchy".

The fact that there is no state-level Ministry of Culture is a third adverse factor impeding the introduction of effective heritage protection mechanisms; the process is simply being left to the will of individuals. This is at its most obvious in the entity government of the Federation of Bosnia and Herzegovina, which – as the only relevant institution –

began systematically to allocate funds for heritage protection in March 2001. Since then, the federation government has allocated between 5 and 6 million convertible marks (BAM) for heritage protection. The government of Republika Srpska made no budget provisions for heritage protection until 2004, when the budget provided for the sum of 500 000 BAM for heritage protection. Moreover, when the funds were distributed, the government did not respect the list of priorities drawn up by the Commission to Preserve National Monuments of Bosnia and Herzegovina, as an institution of state, which is also often true of the federation ministry.

Apart from international organisations and the governments of certain states, the religious communities of Bosnia and Herzegovina, who are also the largest owners of cultural property, have provided most of the funding for heritage reconstruction and rehabilitation since the end of the war. However, in some cases they have made such serious errors that some monuments have completely degraded, and been stripped of their status as protected properties.

This, then, is a brief description of the state of affairs out of which emerged the initiative to draft a new state-level heritage protection law in Bosnia and Herzegovina, designed to bring about a structural turning-point in this field.

5.2. Developing a role for private owners and the problem of restitution

In the quest for specific legislative provisions concerning the role of private owners of cultural properties in this new law, the commission was guided by the fact that there is still no law on property ownership in Bosnia and Herzegovina. In broad terms, the process of transition from social to private ownership is not yet complete. This means that there are currently no cultural properties owned by the state of Bosnia and Herzegovina, but that ownership is in the hands of the municipalities, cantons, entities, District of Brčko and religious communities. Only a small proportion of cultural properties are now in private hands, but the process is still in its early stages and the new law should provide it with further impetus. This also means that the new law will be the first legislation to govern the finer details of private ownership of cultural properties. At the same time as this is being done, the exact proportion of cultural properties currently in private ownership must be determined. The survey of the built heritage conducted in 1986 by the Federal Statistics Institute in Bosnia and Herzegovina noted that: "of the total number of protected properties, 349 (48%) were socially owned, 195 were owned by so-called civic-juristic persons, and only 114 (15.8%) in private ownership."

Although not guided by political considerations in its operations, the commission has had to take into account the current political situation in Bosnia and Herzegovina and the lack of political will to address the question of legislation designed to strengthen the central institutions of the state at the expense of entity institutions and control. The fact that there is no law on restitution is the direct outcome of this lack of political will, constituting a further delay to private initiative and the adoption of heritage protection legislation, including financial and other measures. Furthermore, even the old heritage protection law (1986) did not detail the rights and obligations of private owners of cultural properties. This means that here, as in so many other domains, Bosnia and Herzegovina is starting from scratch. On the one hand, this is a handicap and an additional burden, but on the other, it offers a certain advantage, in that it provides a chance to adopt effective, long-term legislation.

The draft law has a total of 102 articles, with the chapter on the rights and obligations of the owners of protected properties consisting of Articles 77 to 96. This chapter of the law governs the following matters:

- ownership of protected property;
- restrictions on ownership rights;
- expropriation (divestment of ownership) of protected property;
- concessions.

Bearing in mind that European experience in this field varies from country to country, in working further on this section of the law particular attention should be paid to the introduction of legal and financial measures designed to encourage the owners of cultural property, be they legal or physical persons, to maintain, renovate, reconstruct and rehabilitate their property and to make it available for educational purposes and tourism.

5.3. Enabling the private sector through financial tools

In general terms, the cultural heritage of Bosnia and Herzegovina is a significant economic resource and should therefore become a development factor. To this end, the following mechanisms should be developed and incorporated into the law.

- Tax incentives should be provided for donors, particularly small businesses or groups of sponsors. This is of particular importance for Bosnia and Herzegovina given that current taxation policy provides far greater incentives for investment in new buildings and commercial structures than in heritage properties. This would also encourage business start-ups in an economically backward country that even nine years after the end of the war has regained only 40% of its pre-war gross national product.
- Heritage protection partnerships should be encouraged by recognising their legal status, including financial independence and tax concessions.
- The conservation process of old buildings should be advanced by means of concessions and enabling them to become self-sustainable.
- International and local financial institutions should be encouraged to provide loans for the renovation and rehabilitation of the cultural heritage.
- All these mechanisms could include both individual monuments and groups of protected sites of particular cultural value.

- Revolving mechanisms should be set in motion of the kind that have already, although only recently introduced, shown themselves to be effective in the case of the Foundations set up by the Government of the Federation of Bosnia and Herzegovina for publishing and films.
- Investors should be encouraged to reinvest profits when using a cultural property as commercial or catering premises or for multimedia presentations (exhibitions, theatre performances, lectures, concerts, literary evenings, academic symposia, etc.).
- A system should be implemented for renting out cultural properties for fixed terms, on the expiry of which they would revert to the owner, with the option to renew the lease to generate revenue.
- The present entity and cantonal regulations should be harmonised with the state-level law, by creating legislation which does not conflict with or negate new provisions.

The Council of Europe, as an unchallengeable authority, should prescribe these and other measures relating to matters of ownership of cultural properties. If this is not done, the bill could undergo such extensive amendments during the parliamentary procedure that it could lose much of its effect and be reduced to a merely cosmetic piece of legislation.

5.4. Conclusions

The Commission to Preserve National Monuments of Bosnia and Herzegovina expects the committed support of the Council of Europe, the Office of the High Representative in Bosnia and Herzegovina (OHR), the International Monetary Fund and the World Bank – in other words, those international institutions that have a major influence on the drafting of budgets at all government levels and on the expenditure of budget funds – to ensure the effective implementation of all the measures proposed, and also of those governing the private and other ownership of cultural property in Bosnia and Herzegovina. All the members of the commission (three local and two international experts) are unreservedly in favour of the adoption of such a law that, in both existing and foreseen circumstances, will ensure effective heritage protection in Bosnia and Herzegovina, as an integral part of the European and world cultural heritage.

6. Summary of questions and views

The following views were raised in relation to the presentation of papers on Theme 3:

Issue 1 – In Belgium only 30% of the cultural heritage is publicly owned. It is different, therefore, to the countries of South-East Europe. Moreover, private owners are supported financially in Belgium. The important point in relation to Theme 3 is that there is a delegation of responsibility to private owners (and, therefore, a reduced cost to the public budget). Furthermore, there is a partnership between the public and private sectors in managing the heritage.

Issue 2 – There is a great difference between western and eastern Europe in terms of ownership. This situation is accompanied by a relatively centralised organisational structure. Also in the east, funding from national budgets is currently decreasing. One way of resolving the funding problem is through the concession system – but this has its own problems. It is a lease on public property – it does not change the ownership status of public property and, therefore, does not change the ownership structure. There is a lack of will to understand the need to change this. Moreover, in general terms property in public ownership is not effectively managed.

Issue 3 – In the French experience, there are a few examples of the use of the concession system in relation to isolated monuments. For example, in the city of Avignon the local authority granted a concession to a private company which uses the monument for private business purposes. This is not the usual approach in France. A different example is the impact of civil society on the maintenance of ensembles. We cannot intervene every time through grant aid, but tax relief can sometimes be given. It is, therefore, about the role of private sector involvement – from as early as the formulation of the urban development plan. Otherwise, safeguards will not be maintained. But we cannot police everything. For example, some private owners install UPVC (plastic) window frames, replacing the traditional design in favour of energy efficiency. Whilst this is not allowed, it is difficult to check on every action taken by private owners. It is important, however, to give guidance to private owners about proper approaches.

These issues will be further developed through Theme 4.

Theme 4 – Financial and other incentives, sanctions and coercive measures

1. Introduction

As we have considered in earlier themes, a law on cultural heritage should, in the wider public interest, aim to regulate the actions of citizens which impact on the heritage. By moving towards a system of greater involvement of citizens, including private owners and investors, it is necessary for a law to be balanced, including control and regulation of activities supervised by official institutions (negative measures) and assistance and incentives to help support private owners to conserve, restore or rehabilitate their properties (positive measures). A law that is purely a mechanism for protection and control will not have the desired effect in terms of engaging citizens in the process of preserving cultural heritage. This paper, therefore, considers these two aspects – the balance between positive incentives and the negative aspects of control and regulation.

This paper also concentrates on the architectural heritage, as this is where there is the greatest need for financial assistance. Notwithstanding this fact, it may be important to consider providing a balance of tax incentives or other financial assistance for cultural goods in private collections for their conservation/restoration, as well as sanction measures.

2. Financial measures

2.1. Problems concerning finance

Most of the draft laws from South-East European countries that have been considered by the LSTF have little information on ancillary financial measures – which leaves these laws as little more than a prescriptive set of rules. This will do little to encourage private action or a positive view of the heritage. Owners will see the law as being very restrictive and negative.

There are, however, recognised limits on state budgets and, in this context it is difficult to argue for support, particularly if the preservation of the heritage is seen as a specialist activity for the benefit of a few rather than in the wider interests of society. Yet, this is not specifically a problem for South-East European countries – there is never enough finance even in western Europe. The way forward may be to find arguments for persuading governments to give a bigger slice of the state budget.

The approach that is being considered in some South-East European countries is to attempt to raise revenue from the commercial exploitation of the heritage.

2.2. Charging for commercial exploitation

The recent Kosovan draft law (June 2004) considered this approach in Article 52 but only in relation to movable cultural goods (and not in relation to the archaeological or architectural heritage). The idea is that the use of cultural goods in photographic publications, panoramas, postage stamps, signs, souvenirs, posters, television advertisements and the publication of other printed materials including clothing could be subject to a 10% charge on the use of the image. This may, however, be viewed as a restrictive control over property and may actually deter the use of such images. Moreover, in other countries this approach would be regarded as being unconstitutional (limiting a constitutional right to use property). Furthermore, it was proposed that this would be a retrospective charge (dating back to 1999) to which the issue of "reasonableness" should be raised.

This idea of charging for the use of the image of cultural property is also considered in Article 189 of the recent draft law in the Republic of Montenegro. Moreover, in Articles 191 and 192 of the draft law, the idea of a "monument rent" has been considered for certain business activities carried out in immovable heritage property or within a "cultural historic entirety" (e.g. hotels and restaurants, taxi services, wholesale of machines, equipment and accessories, banks, etc.). Private individuals and legal entities that pay income or corporate tax in this situation would be liable to pay a rent at a yet to be defined percentage on income and according to the area of the premises. This money would then be directed to a "competent administration body" and the local government.

Initially, these approaches would seem to be very negative and restrictive and it must be questioned whether they will actually achieve the desired effect – that is, that owners and occupiers will safeguard their heritage property. The actions proposed by Montenegro and Kosovo are more concerned with protection than a positive approach to preservation, rehabilitation and creating a living heritage.

However, these types of mechanisms can already be found within Articles 108 to 114 of the Croatian Law on the Protection and Preservation of Cultural Goods (enacted in 1999). In this respect, the use of heritage images in photography, publications and suchlike is liable to a 10% charge; the use of an image in film, billboards and other advertising is subject to a defined monetary charge; and the use of heritage property as a business premises or for tourism/accommodation is liable to a 2% charge on profits from the activity (NB: recommendations for increases in these amounts may now have been approved).

The money derived from these different types of "monument annuity" either go directly to the state or are divided between the state and city or municipal authorities. However, it is important to note that all revenues collected in this way are paid into a specific fund that can only be used for the protection and preservation of the cultural heritage. Moreover, whilst it is the responsibility of the owner of a protected heritage asset to ensure that it is maintained for future generations, the specific fund is created to assist such owners that pay the annuity.

"…where measures prescribed for the protection of a cultural good [including immovable property] significantly limit ownership rights, or where the owner is exposed to additional expenses that significantly exceed the regular expense of the good's maintenance and exceed any income or other benefit the owner may gain from ownership of the cultural good…".

It is not clear whether the Croatian law actually specifies the types of financial measures that are offered and certainly the draft law of the Republic of Montenegro, whilst attempting to follow the Croatian model, fails to do this.

Nevertheless, the Croatian law presents a fairly balanced approach (balancing incentives against coercive measures). Assistance is provided as compensation for the additional restrictions that result from owning protected, as opposed to ordinary, property. At the same time, the basis of the provisions are that if an owner is unable to meet the obligations required by law the responsibility still remains, which may result in the owner being required to sell or relinquish the property. In theory, this is justifiable, but any such procedures should be reasonable (with appropriate grounds of appeal and/or fair compensation procedures for the loss of property).

The balanced approach is the right approach to achieving a successful law. However, the opposite will result if the restrictions outweigh the incentives. For example, it has been reported that NGOs that wish to financially assist conservation and restoration action within Bulgaria are subject to tax on the donations offered. The result is that NGOs are discouraged from making such investments!

2.3. Charging for concessions

Another means of raising finance for the cultural heritage is through the concept of offering concessions. This is developed in the recent draft law from Montenegro (Articles 89-100) and the draft law produced in Bulgaria (Articles 73-77). The Bulgarian concept of offering concessions in relation to the cultural heritage is developed from more general provisions through the Concessions Act of 1997. In effect, the concession is a "right to use" for a monetary payment – a contract between the state (or local government) and the occupier or user of public property (including heritage assets). It creates obligations on the concession holder, which could include a requirement to perform conservation or restoration activities on a monument.

For example, an archaeological site near a highway could provide an opportunity for cultural tourism. A concession could allow the possibility of tourism development (hotels, signs, etc.) in return for a payment towards the cost of archaeological research. Another example would be in relation to historic buildings in a mediaeval town where the concession would allow the use of buildings for tourism (or theoretically, other business purposes) for a fee, with the payment being used to assist the conservation/restoration of the buildings.

There are differing opinions between heritage experts in Bulgaria as to whether the concession concept is a good idea. Certainly, it would be a means to open up heritage to the private sector, but there remains resistance to this – in the belief that the private sector is not capable of managing it properly (the issue of Theme 3).

In the absence of adequate financial support measures, the concept of concessions would seem to be a plausible approach to using the heritage with appropriate safeguards – which could be specified in contractual terms, although normal procedures of control that should apply to monuments may be sufficient. At the heart of the issue is the question of whether the concession concept is philosophically acceptable, in that the concession system may be used as an argument to retain property in public rather than private ownership. Moreover, the concession approach should not be a way of replacing financial support mechanisms, the need for which is identified in the Granada Convention (1985). In order to encourage private sector involvement, subsidies and other financial incentives and support measures should be made available. Moreover, these are identified in Council of Europe documents. In addition, it is also important that sufficient information and technical guidance is provided to assist private initiatives and owners in preserving the cultural heritage.

3. Council of Europe: the Granada Convention and the Council of Europe recommendation on funding and associated measures

Article 6 of the Granada Convention (1985) defines a number of ancillary measures that each country should undertake to provide (as parties to the convention) in order to encourage private initiatives for maintaining and restoring architectural heritage. This includes financial support measures (subsidies, loans, etc.), as well as fiscal measures to facilitate conservation action. This article does, however, recognise that there is a limitation on the budgets of public authorities.

Article 14 of the Granada Convention defines further measures for the participation and action by organisations other than the public authorities. Linked to the question of financial support, it identifies the need to foster the development of sponsorship and non-profit-making associations working in this field.

Furthermore, reflecting on the fact that rehabilitation and conservation/restoration work is not generally attractive enough for private investors in comparison to new construction (which offers a higher degree of profitability and fewer risks), a Council of Europe recommendation has sought to identify measures to promote action by the private sector. Recommendation No. R (91) 6 of the Committee of Ministers to member states on the measures likely to promote the funding of the conservation of the architectural heritage recognises that there is a need to attract more private funds and promote action by:

- creating favourable conditions to stimulate conservation projects (legal, administrative and other measures e.g. strategies for managing rehabilitation and the regeneration of historical centres; informing potential investors about resources that exist for putting the heritage to use; providing project co-ordinators to assist in overcoming administrative and financial complexities involved in major projects, etc.);

- using limited public funds more effectively to generate private investments (including specific measures to promote partnership between the public and private sectors);

- making private investments more profitable and diminishing their risks;

- promoting sponsorship.

It is, therefore, still important in law to create financial support provisions (whether or not the limited budgets will enable the provision of such finance) and also to provide technical assistance and guidance. It may also be useful to consider different arguments and methods of raising finance and to examine the approaches adopted in other countries where finance provisions are more developed.

4. Other means to raise finance

4.1. The use of lotteries

Lotteries can provide a useful source of finance, as in Italy (for restoration of important monuments). In Germany, one third of the income derived from a television lottery (*Glücks-Spirale*) is given to the Deutsche Stiftung Denkmalschutz foundation, raising as much as €15 million per year (at 1999 levels) for the built heritage. In the United Kingdom, the National Lottery has transformed funding since it was set up in November 1994, providing 16.67% of the income raised for the Heritage Lottery Fund. This fund has provided a staggering £3 billion (equivalent to €4.5 billion) to support the heritage sector in its first ten years of operation (up to 2004).

4.2. Sponsorship, foundations, funds and non-profit agencies

There are a number of different systems to encourage sponsorship (usually through tax relief on company profits/donations given to foundations), as well as fund mechanisms that have been established to support non-profit-making organisations (relieved of tax), in relation to conservation, restoration and rehabilitation work. An ICOMOS report (produced by the German National Committee in 1997) entitled "Legal Structures of Private Sponsorship" highlights some examples from different countries.

To encourage commercial and industrial firms in France to sponsor culture, particularly heritage, a legal framework known as the Fondation d'Entreprise (Enterprise Foundation) was implemented in 1991. Such a foundation is set up for carrying out (for profit) work in the public interest that cannot be funded through donations, bequests or public appeals. The encouragement of firms wishing to develop their sponsorship policy has subsequently led to the establishment of other types of foundation (e.g. the Fondation du Patrimoine). In Denmark, private companies can set up charitable foundations (a number of which support heritage), that can top-up state grants for approved schemes of works set up by private enterprises. Deutsche Stiftung Denkmalschutz, the German foundation, raises just under half of its yearly funding from private donations. The foundation supports requests for assistance from monument owners, provides assistance where there are social problems and a need for community support, and can assist smaller specific building foundations. These foundations do not pay taxes on the first €30 000 (approximately, according to 1999 figures) profit – at this level it is possible to support a holding company working on a non-profit basis on buildings in need of action. Limited holding companies also work on a non-profit basis in the Netherlands – for example Stadtherstel, which restores and adapts historical buildings, using the subsequent rent received to assist in funding new projects.

In the United Kingdom the Architectural Heritage Fund was set up in 1975 (with an initial fund of £1 million – approximately equivalent to €1.5 million). This fund now amounts to over £13 million (€20 million). It provides feasibility study grants, project administration grants, project organiser grants, refundable project development grants and low interest loans (at 4%) to building preservation trusts (of which there are nearly 200 in the whole of the United Kingdom) for the non-profit activity of rehabilitating historic property. Most of these trusts work on a revolving fund basis (using the proceeds of sale from a rehabilitation project to fund the next project or by retaining ownership and raising finance for further projects from income from lettings or using the capital value as a basis to secure loans). Revolving funds, operating with charitable status, are even more highly developed in the United States. The Nationaal Restauratiefonds was set up in the Netherlands in 1985 due to the fact that there were insufficient resources available for restoration. It also works as a revolving fund, issuing loans at reduced interest rates, usually 5% less than normal bank rates (recently as low as 1%), with the loan acting as a mortgage by being spread over a long period of time (up to 30 years), with payments on such loans being repaid into the fund as is the case with loans to building preservation trusts from the Architectural Heritage Fund.

There are many different models of financial support that can be identified and should be explored for possible use in the South-East European countries-in-transition.

4.3. Conservation economics

Moreover, based on the premise that financial resources are finite and that most governments are unable to provide as much funding as may be necessary or desirable bearing in mind other needs of society, it is relevant to consider the direct and indirect benefits to be gained from financially supporting heritage in order to provide an argument in favour of the provision of public funds.

Studies have been carried out by ICOMOS[1] and some countries (notably the United Kingdom, Germany and the United States[2]) and reported by the EU, which reveal the direct and indirect benefits to be gained from financially supporting heritage. Direct benefits include the conservation, restoration and rehabilitation of heritage property: long-term preservation. The indirect benefits are much wider. These include, for example, the provision of accommodation for living and working; tax revenues gained as a result of occupation; supporting traditional craft techniques and professional employment; tax revenues gained through people employed in conservation work; tourism and associated employment, income and tax revenue; as well as the improvement of facilities and an enhancement of the environment to the benefit of society as a whole. Moreover, these studies have consistently shown that public investment in heritage usually levers a considerably higher amount of investment from the private sector (with resultant tax revenues for the public budget) with an overall benefit for the built heritage and for society.

These types of studies are now being used as an argument to generate financial support from public budgets – principally because of the overall benefits that can be achieved. However, it is important that funding is directed in a way that will benefit wider society: not necessarily those built assets that are of great importance, but those that are endangered. For example, the rehabilitation of older buildings can create opportunities for good housing (as well as preserving a heritage asset). Thus, if it can be argued that the preservation of the architectural heritage will benefit wider society (rather than it being an elitist activity to the benefit of a few), this is more likely to encourage government financial support.

Thus, it may be useful to develop indicators of benefits (not just relating to the preservation of heritage) that can be gained from financial support for heritage, which could be statistically analysed and presented when government budgets are being considered. The possibilities for cultural tourism, the development of businesses, jobs and living accommodation, the benefits of an improved environment, the resulting tax revenues and suchlike, should be considered. This would fit in well with the aims of the Regional Programme for South-East Europe with regards to the aim to implement social and economic sustainable development as well as enhancement of the heritage. Moreover, the programme aims to assist in the implementation of long-term sustainable activities "in order to act as a catalyst for the attitudinal changes required at all levels".

---

1. ICOMOS (1993): *Conservation Economics: Cost Benefit Analysis for the Cultural Built Heritage: Principles and Practice*. This study identified a wide range of benefits that may be derived from conservation action enforcing the concept of different values.
2. English Heritage, Town Centres Ltd. and London School of Economics (2000): *The Heritage Dividend: Measuring the Results of English Heritage Regeneration*, 2nd ed.; Hawkins, H. C. et al. (1997): *Economic Impacts of Historic Preservation, US Department of the Interior, National Park Service, National Centre for Preservation Technology and Training*, Publication No. 1997-05; Kirschbaum, J. and Klein, A. (eds) (2000): *Denkmalpflege und Beschäftigung [Heritage Conservation and Employment]*, Proceedings of an International Conference in the framework of the German EU Presidency 15/16 April 1999 in Berlin, Schriftenreihe des Deutschen Nationalkomitees für Denkmalschutz.

5. Financial measures to promote conservation and restoration action: some examples[3]

In consideration of the different possibilities for financial assistance measures, there are three principal methods of providing financial support: subsidies (grants), loans and fiscal (tax) relief. Some countries rely on one of these methods as the main source of funding, whilst others use them in combination or separately. In most cases, financial support is subject to an agreed plan of works for maintenance, repair or restoration work. Grants can be prioritised according to the quality or condition (or disrepair) of protected assets. Financial support may also be linked to other activities such as rehabilitation programmes (improvements/alterations particularly for residential use) and other activities to regenerate historical centres including partnerships between public and private sectors. Private and charitable foundations and trusts may also play an important role in providing financial support. The benefits of such co-ordinated measures, especially when linked to management strategies for historical centres, should be examined to find options that may be relevant to South-East European countries-in-transition. Some examples of the different methods in use can be identified.

5.1. Subsidised surveys – Monumentenwacht

Based on the principle that "prevention is better than cure" (regular maintenance is more efficient compared to costly restoration/repair schemes), the subsidised (low cost) survey system operated by the *Monumentenwacht* (Monument Watch) organisations in the Netherlands and Belgium helps owners to prioritise works on historical buildings. A team normally consisting of two members (usually an architect and a stone mason or other building craft specialist) provides a technical report for owners of historic properties concerning different priorities of work that should be undertaken. This professional report is provided at a subsidised price to encourage owners of historic buildings to take up the service. The report can be linked to grant aid schemes (or tax relief) to support action. This approach could provide direct help to owners of private properties in transition countries.

5.2. Direct financial assistance (grant aid and other subsidy assistance)

Grant aid is the primary source of support in the United Kingdom. In France, 30-50% towards costs can be given for all classified property, and 15-20% for those on the "supplementary" list, municipal authorities can also give money for other historical properties. In Belgium, grant support is given for both maintenance and restoration work

---

[3]. Pickard, R. and Pickerill, T. (2002) "Conservation finance 1: Support for historic buildings" and "Conservation finance 2: area-based initiatives and the role of foundations, funds and non-profit agencies", in *Structural Survey*, Vol. 20, No. 2, at pp. 73-77 and 112-16.

(40-90% with provinces and communes contributing). In Denmark 20-50% is given, whereas in the Netherlands, the range is slightly greater (20-70%). Most German states provide grant aid, and in Ireland a recently initiated grants programme provides small grants up to a maximum ceiling figure (approximately €6 700 and double this in exceptional cases).

5.3. Tax incentives

In addition to grant aid, income tax relief is given (for maintenance/restoration works to protected buildings) in France, Belgium, Germany and the Netherlands and tax relief is the main source of assistance in Spain. A special income tax relief has been developed in Denmark for "listed houses" (protected buildings originally constructed as houses) according to a formula based on a survey of materials and features of such buildings and an assessment of "annual decay". Lower rates of VAT (on building operations and materials) apply to heritage properties in Italy (10% instead of 20%) and in the United Kingdom for rehabilitation work (alterations can be zero rated – but this does not apply to repairs) and a lower rate of tax (at 5% instead of 17.5%) is applied to historical religious buildings and for the conversion of existing properties to residential use. Other forms of fiscal support include capital allowances/tax credits, and relief from inheritance and real estate taxes. In the United Kingdom, relief from property taxes is given on unoccupied protected buildings to encourage action.

In the United States, an innovative system has linked the "rehabilitation tax credit" (a 20% tax credit against costs for certified heritage properties) with a special low-income housing tax credit (at 9% annually for a period of ten years). This has induced many developers and traditional property investors to work in the heritage sector, often in partnership with community organisations (creating a social benefit), particularly in deprived downtown areas. Such action has been found to act as a catalyst to neighbourhood revitalisation. So, this is actually beneficial for the heritage and also for the local economy and society. It has created a market for investors to rehabilitate old buildings and protected structures for the particular purpose of providing good and affordable homes in historic buildings.[4]

5.4. Heritage led rehabilitation and regeneration strategies

The rehabilitation of old parts of towns in France is supported through Opérations programmées pour l'amélioration de l'habitat (OPAH) [Planned Housing Improvement Operations]. Since 1977, when the OPAH programme was introduced, to 1999, over 3 000 improvement operations were carried out, resulting in the rehabilitation of over 600 000 dwellings (mostly in old quarters and historical centres). The main body for

---

4. Pickard, R. and Pickerill, T. (2002): "Real Estate Tax Credits, Investment and Finance in Historic Preservation in the USA" – in *RICS Foundation Research Paper Series*, Vol. 4, No. 17.

grant provision is the *Agence nationale pour l'amélioration de l'habitat* (ANAH) [National Housing Improvement Agency], which subsidises work undertaken by private landlords. The rules of the agency also allow for the possibility of additional funding for buildings of architectural interest located in *secteurs sauvegardés*, ZZAUPs (protected architectural, urban and landscape zones) and OPAH areas with a heritage component. The state and municipalities can provide additional funding for OPAHs.

Programmes have been developed recently in Ireland to provide income tax relief through urban renewal programmes in older areas (based on integrated area plans) and a Townscape Restoration Scheme.

In Denmark, urban renewal programmes can support local building maintenance, restoration and rehabilitation action for listed houses and those "worthy of preservation" based on matched funds from the state and a municipality.

In the United Kingdom, the Heritage Lottery Fund's Townscape Heritage Initiative provides a capital grant (20-50%) to local partnerships that manage a common fund (from which individual grants can be given to property owners often at a higher level than normal conservation grants). This type of funding is directed towards deprived historical areas, where conservation and regeneration action forms part of a wider strategy of economic and social regeneration involving the local community. Furthermore, grants through the Heritage Economic Regeneration Scheme have been targeted at a wide range of conservation issues where there is a demonstrable need for public intervention due to economic and social deprivation (rescue/reuse of historical buildings, creating new employment opportunities, renewing the economic base, etc.).

In Germany, the federal *Städtbaulcher Denkmalschutz* programme (preservation in the context of the town), which operated in the 1990s in new states of the former East Germany, had advantages over normal state assistance programmes as it could tackle problems in a comprehensive manner (monuments, the context of monuments, streets, environment, etc.). Funding was shared between federal, state and local authorities. Repair grants made to individual building owners were as high as 90% of costs, which could be combined with financial support from other programmes (for example, for modernisation/rehabilitation).

Thus, these are integrated conservation approaches linked to urban planning mechanisms and with the aim of using the heritage environment as a basis for rehabilitation action.

6. Sanctions and coercive measures

The Granada Convention identifies a number of "statutory protection measures" in Articles 4 and 5. These include appropriate supervision and authorisation procedures and measures to prevent damage or demolition. In addition, Article 4 also refers to two types of coercive measures:

- permitting public authorities to require the owner of a protected property to carry out work or to carry out such work itself, if the owner fails to do so;
- allowing compulsory purchase (expropriation) of a protected property.

Furthermore, Article 9 of the convention refers to the need for sanction measures against infringements of the law – which should be met with "a relevant and adequate response" (either through administrative or criminal law or both).

It has to be remembered that if restrictions are going to be placed on the owner's right to use the property, this must be in the public interest (i.e. the purpose of law is to safeguard the heritage in the wider public interest) and reasonable (i.e. to have reasonable measures to oblige the owner to safeguard the heritage balanced by financial and technical support measures). However, many of the new law proposals being developed by South-East European countries have a heavy bias towards often onerous, and possibly unreasonable, obligations (made worse by inadequate financial support measures). This will not have the desired effect. Moreover, in some cases there is a desire to restrict ownership of heritage assets (or to have a first option to take such assets into public ownership if they are sold). This is unduly restrictive.

What then are appropriate coercive and sanction measures? This can be examined by reference to practice elsewhere. Countries in western Europe that have signed and ratified the Granada Convention can be used to illustrate this.

6.1. Rights of entry

In general terms, the law could provide for a "right of entry" for heritage officials to the property to check both on the condition and for any unauthorised work. However, such a requirement should be reasonable, which includes a proper notification procedure – at the same time an owner should allow reasonable access to officials. Such rights of entry are in operation in France, Germany and the United Kingdom, for example.

6.2. Restoration

The differences between restoration (restoring missing items or changes) and conservative repair should be highlighted. It is important to ensure that the restoration does not mean "conjectural restoration" (International Charter for the Conservation and Restoration of Monuments and Sites: ICOMOS Venice Charter). Care must be taken in legal procedures in this respect. Some draft laws have devised requirements to return buildings to their "original condition" (both Serbia and Montenegro, for example). Conservation philosophy today suggests that restoration as such is likely to be conjectural unless there is "sufficient evidence to define the earlier state". Moreover, it is almost impossible to define the "original" state as most buildings change over time and, in fact, changes made to a structure throughout its history may add further value and may merit protection. Therefore, the emphasis should be to "conserve as found" and to maintain it as an asset for future generations. This is a more reasonable proposition for a building owner – rather than insisting on an expensive restoration (which may falsify the past).

6.3. Maintenance obligations

Some countries provide a duty to keep a property in good repair (and using appropriate conservation techniques), whilst in others there is no "duty" as such, but measures can be used to require owners to take action. This can sometimes be divided between two types of action: urgent or emergency repairs or more detailed conservation/repair work (restoration work will be more extensive and onerous and must be supported by financial and technical measures).

6.4. Urgent works, repairs and expropriation measures

In some countries, the relevant authorities can enter premises to carry out urgent repairs after official notice to carry out necessary works has been served on the owner to no avail. This type of action is to ensure that a protected building is safeguarded (for example, repairing a roof, or providing temporary support where the structure is suffering from subsidence, or preventing damage by vandals where a property is not occupied by boarding up windows).

In France, half the costs can be recouped from the owner where the property is in jeopardy. In Germany, this action is rarely taken because of the difficulty in recouping costs (which is something to bear in mind). In the United Kingdom, the full cost of emergency repairs can be recouped but the procedure is subject to appeal. Grounds include "financial hardship" (the owner cannot afford to pay), or that "the works are not necessary (over and above those required), and otherwise unreasonable". In fact, grant aid is usually offered to an owner to overcome the problem of financial hardship. This highlights the need to have a balanced approach of positive incentives and controls. Moreover, in Denmark, the preferred approach is to use counselling and technical assistance with the offer of subsidies or loans to correct the situation.

In the United Kingdom, a "repairs notice" (a legal provision) can require that a detailed schedule of works must be carried out with the ultimate sanction of compulsory purchase (expropriation) if the works are not undertaken in a specified period. Such notices are rarely served, but the threat of such action is often enough to prompt the required works to be carried out. Moreover, care has to be taken in the use of this procedure – as it will result in the local authority having to pay compensation and public authorities generally do not wish to waste their limited budgets in this manner. However, should expropriation follow, there is the ultimate sanction of a "minimum compensation order" if "deliberate neglect" can be proved. This is applicable where it can be proved that an owner has deliberately allowed a property to fall in disrepair so that it may be argued that the condition is so bad that the property should be demolished in favour of new development (but in practice this is rare and very difficult to achieve in law).

An example of this may be given in relation to the protected country mansion of Pell Well Hall in England. The owner of this protected building first applied to the local planning authority for listed building consent to demolish the building in 1978 and sought to achieve this aim through various subsequent court hearings. In 1990, after the building had deteriorated and following the confirmation of a "compulsory purchase order" with the stipulation that minimum compensation should be paid, the price set for compensation for expropriation of the house and about two hectares of land was set at the minimum figure of £1 (approximately €1.5). The owner was also required to pay the legal costs of the local authority.

Expropriation provisions also apply in countries such as the Czech Republic, France, Georgia, Germany and Spain but are generally only used as a last resort. Any system of compulsory purchase must be "reasonable" and provide for "fair compensation" at the market value of the expropriated property (the value should reflect its condition/state of repair). The draft laws of countries-in-transition rarely account for this. Furthermore, it also has to be borne in mind that if an owner has to be compensated for the loss of the property then this will be a large drain on the already limited resources of the available budgets – which is one of the reasons why the procedure is only rarely used in the United Kingdom. In fact, it is likely to be less expensive to provide a subsidy – emphasising again the need for appropriate financial measures!

6.5. Legal action concerning unauthorised action

Action to stop activity damaging to protected heritage assets can be quite effectively pursued through legal mechanisms other than those provided for in heritage legislation, such as with the assistance of the police in France and the Netherlands. A system of "enforcement" could be specifically identified in the cultural heritage law (enforcement officers in the United Kingdom are employed by local government for this purpose). This will require a "stop" procedure – a legal procedure to require an immediate stop to the activity backed up with fines or penal measures. ("Stop notices" can be applied to unauthorised development activity and legal injunctions can be applied to unauthorised activity on protected heritage assets in the United Kingdom, the contravention of which is subject to a fine at the discretion of the courts.)

Enforcement action can include procedures for reparation measures, that is, to reinstate the situation that existed before unauthorised work was carried out (for example, in Belgium, Denmark, Ireland, the Netherlands and the United Kingdom). These can be backed up by criminal proceedings, though this is generally a last resort. The maximum period of imprisonment applied in Europe varies between six months and five years.

Fines and criminal measures may be mentioned under a separate penal code (rather than in a law on cultural heritage), in which case reference should be made to these separate measures (for example, by reference to specific articles) in the law on cultural heritage.

The important point is that any measure should be designed to penalise and act as a deterrent. In the United Kingdom, every unauthorised action can be subject to a fine. For example, in the case of a listed building in Soho, London, a developer was fined £1 000 (approximately €1 500) for each of 14 separate issues (i.e. £14 000 in total) for stripping out timber panels and other interior features of a listed building. By taking action on each feature removed without consent, it was possible to go beyond the then maximum fine of £2 000. Moreover, the defendant was also ordered to pay the court costs of the local authority and the fines could have been much higher but for the fact that the developer pleaded in mitigation that he had subsequently instituted a repair scheme costed at £80 000. Since this case, reported in 1990, the law has been amended so that the maximum fine is now set at £20 000 (approximately €30 000) for any single unauthorised action.

Moreover, as previously stated, in most countries there are possibilities to imprison offenders, with maximum prison sentences generally in the range of six months to five years. But these types of measures should only be used for the most extreme cases to serve as a deterrent to other potential offenders. An example of this can be provided in a case in England that received a great deal of coverage in the national press. A developer was sentenced to four months in prison (and his accomplice to 28 days) for the bungled blowing up of a listed Wesleyan Chapel using explosives. The plan had been to put a crack in the building, rendering it unsafe so that there would be grounds to obtain permission for its demolition (as it would be regarded as a dangerous structure). However, the action misfired causing the whole of the front of the building to be blown out.

6.6. Problems concerning sanction and coercive measures

Apart from the issues of reasonableness and onerous requirements mentioned in relation to countries-in-transition, one problem that exists generally is that there is evidence that sanctions and coercive measures are ineffective due to the fact that they are often not applied, for example in Denmark (although juridical orders are increasingly being served) and France (where the provisions have been reviewed). In some countries-in-transition difficulties can result from a lack of precedents of prosecution cases (and especially if specific measures have not been enacted). Another problem is the low level of fines (Czech Republic) or the fact that the level of fines is not sufficient to act as a deterrent (Germany). In Ireland and the United Kingdom, the level of fines has increased in recent years. The maximum level of fine in Ireland (approximately €1.5 million) for carrying out a development without permission or for not carrying out specified work on protected structures would seem to be a significant deterrent, but much damage occurred before this strengthened regime of protection commenced.

7. Conclusions

It must be reiterated that there is a need for balance between financial and technical support on the one hand, and obligations and sanctions on the other. The idea that we safeguard the cultural heritage for the benefit of society as a whole means that there will be restrictions on the normal right of property owners to enjoy their property. In order to compensate for such restrictions, other incentives should be provided – the most significant being financial assistance.

Any law that consists of a long list of restrictions and controls seeks, in reality, only to protect – not to preserve. However, there is no point in having a protected but damaged heritage. In order for private owners of heritage assets to safeguard them they must be provided with assistance.

Whilst budgets are limited, the effective use of the heritage can ensure that it pays its way in social terms, not just as a heritage asset but also for other purposes (a living heritage). This, in turn, provides benefits for society and the economy, for example through employment, housing and tax revenues. It is these arguments that should be explored to try to establish more support.

In other respects, it is important to make statutory provisions for support in law and to ensure that all other procedures that limit the normal rights of an owner are reasonable.

8. The case of "the former Yugoslav Republic of Macedonia"

A new law to supplement the Law on Protection of Cultural Monuments (1973) has been influenced by the provisions of some 50 different kinds of regulations (for example, the laws on crime, spatial and urban planning and investment project development) in force by the end of 2004. The new Law on Protection of the Cultural Heritage was passed in April 2004, and came into force on 1 January 2005.

For the first time, the new law considers several very important issues concerning the protection of the cultural heritage in "the former Yugoslav Republic of Macedonia". The scope of interest has been expanded in relation to two different groups of cultural heritage: the material (immovable and movable) as well as the intangible heritage. A number of issues and financial measures to safeguard the heritage can be highlighted.

8.1. Illegal activities, armed conflict and natural disasters

Particular parts of the new law consider the protection of the heritage in relation to illegal activities (Chapter 7, Articles 102-105) and armed conflict and natural disasters (Chapter 8, Articles 106-110). The latter provisions were derived from international agreements and documents, accepted by "the former Yugoslav Republic of Macedonia", as well as from the negative results of the 2001 armed conflict.

Previously, there were many illegal excavations on archaeological sites and thefts from churches (stolen icons and church artefacts), particularly in the rural areas. "The former Yugoslav Republic of Macedonia" is not in a position (concerning the current economic situation and administrative structure) to establish a particularly educated service to control illegal activities (such as the "police/army of protection" in Italy), but the new law contains many instruments regulating this matter. In the new Department for the Cultural Heritage Protection within the Ministry of Culture, a particular office for prevention, planning measures and controlling the implementation of the propositions for the security of the protected heritage has already been established. This department has also established an office for preparatory measures and monitoring in cases of armed conflict and natural disasters.

Also, according to the new law, the government is obliged to create a National Action Plan for the prevention of the criminal activities (Article 103). In relation to this, there is new chapter – "Protection of the heritage from the pollution of its environment/surrounding" (Chapter 9, Articles 111-112) – which is designed to establish co-operation between the Ministry of Environment and Spatial Planning, local authorities and the Ministry of Education and Science.

8.2. Integrated protection

A strategy of integrated protection is developed in the new law, providing many control mechanisms regarding spatial and urban planning and relevant legislation relating to this. For example, within the Law on Investment Project Development the protection of heritage is treated in only one article which requires that the investor provides technical documentation (prepared or approved by the responsible institute) only for the buildings protected by this law. (This means that the heritage in the process of valorisation/evaluation could not be taken into consideration.) Within the Law on Spatial and Urban Planning there is no obligation, beyond notification of proposals, for planning institutes to collaborate with those responsible for cultural heritage. As a result, there are many problems with illegal construction, with many interventions by investors being granted by the planning institutes, particularly in urban areas.

The new law will return decision-making powers to the Ministry of Culture (elaborated in Chapter 3, Articles 69-81: 13 articles). This returns the situation to that which existed before the Law on Investment Project Development was brought into force (1999), and the ministry will be in a position not only to comment on urban planning proposals, but also to approve them.

The objective will be to improve the mechanisms and the co-operation between the two disciplines (protection and planning), promoting heritage as a factor of development, not as an obstacle in the creation of the urban and spatial plans.

8.3. The use/occupation of the cultural heritage by concessions

The new law established a legal framework for the use/occupation of the cultural heritage by concession, which has provoked great interest (Chapter 11, Articles 117-120). So, even though the law is not yet in force, some initiatives have already been submitted. Property that may become subject to a concession is limited to immovable monuments in state ownership (not including reserved archaeological zones, memorial objects of important events and religious buildings of outstanding importance which are in use). A concession can be awarded to a domestic or foreign legal entity or individual, under regulated conditions. The concessionaires should possess the appropriate financial and technical capabilities to implement the activity, to offer a programme for revitalisation and a management plan. For the use of cultural heritage subject to a concession an annual fee will be paid. The amount of the fee will be determined by the concession contract. The period for which the concession is awarded will be:

> "up to 10 years for the performance of a production activity and up to 15 years for the performance of other activities regulated by this Law" (Article 117).

8.4. Financial support measures in the Law on Protection of the Cultural Heritage

In order to incorporate the owners of cultural heritage as participants in the protection process, the new law regulated their rights and obligations more strictly and clearly than the previous law (Chapter 5, Articles 123-141). The new aspect in this regulation is that the owners have the right to request financial support on account of limited activities on their cultural property (depending on the regime of protection), or if they had spent unpredicted amounts for the protection of the heritage. There is also an article (Article 127) where some benefits/exemptions (customs or other tax-free benefits) are provided for the owners of heritage. However, this has not yet been developed due to the necessity to work in harmony with the other authorities on this subject (particularly with the Ministry of Finance). Furthermore, there are some financial incentives for private collections in relation to the public presentation of such collections within the governmental institutions.

8.5. Tax measures and foundations provided by other laws

According to the Law on Culture (passed in 1998/2003), there is a possibility of establishing funds and foundations in this area. Also, there is a law on income tax which provides that donations and grants for cultural purposes are exempt from the payment of taxes up to 3% of the total income if these are invested in public cultural institutions financed by the state budget. There is a need to underline that this measure concerns foundations for different kinds of cultural activities – not just those for the protection of heritage. Whilst these examples indicate that there are some tax provisions that can benefit the treatment of the cultural heritage within the framework of other laws, compared with the legislation of other countries the tax policy is not favourable. This is the reason for the many activities by the Ministry of Culture aimed at changing laws to establish a more acceptable status for the cultural heritage.

8.6. Investment in the cultural heritage

Investments in the cultural heritage are still insignificant and most of them come from foreign donors. Therefore, a central body responsible for co-ordinating and registering all foreign investments and interventions has been established within the government. Within this scope, there are a number of continuing projects developed by the Institute for Protection of the Cultural Monuments of the Republic of Macedonia in association with the European Centre of Byzantine and Post-Byzantine Monuments (Thessaloníki) on research and documentation of relevant monuments.

- In the previous period there were several projects from PHARE programmes: on the archaeological sites of Vardarski Rid and Stobi and on the rural ensemble of the Aroman village of Malovishte (near Bitola), such as projects for cross-border co-operation in terms of economic development, cultural and ecological preservation.

- Another two internationally funded projects have been established in response to damage to churches incurred in the 2001 conflict. The European Agency for Reconstruction is financing the reconstruction of the 19th century church at the monastery of Lesok (Tetovo) and the Dutch government is financing the conservation of the monastery church of Matejche (Kumanovo) from the 14th century.

- In the previous year, the World Monuments Fund gave a grant of US $50 000 for preventative conservation of and research into the wall paintings in the 13th century cave church of Radozda (near Struga).

8.7. Cultural tourism as an economic resource

The most important resource for investment, protection and revitalisation of the cultural heritage in this exceptionally difficult economic situation in the country is tourism. In the scope of the National Programme for Culture (2004-2007), cultural tourism is one of the top objectives in the strategy for cultural development. But, unfortunately, the Ministry of Culture was not involved in the creation of the tourism taxation policy. On the other hand, the ministry has made a great effort to introduce "income for monuments" as Croatia has already done (in the document "Changes and amendments on the Law on Protecting the Heritage" dating from 2003).

The right way to make the cultural heritage a prospective economic source (not for all types of monuments) and to create a respectable fund for its protection and revitalisation (beside the state budget) is to implement cultural tourism projects. It is obvious that to consider heritage for tourist exploitation is a very complex and expensive activity. So, more long-term action in this field could be achieved by the development of cultural tourism through rural tourism on rural ensembles (a type of living heritage), which will underline several aspects: revitalisation of the rural areas abounding with cultural heritage assets (which has also been a demographic problem for a long period of time); protection of the monuments, in time; job creation; profitability for the owners/users; and providing budgets for heritage protection. The Law on Protection of Cultural Monuments gives a framework in relation to this issue (Article 5, paragraph 8; Article 6, paragraph 2).

One of the most important, long-term projects in progress in this area is the Community Development and Cultural Project (2002-2005, but with great likelihood of being continued), financed by the World Bank, carried out by the established Project Co-ordination Unit as an independent body for this issue and with the permanent collaboration of the Ministry of Culture and its institutions.

The purpose of Component 1 of this project ("integrated communities development") is to give incentives for production and other cultural activity development in less developed regions (for maintaining craft skills or traditional methods of construction), as well as projects for protection/conservation of cultural heritage. This phase of the project is implemented in seven different regions, particularly in the east and west of the country.

There are three types of grant:

1. *associative grants of US $200-20 000* for implementing projects on the cultural and natural heritage with the participation of the local population (through established local associations);
2. *grants for other needs of the communities* (several small grants of US $500): as fellowships given to children, pupils, students for their environmental refining activities (for example: gardens, school yards, trees);
3. *grants from the Ministry of Culture - as a financial support (max. US $100 000)* for projects concerning the protection of different types of cultural heritage according to the Prioritised Intervention List prepared by local and international experts at the World Bank.

Component 2 of the project is called "institutional development at national level". The priority of this section is to support local level activities by implementing activities at a national level such as: a national action plan on tourism focusing on cultural and eco-tourism; an evaluation and craftsmanship action plan; and the modernisation and digitalisation of the current inventory system for the cultural heritage.

For example, this project will enable:

– new job openings, attracting more visitors/tourists and investments into areas with cultural monuments, situated in less developed regions of the country;
– improvement of the efficiency of the national and local authorities/the communities in: cultural heritage management through mutual activities; partnerships between the public and private sector that could produce appropriate local development strategies; increasing the technical capacity; and achieving better conditions for the cultural heritage and its presentation and revitalisation.

8.8. Conclusions

The first steps are now being made to provide financial incentives for different types of activities within the new legislative regime for the cultural heritage resulting from the Law on Protection of the Cultural Heritage 2004 and some other laws and with the assistance of the World Monuments Fund, the PHARE programme and the European Agency for Reconstruction and other bodies. There is a need to co-ordinate tax policy in this field with the Ministry of Finance. Further work is needed to integrate the management of the cultural heritage with development and investment strategies. Similarly, progress has been made to curb illegal and resolve other damaging activities, but further work is needed.

9. Summary of questions and views

The following issues of debate and responses were raised in relation to the presentation of papers on Theme 4:

Issue 1 – The development of cultural tourism is important but ministries that have a responsibility for the cultural heritage are often kept out of any tourism taxation strategy (which is usually under the remit of ministries dealing with the economy, investment and trade). There is a Council of Europe recommendation on cultural tourism which states that the cultural heritage could be a social and economic resource. But in the Republic of Serbia there are a lot of problems between the ministry dealing with the heritage and the ministry dealing with the economy.

In the development of a new law for tourism, the Ministry of Culture has intervened, trying to include the idea of using some percentage of tourist taxation for repairing and maintaining the cultural heritage.

> *Response*
>
> Cultural tourism is an issue for both ministries to consider. It is important to develop co-operation between many different ministries when considering integrated mechanisms – at the earliest stage possible. Moreover, it is important to develop an interministerial dialogue. There is a need to educate other ministries that the cultural heritage is relevant to tourism. This is the first step. The next step is to attempt to co-ordinate a strategy for cultural tourism, but the practicalities of this are another issue.
>
> Statistical analysis of actual revenues that have been generated from the cultural heritage as a tourism resource would help to prove the argument for more financial resources. This involves a lot of work and the co-ordination of issues. But if it can be shown that the cultural heritage is providing a financial benefit to society then this could be used to argue for more funds to assist the cultural heritage. The gathering of this information could help to provide evidence. This could be a way of putting more pressure on the relevant ministry dealing, for instance, with revenue, investment and economy, to provide a greater slice of the national budget for heritage.

Issue 2 – There is a problem that relates to all the countries participating in the regional programme. Once they were socialist countries – but now they are countries-in-transition. Now there is both public (and state) ownership and private ownership. Many cultural monuments have had work done on them. Many have been returned to private ownership. There are many new owners. Such owners may now wish to sell sites that are in poor condition. They leave them to deteriorate and ruin. What can be done to prevent this? In Bulgaria it is a vicious circle – any repressive sanctions need to be made with all the strength necessary – but in reality this does not happen?

Response

France can be given as an example to answer this question. There are two approaches to improve the sanction system.

First, temporary measures to stop construction works – in France a representative of the mayor can stop any development work that is damaging to a protected monument. This can be a very effective measure.

Secondly, there are some traditional sanctions, for example, monetary fines. However, these are not always effective as judges very rarely apply the maximum level of fine. Therefore, we need other ways to have an impact. There is the case of a developer who applied for permission to build a 200 square metre house on the Cote d'Azur. Consent was given for this. But the developer then constructed a 2 000 square metre hotel. The developer was subsequently forced to demolish the illegal over-developed site. Another example is that of a person who demolished a protected mediaeval tower situated on his land – he was sentenced to restore the tower using the same materials. A further example would be the unauthorised installation of escalators in protected buildings (which can destroy original staircases and decoration) and in this situation it is possible to insist that these features are reinstated.

Issue 3 – As regards tax relief and other financial incentives, it would be useful to have a positive example of direct crediting, in the sense of investment credits, which could be granted if good credit lines are available, or a preferential relief in the cases concerning direct investment for protection or conservation of monuments or other types of cultural assets. In Bulgaria, investment banking is already quite well developed, and they support small and medium-sized businesses with projects concerning agriculture, infrastructure or even tourism, but not directly related to cultural objects/sites. If there are any good models it would be useful for us to know them, because it should be possible to use a credit with a relief regime.

Response

In the United States, a rehabilitation tax credit is provided in relation to certified historical structures. The United States is not a country well known for its heritage, but it does have a system of protected heritage buildings and districts. More significantly it has much more highly developed systems for financial management. The tax credit system for rehabilitating historical buildings (at 20% against tax) can be combined with the tax credit for providing affordable low-income housing (9%). It is a very good system because it has actually encouraged a market for investors and developing companies away from their normal large office buildings or other types of investment – they actually want to invest in old buildings. They are not only restoring and rehabilitating those buildings, but they are creating social benefits. Many downtown areas had become ghettos when other activities moved out of town. Now they are coming back to life, and the community is improving around that. Sometimes this results not just in the rehabilitation of the building itself, but also the land associated with it. So the community can meet and it generates a good communal spirit. So, this form of tax credit is very positive because otherwise it is usually very difficult to try to encourage investors to invest in heritage buildings – but this is a way of drawing them in. Similarly in France and the United Kingdom, financial incentives are given to area-based initiatives centred on areas of old buildings and old houses suffering from deprivation.

Another example can be given in relation to building preservation trusts operating in the United Kingdom which are able to obtain loans at preferential (low) interest rates from the Architectural Heritage Fund (a kind of foundation). All borrowers must offer adequate security, which is usually in the form of a first charge on the building once a rehabilitation project has been completed or it could be by a repayment guarantee from a commercial bank. Furthermore, some building preservation trusts keep their completed projects rather than sell them. This enables them to let the property for an income. Moreover, the increased capital value of the asset after rehabilitation can be used to raise credit from a bank for further rehabilitation projects (via loans similar to a mortgage). Similarly, the National Restauratie Fonds has been mentioned in the presentation. This is a subsidiary of a commercial bank operating in the Netherlands, which gives long-term loans at low rates of interest for work on historical buildings.

Issue 4 – Further knowledge is needed of incentives and creating funds/fund-raising. It is acknowledged that an owner should preserve and maintain – but it is rare for a private owner to be able to afford the maintenance costs. Property interests have been restored to private owners but these new owners do not have the money to rehabilitate. How can we encourage the owner of an old building to take action instead of selling to a developer who may sell apartments before they have even been completed?

Response

One way to stop an owner selling to a developer would be to provide specific incentives for the owner to maintain, restore and rehabilitate. Apart from financial tools, there is also a need to give guidance and assistance. Building owners should be able to obtain advice, for instance on how best to undertake improvement works, how to conserve, how to repair, what materials to use or what colour of paint to use. The emphasis should be on using and rehabilitating buildings with positive encouragement. Moreover, once a building has been conserved or restored it will have added value. There are many examples in the United Kingdom where financial assistance has been given for specific projects – not just to support work on that building but also to act as an example to others. Once a building has been brought back to life other people and owners can see the benefit of the restored/rehabilitated building (aesthetically and financially – a restored building may have added value). This type of action has, in many cases, encouraged others to take action – particularly if it is through an area-based heritage regeneration strategy. Motivation is a key factor.

Another way of dealing with this would be to consider that buildings depreciate (they are "wasting assets"). Where buildings are owned by private entities/businesses, then in Belgium and other countries everything that is invested can be depreciated against tax (business/corporate tax on profits/business income). Therefore, the cost of works to historical buildings used as a business can allow for the recovery of costs against income tax.

Furthermore, it depends on the status of the building. If it is protected then it should require consent for demolition. Even buildings that are not individually protected could be safeguarded if they contribute to an area. For example, disregarding protected listed buildings, all other buildings within a designated conservation area in England require conservation area consent for their demolition. Such consent is only usually given if the proposals to replace the older building "preserve and enhance the character and appearance of the area". Moreover, in England, policies can be established in development plans to ensure that the character and appearance of areas is safeguarded. Thus, by some controls it is possible to stop an owner selling an old building so that new apartments can be developed. This approach results from an integrated process.

Issue 5 – If the state institutions are involved in work on cultural heritage, private investors will not be involved. Therefore investors are disadvantaged. How can we combine action by both the public and private sectors? Is there a way of providing long-term credit at low interest rates to support investment?

Response

At the moment there are loan facilities in Bulgaria for short-term financing, as well as for in the long term: for example for the purchase of buildings, for new constructions or the rehabilitation of buildings. There is no direct preference for restoration activity with a low interest rate. A museum is a legal institution – and can elaborate a business plan, because it raises an income from its activities and from this an investment credit could be possible.

A conference took place in Strasbourg in November 2002 with representatives from the European Bank for Development, which for the first time paid some attention to the cultural industries by expressing interest in investment in cultural industries on the basis of business plans. Thus the road is opened. With a good business plan it may be possible to apply to the European Bank. However, it does not make direct investments. It has to find a bank correspondent in a country to undertake these obligations. Furthermore, the preferential interest rates that the European Bank could offer will grow if it is necessary to proceed through a national commercial bank, which could cause problems. Therefore, unfortunately, the issue of low rates of interest may not be resolved.

Issue 6 – Does the institutional control regarding investments and investors favour the investor over the cultural heritage? In other words, investment often results in the cultural heritage being demolished or abandoned. This is particularly the case where permission has been granted for commercial development and where, during the course of development, archaeological remains are found. Even if sanctions are envisaged, will a developer delay the works to allow an archaeological investigation? If the developer is to be put in an unfavourable financial situation due to a requirement to investigate (a delay or stoppage of the development works) will this happen? How is it possible to come out of this situation, bearing in mind the specific interest of the investor, and the specific protection and preservation of the cultural heritage?

Response

A number of examples can be given. First, in Spain it is possible for the authorities to declare a site as an archaeological reserve and, therefore, not to be destroyed. It is possible to give another site in exchange to allow for the development to occur. Similarly in Hong Kong, Israel, the United States, Canada and some other countries there is a system known as the "transfer of development rights" (TDR). In New York, for example, there are quite of number of 19th century buildings that are designated landmark buildings – some are churches – which are surrounded by skyscrapers. The land on which such buildings are located has a high development potential and a high development value. The TDR mechanism operates by allowing an owner to sell rights to develop to a receiving site elsewhere, in other words by transferring the right to develop. Within this arrangement there is usually a requirement for a preservation easement, which means that the authorities will allow this development to occur elsewhere as along as the developer provides a regular sum of money to maintain the heritage building in perpetuity. This is usually managed by a specific organisation.

Theme 5 – The living heritage: a sustainable approach

1. Basic principle: sustainable development

1.1. Definition of the concept of sustainable development

Like integrated conservation, sustainable development is one of the major basic principles of heritage policies advocated by the Council of Europe.

This concept is, however, more recent since it was cited for the first time at international level in 1987 by the World Commission on Environment and Development and developed subsequently in 1992 at the UN Conference on Environment and Development in Rio on the theme of the future of the Earth (the "Earth Summit").

According to the Rio Declaration, adopted at the end of the Earth Summit, sustainable development is "development that meets the needs of the present without compromising the ability of future generations to meet their own needs".

This basic principle rests on three, equally important pillars:

- economic development;
- social cohesion;
- protection of the environment and the cultural heritage.

Applied to cultural and natural heritage, sustainable development means the ability of the heritage to adapt to the new demands and needs of society without interruptions, phases of obsolescence (prolonged deterioration) or interventions likely to upset the balance of its environment.

Sustainable development may, therefore, be seen as a new phase in modernity that restores tradition to a position of importance.

It introduces the notion of shared responsibility for the future of the planet that suggests a change in ways of life and modes of production, stressing the importance of recycling and the restoration of old buildings in order to avoid wastage and waste.

It also presupposes the implementation of "careful policies" that respect the principle of precaution with regard to the environment in which we live.

The Council of Europe included the principle of sustainable development in a reference document on spatial planning entitled Guiding Principles for the Sustainable Spatial Development of the European Continent, adopted at Hanover on 8 September 2000 by the European Conference of Ministers responsible for Regional Planning (CEMAT).

Sustainable development is also the intellectual basis of the Framework Convention on the Value of the Cultural Heritage for Society[5] at present under discussion by the heritage authorities of Council of Europe member states.

1.2. Practical implications of sustainable development

Implementation of the principle of sustainable development in heritage policies means that new approaches at economic, social, environmental and cultural levels are needed. It also leads to the introduction of new management styles. These changes, the results of which are just beginning to make themselves felt, may be summarised as follows:

With respect to economic development

1. Sustainable development offers a new development model based on enhancement of the status of the heritage rather than simply on the production of goods and economic profitability.
2. It mobilises the economic potential of the cultural heritage through active management, while at the same time continuing to protect its cultural (historical, aesthetic, technical) value.
3. It acts as a driving force in local development policies for which local authorities are now required to assume greater responsibility, including their practical management (previously under the authority of national government).

With respect to social cohesion

1. Sustainable development contributes to the improvement of the social fabric by improving the urban or rural fabric through targeted interventions on built heritage (social) housing and public spaces.
2. It confirms the role of the heritage as a factor for integration and social cohesion since its conservation (change of use, maintenance, restoration and enhancement) improves the conditions and quality of life of local communities.

With respect to protection of the environment

1. Sustainable development enhances the quality of the living environment and the well-being of society by responding to the need to live in a place that is at once dignified, clean and pleasant, whatever its members' resources.
2. It protects and develops biological and landscape diversity by conserving the natural heritage, introducing new cultural landscape management policies, promoting tourism respectful of the environment and reducing environmental damage (pollution and waste).

---

5. The convention was opened for signature in Faro, 27 October 2005.

3. It fosters territorial cohesion between town and countryside, as well as between the neighbourhoods of a particular town, through balanced development and the promotion of better access to the whole territory.

With respect to enhancement of the cultural heritage

1. The principle of sustainable development preserves the collective memory and cultural identity of communities by conserving and enhancing the heritage in the broad sense of the term.
2. It preserves and enriches the diversity of cultural environments by integrating the various forms of the cultural and natural, movable and immovable, tangible and intangible heritage and by simultaneously encompassing its market, social and cultural values.

With respect to policy and management methods

1. The principle of sustainable development goes still further than the principle of integrated conservation in so far as it implies close collaboration among heritage actors, not only with those involved in spatial and urban planning, but also with economic, social and environmental players. Co-operation mechanisms, therefore, need to be established between these different partners in order to guarantee the success of sustainable development projects.
2. The energetic management of the heritage that sustainable development implies also requires a more flexible and open attitude on the part of its managers (political authorities and civil servants) to changes of use of the heritage and the physical changes necessary for its current use.

In the final analysis, application of the principle of sustainable development positively encourages a living heritage rather than a museum-type heritage through:

- urban rehabilitation and local rural development programmes;
- a use of the heritage that produces economic and social benefits as much as cultural benefits;
- enhancing the heritage in order to respond to the current needs of society rather than for the benefit of a few specialists or art enthusiasts.

2. Main problems

2.1. At a legislative level

By and large, the legislation of South-East European countries exhibits an extensive notion of heritage as suggested by sustainable development (cultural and natural, movable and immovable, tangible and intangible heritage). The notion of cultural environment does not yet appear very clearly in definitions.

Furthermore, the sections on heritage management reflect an approach that focuses too much on monuments in the traditional sense of the term. Given that a group of buildings, a natural site, a cultural landscape or an archaeological site are not managed in the same way as an individual monument, the provisions on these categories of heritage should be more specific and presented in separate sections.

As for the concept of sustainable development and the related principles, such as shared responsibility, careful management, social cohesion and improving the economic and social potential of the heritage, they are virtually absent from the legislation.

2.2. At an institutional level

It should be recognised that sustainable development is more a matter of attitude, approach and a favourable institutional context than legislation. It is essential to guarantee – to heritage players and their project partners – a sufficiently clearly defined and flexible institutional framework to enable them to work in a truly integrated, co-ordinated way.

It would seem, however, that the institutional framework of the countries of the region does not at present provide the linkages and co-ordination mechanisms needed for the realisation of a sustainable development project.

2.3. At a political level

Similarly, clear affirmation of the political will to carry through this type of project – that is, in the medium or even long term – is crucial to the success of any sustainable development project.

The development strategies of national authorities as well as the action plans arising from them, would benefit from an explicit reference to the principles of sustainable development and the will to promote a "living heritage" through a flexible, open approach to adapting it or changing its use.

3. Possible solutions and examples of good practice

3.1. Direct participation in the drafting of development plans

A development plan is a strategic legal instrument (giving broad guidelines rather than hard-and-fast rules) which sets out medium-term general development strategies (usually for a period of five to ten years).

A development plan is approved by national or regional authorities, according to whether it is general or particular, and consists of three parts: an assessment of the existing situation (strengths, weaknesses and major trends), strategic issues and objectives and an action plan with priorities.

It is particularly useful if defenders of the heritage participate in the drafting of this type of instrument – traditionally managed by spatial planners – in order to ensure that the heritage is indeed among the government's (or local authorities') basic political priorities and will, therefore, be taken up in practical action plans and those "lower" in the hierarchy of plans.

It is also important to ensure that heritage is appropriately linked with the other (sustainable) development priorities in economic, social and environmental policies.

3.2. Participation in urban rehabilitation and rural development programmes

In addition to being involved in the drafting of development plans, the authorities responsible for heritage have a major role to play in the implementation and follow-up of urban rehabilitation and rural development programmes in order to guarantee the enhancement of the cultural heritage, economic development and improved living and social conditions for all the populations affected by those programmes.

For example, in the Karst region of Slovenia there is a rural development programme based essentially on the protection and enhancement of endogenous resources characterised by a very rich cultural and natural heritage, and by its food and a high-quality culinary tradition. The expected practical outcomes include the development of tourism (bed and breakfast, agrotourism, local gastronomy, cultural activities), the restoration and enhancement of the cultural heritage (for example the exceptional Skocjan caves, historical villages and old farms), water management (supply and treatment), improved agricultural production (higher quality, ecological) and increased local employment, thus reducing unemployment among women and the unskilled, which is endemic in this rural region.

3.3. Providing an appropriate legal framework for such programmes

In the framework of development programmes conducted in co-operation with the private sector, those responsible for the heritage and their institutional partners need legal instruments in land and urban planning policy, in particular in order to give "developers" the framework and legal security for their work that is essential for the implementation of any large-scale project.

With respect to land policy, the public authorities should, in particular, have expropriation and compulsory purchase procedures (for public-interest reasons) for acquiring certain private properties in a critical condition or, again, concession or long lease procedures to enable public property to be privately managed. This legal framework, combined with heritage protection instruments, would enable them to conduct a genuine policy to control land and real estate transactions in co-operation with the private sector.

With respect to town planning, in addition to the adoption of development and land use plans and urban planning regulations (concerning the urban or rural area covered by the development project), the authorities responsible should also have available to them legal instruments enabling emergency work to be carried out, if necessary despite the owner's refusal to do it, control procedures to be implemented and penalties imposed for work carried out without a permit or for allowing buildings to fall into disrepair. This is particularly important for the conservation of the cultural heritage in countries where there are innumerable illegal interventions and buildings left to wrack and ruin.

3.4. Assisting programme partners by giving technical and financial support

The legal framework for development programmes should also include public finance mechanisms to support the partners and encourage them to comply with regulations (the carrot and stick principle). However, because of the numbers involved, it is difficult to envisage funding being made available under heritage policies for properties other than individual listed monuments.

Other modes of financing regional development, therefore, need to be found, such as policies on urban rehabilitation, housing, assistance for small and medium-sized enterprises (SMEs), change of use of abandoned buildings, the provision and maintenance of public spaces, infrastructure and nature conservation.

It is also important to look for creative, low-cost solutions favourable to the restoration of the heritage rather than new building.

For example, in Wallonia (Belgium), heritage legislation provides for the financing of the excess cost engendered by the change of use of listed buildings, even if the work is not going to be carried out on old elements of a building (for example the installation of new bathroom facilities, an alarm system, kitchen or lift). Similarly, the authorities publish and make available to the public leaflets containing information on all the various types of financial and fiscal support available in the framework of conservation and restoration programmes.

Furthermore, the authorities responsible may also provide decisive technical support through speedy, efficient administrative procedures (particularly with respect to issuing permits, financing and inspecting work) and public information.

In the Brussels-Capital Region (Belgium), for example, the Monuments and Sites Department makes available to developers and the owners of listed properties a list of (registered) specialists in the various techniques needed for the restoration of the cultural heritage. It also publishes a (regularly updated) list of unoccupied historical buildings that could be reused by companies, promoters or private individuals for professional or private purposes. The list is also circulated abroad through chambers of commerce, consulates and embassies.

3.5. Setting up institutional co-ordination mechanisms

Finally, urban rehabilitation and rural development programmes also require a comprehensive approach to the complex problems connected with the functioning of towns and villages. Fully integrated management that seeks a comprehensive and detailed understanding of situations and the mechanisms that have produced them is essential.

The multisectorial partnership approach to development programmes, therefore, involves the setting up of co-ordination mechanisms at both institutional and legislative levels:

- *horizontally*: the formation of multidisciplinary teams and the co-ordination of a multitude of interacting competencies (heritage, spatial planning, urban planning, housing, the environment, agriculture, tourism, transport, the economy, social affairs, culture, education, etc.);
- *vertically*: co-ordination of actions conducted at the different levels of power (European, national, regional and local) and respect of the complementary nature of these levels of power according to the principle of subsidiarity;
- *territorially*: co-operation among the urban neighbourhoods or villages covered by projects and with the neighbouring territorial authorities to enable productive communication between projects and their territory.

4. Conclusions

i. Sustainable development requires clear, firm political commitment from the outset and constant management to ensure the success of urban restoration or local rural development programmes.

ii. It applies to heritage in the broad sense of the term according to the notion of the cultural environment, including the cultural and natural, movable and immovable and tangible and intangible heritage. Thus, sustainable development reflects the new notion of the cultural environment.

iii. It aims to guarantee the sustainable conservation of a living heritage through its use and enhancement in order to produce economic, social, environmental and cultural benefits, at the same time as responding to the current welfare needs of society as a whole.

iv. It can only be achieved in the framework of comprehensive policies that integrate the plethora of competencies concerned (heritage, regional planning, town planning, housing, the environment, agriculture, tourism, transport, the economy, social affairs, culture, education, etc.) and foster partnership with the private sector.

v. It requires institutional reforms establishing co-operation mechanisms that ensure at once horizontal co-ordination (between the authorities responsible), *vertical* co-ordination (between the different levels of power) and territorial co-ordination (between territories concerned and neighbouring territories).

vi. It involves legal reforms and the establishment of an adequate legal framework, particularly with respect to land and town planning policy, in order to provide "developers" with the framework and legal security that are essential for the implementation of any large-scale project.

vii. It justifies technical and financial support of the partners involved through public finance mechanisms (subsidies, tax breaks, and low-interest loans) under the various policy areas concerned, as well as through speedy, efficient administrative procedures and an efficient public information system.

5. Summary of questions and views

The following issues of debate and responses were raised in relation to the presentation of the paper on Theme 5:

Issue 1 – To illustrate point 3.2 of the presentation (Participation in urban restoration and rural development programmes), the Regional Development Plan (RDP) of the Brussels-Capital Region, adopted in 1995, set out a "city project" which boiled down to 10 main objectives to be met by 2015, thus allowing 20 years for these to be achieved. Among the 10 objectives, 3 were concerned directly with the cultural heritage, the aim being that development in Brussels should respect and exploit the value of that heritage.

The first objective was to rehabilitate the historic heart of Brussels and the old centres of the 19 communes which had been incorporated into the city over time. This enhancement of the urban fabric was to be achieved by strengthening local identity.

The second objective was to strengthen the identity of the city by managing, enhancing or newly creating parts of the urban landscape. Gradually, the city had in fact lost its sense of what it should look like, with streets being widened, whole blocks being torn down, and so on. It was, therefore, decided not only to restore the older parts which were significant in terms of the image of Brussels, but also to create features that would be of symbolic importance to the city, such as newly designed "gateways" into Brussels on the major roads leading into the city. So that these gateways would have a genuine aesthetic quality and would offer visitors a positive image of the city, a system of competitions was introduced to attract artists.

The third objective was to undertake cultural projects which would provide information about the Brussels Region for tourists: upgrading of museums, live performance and opera venues and, more generally, greater use made of various cultural activities for tourism in the broad sense of the word.

In reality, these three objectives are mixed up with the other seven objectives of the RDP concerned, for example with mobility, infrastructures, restructuring of the former industrial fabric and protection of housing (under great pressure from offices, which are far more profitable than housing).

This kind of plan or general development strategy has succeeded in unlocking budgets belonging to the entire urban community to carry out heritage projects which could not have been funded by cultural budgets, and has done so thanks to the fact that three of the ten development objectives are concerned with the cultural heritage.

Issue 2 – To illustrate point 3.3 (Providing an appropriate legal framework for such programmes), let us look at the possibility of carrying out emergency work automatically, which is a common practice with many of us. It generally takes one or sometimes two years in Wallonia (Belgium) to process an application for a grant or a permit to carry out restoration work, during which time buildings continue to deteriorate or even collapse. In cases of emergency, when buildings are likely to fall into ruin, it is vital to have fast-track legal procedures and emergency systems for authorising work. In Belgium, if an owner contacts the department of the Walloon Regional Government responsible for monuments and sites, for example, and says that there are stability problems, water penetration or dry rot in a listed building and that it is in danger of collapse, it is legally possible in such cases to obtain "fast-track" permits and funding (i.e., within 15 days). A (simplified) file is drawn up within a day by department staff, it is passed to government within a week, notice is given immediately of the government decision, and the owner can start work the following week.

Issue 3 – Developments in France have clearly been similar to those in Belgium in that there are now so-called "coherent planning schemes" (Schémas de Cohérence Territoriale, SCOT) covering a city and its suburbs, or a medium-sized town and its rural environs. These planning guidance schemes cover a 15- to 20-year period and take into account all data associated with (sustainable) development, including the protection of the natural and cultural heritage. The schemes apply at the level of the local "spatial plan" and genuinely bring together all the policy areas concerned with development: land use policy, of course, but also policy on architecture, transport (they take particular account of so-called urban movement plans), protection of the natural environment, trade (some commercial schemes try to achieve a balance between small shops and major retailers) and so forth.

Furthermore, "local habitat programmes" (Programme Local d'Habitat, PLH), take account of the social dimension of housing by trying to create a satisfactory balance between different urban areas. In other words, the goal is to achieve coherent planning policies (for areas of the order of 100 000 to 300 000 inhabitants as well as smaller areas) that take all kinds of data into account and contribute to sustainable development – once again covering both the economic and social fields, the transport infrastructure, trade, and the natural and cultural heritage.

Issue 4 – In France, they have plans for the development of towns which are a kind of agreement between the Ministry of Culture and the towns (local government) relating to preservation and rehabilitation. Is this mechanism still in use and is it legally regulated?

Response

In addition to coherent planning schemes and local habitat programmes, there are also urban areas with a particularly rich heritage that are known as "safeguarded sectors" (*secteurs sauvegardés*), for example in Paris, Lyon, Nice, Toulouse and Bordeaux. The state draws up the Safeguard Plan and finances the operation, which is very expensive, since it costs an estimated €1 million to implement a Safeguard Plan (over several years). The local authority then takes over, being responsible in particular for the restoration of public spaces, which is very important in the process of urban renewal. When a local authority carries out restoration work, by pedestrianising an area full of cars, for example, removing electric cables or planting trees, in order to improve the quality of public spaces, there is a significant knock-on effect on inhabitants and investors.

There is also another form of agreement for historic towns known as ZZAUPs. Local authorities take certain responsibilities for maintaining a certain quality level concerning the local cultural heritage and plan for the promotion of different types of activities.

Lastly, there are so-called "cities of art and history" (*Villes d'art et d'histoire*) agreements, under which cities give an undertaking to the National Monuments Centre (a public agency responsible for managing a number of state monuments) to improve the quality of their heritage and to use it for tourism (through guided visits, leaflets, perhaps Internet sites, etc.), in exchange for financial support.

Issue 5 – For a year now in a municipality in Bulgaria the local authority has tried to persuade the government to develop a sustainable strategy for environmental, economic and social development. There are 60 archaeological sites in the area (the Rhodopi area), one mediaeval complex of buildings of European significance and three natural phenomena – including "stone wedding gates" as they are called. The area is the home of 60% of plant species and 50% of animal species in Bulgaria and the environment has sustained these species. The new local authority has adopted a programme for the cultural and natural heritage. However, 20% of the population in this area is unemployed and only recently has tourism started. Conditions have to be improved for museums, tourism and the infrastructure for it.

We are happy that tourism agencies have initiated interest in the area. People are starting to take interest in hotels. We expect the municipality to adopt a 10-year strategy but we cannot rely on the government.

There are many different communities here in Bulgaria – Muslim, Orthodox and Armenians, among others. We want to stop migration from the area – so we must use it as a resource. On a separate but connected issue, it is important to mention again the need for long-term investment credits for sustainable development strategies. In the border regions such as with Greece we need a cohesive strategy.

Issue 6 – A brief comment on another municipality in Bulgaria, where the concept of sustainable development is fashionable. Many municipalities want to have an integrated approach but there are a number of problems:

First, a stable legal framework does not exist. This adds to the burden of synchronisation of activities between institutions. For example, in this municipality there has been much restitution of architectural monuments to private owners. Before this occurred there was an exhibition of the life in the town in the 19th century (to show people how the area used to look). In discussion with owners we compensated the owners with another property – so we can keep the architectural monument in a unified form.

Secondly, two years later another problem arose – to negotiate with the district authority to transfer the public state property into municipal state property. This also means re-thinking the steps – putting a different emphasis on new uses. We need long-term strategic programmes – but it is difficult when the legal framework is not yet developed. Do we put resources into old schools with leaking roofs or into heritage buildings that need repair?

Thirdly, many new fast food premises operate from private premises. But, sometimes, archaeological remains can be found in their basements. The contract for the sale of these premises included an obligation to preserve. However, these buildings are often sold many times over and the new owners do not observe the obligation.

> ### *Response*
>
> In answer to this first point the concept of "transfer of development rights" (TDR) is well developed in the United States and Canada and in some other countries. The idea is that a developer is given another site to develop on instead of exploiting the protected site but this usually has to be through a legal agreement (such as a "preservation easement") whereby the protected site is handed over to an organisation that will preserve/rehabilitate the site and this agreement provides for a financial sum to assist this (which is often required to be paid in perpetuity).

Issue 7 – Ownership rights and rights of entry by officials have been mentioned in the presentation. A short question – there are twelve old churches in our area. But there are disputes between the religious authorities and the state. Can you give some examples of good practice in regulating religious property of cultural heritage significance?

> ### *Response 1*
>
> In the United Kingdom there is an arrangement known as the "ecclesiastical exemption". For any listed building that is used as a place of worship (for whatever religion: Christian, Jewish, Muslim, etc.) the religious authority can be exempted from the

normal regulations if it adopts a code of practice regarding works to buildings. This allows them to make changes to buildings for the purposes of modern worship (for example, adding extensions for toilet facilities or removing the traditional seating for a more open plan to assist modern forms of worship), and the code of practice should mean that they respect the character of the building.

Response 2

In Germany, ownership of religious buildings is always vested in the church, but there is no difficulty in maintaining them because 10% of income tax is allocated to the various churches. They thus have plenty of money and can maintain their property, under the supervision of the historic monuments services.

In France, the situation is different because the cathedrals are the property of the state, including the movable objects within them, while almost all churches belong to the communes. A distinction is, therefore, made between the ownership and the maintenance/restoration of the building. The churches are assigned to the church, usually Catholic, and the assignee clergy may make unrestricted use of the church building free of charge (no one may charge for entry) and must cover the costs associated with worship (such as lighting, flowers, altars, etc.). However, the law on historic monuments naturally applies as normal to listed churches, and state officials supervise and direct works.

Theme 6 – Classification of museums and the status of collections

1. Introduction

Items of movable cultural property (which are difficult to define when attached to immovable property, as in the case of altarpieces and statues, for example: should they be considered as movable property or as immovable property in terms of the purpose for which they were intended?) may be owned by different entities (public entities, such as the state, local or regional authorities or public institutions; churches; or private-law entities, such as individuals or legal persons such as certain associations, foundations or companies). Their status raises real difficulties. This question also applies in similar terms to archives and libraries.

2. Status of museums and their collections

2.1. Definition of a museum

According to the definition provided in Article 2 of the International Council of Museums (ICOM) statute:

> "A museum is a non-profit-making, permanent institution in the service of society and of its development, and open to the public, which acquires, conserves, researches, communicates and exhibits, for purposes of study, education and enjoyment, material evidence of people and their environment.

> The above definition of a museum shall be applied without any limitation arising from the nature of the governing body, the territorial character, the functional structure or the orientation of the collections of the institution concerned".

Similarly, in French law a museum is considered to be "any permanent collection of items whose conservation and preservation are in the public interest and which is organised for the purpose of the public's knowledge, education and enjoyment" (Article L. 410-1, *Code du patrimoine* – French Heritage Code).

Accordingly, any institution is entirely free to call itself a museum, whether it is set up by a local or regional authority, a company or even an individual who decides to organise a number of objects in his or her possession into a collection.

2.2. Application of a specific label

However, one could also consider that certain museums should be singled out on account of the quality of their collections and the measures they take to ensure their continued existence. While this gives them advantages, such as a quality "label" or tax concessions, it also imposes obligations on them. For example, the recent French law of 4 January 2002 introduced the category "museums of France", a specific title which may be awarded to certain public or private museums (owned by the state, local or regional authorities, public institutions; or non-profit private-law legal entities). This has various legal consequences.

2.3. Rights of recognised museums

Recognition of these museums, which often house old collections, particularly of national museums, requires the prior approval (sometimes on a case-by-case basis, sometimes automatically) of a competent administrative authority (the directorate of museums of the Ministry of Culture, for example). Once the title has been awarded, museums can use it to benefit from various tax concessions available to non-profit-making bodies. For example, they can be exempted from certain taxes (such as local taxes and VAT), and acquisition procedures relating to the most interesting movables can be made easier, using patronage mechanisms. For example, donations can be facilitated by making them completely neutral regarding tax or significant corporate tax concessions can be given to companies buying a work to be donated to a museum.

In France recently, two companies were allowed to deduct from their taxes a part of the financial grant they made to museums to restore their goods: the company – Canon, a specialist in photocopies and photographs – thus financed the restoration of the pictures "The Wedding Feast at Cana" by Veronese kept at the Louvre Museum in Paris, whilst the company L'Oreal, specialist in high quality beauty products, financed the restoration of Louis XV's bathroom at the Palace of Versailles, linking the royal bathroom to L'Oreal's beauty products. This type of tax deduction scheme is found in many European countries (Spain, Italy, Belgium, etc.) as well as in the United States.

Another fiscal mechanism which can produce a rather spectacular effect is a "gift"/ donation whereby, a person may settle a tax bill not in cash but by surrendering a work of art, provided of course that there has been prior recognition of the object's artistic value by a specialised commission.

This is how the French national collections acquired a painting by Vermeer ("The Astronomer"), paintings by Monet, and a commode belonging to Madame du Barry, Louis XV's last mistress. A large part of the Picasso Museum collection also came from this form of giving.

This type of donation may also cover archaeological objects and archives, such as the archives of Lavoisier, a great scholar who was guillotined during the French Revolution, which were handed over to the French state in settlement of a tax bill. The donation may also concern the technical heritage, such as the donation to the state of the first computer (from the 1950s) of the French trademark "Bull", or still more surprisingly, the donation of two helicopters of the 1950s, which played a part in the war in Indochina.

These different fiscal mechanisms work very efficiently. Combined with the mechanisms of expropriation or pre-emption (first option to purchase – see below), they can genuinely lead to a substantial increase in museum collections.

Lastly, solutions inspired by the British "trust" model (the National Trust, for example) can enable semi-public collections to be open to the public, especially through favourable conditions for donations to fund the purchase of works of art.

2.4. Obligations of recognised museums

The specific title awarded to these museums entails a number of fairly important obligations:

- the obligation to keep an inventory – preferably computerised – with precise management of objects, including regular inventory checks, follow-up of loans (incoming and outgoing) and similar;
- the obligation to allow public access (except, of course, for some objects which may remain in the museum's reserve stock, or cannot be exhibited on account of their fragility);
- the obligation to use certain categories of professionals to manage museum collections (curators, etc.); they may be civil servants who have passed specific competitive examinations or they may be selected on merit;
- the obligation to use specialist restorers: the restoration of works of art involves first, a complex ethical decision, which must be made by an inter-disciplinary committee (historians, art historians, curators and restorers, to determine the condition sought – need for restoration of paintwork, etc.) and second, commissioning restorers with proven professional skills to do the work; in this way, a list of restorers can be drawn up who have exclusive authorisation to work on museum collections;
- the obligation of preventive conservation: legislation may authorise the state or the museum's supervisory authority to establish a number of regulations to ensure preventive conservation in museum premises (regulations covering fire and safety precautions, protection from water damage, standards relating to lighting and humidity levels, etc.); such legislation may also allow designated authorities to lay down a number of technical standards and exercise scientific and technical supervision over certain staff members to ensure that they enforce the regulations.

2.5. Legal status of objects

Lastly, we turn to the legal status of objects. In accordance with ICOM's Code of Ethics for Museums, there is a general presumption of permanence of collections; consequently, disposal of objects can only take place in exceptional cases, after consultation of curators and competent legal experts.

In a number of countries, particularly in southern Europe (France, Italy, Spain, etc.), the system of *domanialité publique* (special provisions governing public property) exists; this means that objects belonging to museum collections (but also archives and libraries) are subject to obligations arising from these museums having been designated as being in the public cultural interest (see above). However, they are also protected against any shortcomings of museum staff and/or against theft and illicit transactions. The rule of the inalienability of collections, thus guarantees that, even if they are wrongly put onto the market, the owner can claim ownership of the object and have it returned to his or her collections without having to compensate the buyer, even if the buyer acted in good faith. Furthermore, the rule of *imprescriptibilité* (relating to property that cannot be acquired by prescription) means that this claim can be made at any time, with there being no possibility of reliance on adverse possession provisions in force. In this way, at the end of the 1990s the French state was able to claim ownership of part of the Vendôme Column that had been sold during the revolutionary events of the Paris Commune in 1870. Thus, in the event of theft followed by illicit trade, resulting in a museum collection object being put up for sale on the art market, it is possible – with no time limitation – to claim ownership and, where relevant, without paying compensation. This solution provides very effective protection for museum objects.

There is, then, the question of what objects can be protected in this way. Do these provisions only apply to public property or can they also apply to items of cultural property belonging to private-law entities but governed by the same rules as public museums, owing to the quality of these items and the guarantees they present? For example, some countries (such as Portugal) take into account the public-interest aspect of items collected by bodies which exhibit them to the public (foundations, for example).

This presupposes the existence of specific regulations in criminal law for the protection of public collections, and the provision of specific sanctions in the event of these items being stolen, damaged or threatened.

Nevertheless, even in these cases, disposal of an object classified as public state property may be possible under a specific procedure: Article L. 451-5 of the French Heritage Code requires that this be "with the concurrence of a scientific committee" (… *l'avis conforme d'une commission scientifique*).

It should be noted that, in other cases, it may be that there are no exceptions to the general law for museum objects, in which case, if they are sold or traded on the art market, they may be subject to the usual system of prescription. This mechanism operates in many instances in the United States, where museums "circulate" their works, selling one to acquire another. However, even in countries that do not have the system of *domanialité publique* (such as the United Kingdom[6]), various provisions in the clauses of the

---

6. Aside from royal collections, which are inalienable, protection is provided by the laws specific to the different museums which, while they do not prohibit the disposal of works, subject such sales to strict regulations, with the result that sales are rare.

museums' statutes have the result of effectively prohibiting transfer of ownership. The fact remains that both British and American law follows the rationale of the art market. The usual rules of prescription apply, which means that museums cannot recover their property, regardless of the time period that has elapsed (after six years, in Britain, ownership is transferred from the initial owner to a purchaser having acted in good faith).

2.6. Monitoring of museums

The law must allow monitoring of state museums, museums of local authorities, publicly-owned establishments or private organisations of a non-profit nature, by official state authorities to ensure that the obligations provided for in the legislation are properly complied with in the various fields. Non-compliance with these obligations can result in the institution concerned having its quality label withdrawn.

2.7. Status of private museums

As we have seen, this status can vary. In some cases, because they provide certain guarantees, private museums may be awarded the quality label "Museum of …." They are then covered by the same regulations as public museums, even if the status of their property may differ in some respects, if the system of *domanialité publique* does not apply to their collection. In other cases, private museums are "ordinary" museums, in which case they are governed by the rules of ordinary law, which apply to all private persons in respect of their private property.

The state, therefore, has a clear choice to make in its legislation: it needs to decide exactly what a "protected" museum is, to what institutions this system can apply, and what obligations and protection the system provides for.

3. Protection of movable property

Different kinds of movable cultural property can belong to different public or private entities (including churches), without necessarily always forming part of collections that are open to the public (for example, objects in churches and abbeys, cultural property in public administration buildings, works of art in private historic buildings, etc.). They can be covered by protection provisions based on those governing immovable property of artistic or historical interest. This presupposes the introduction of legal rules governing the following.

3.1. Scope of protection

This relates to what interests may be taken into account for protection purposes (historic, artistic, ethnographical, scientific, etc.) and what reference date for the object should be used (time limitation prohibiting, for example, the protection of contemporary art less than 50 years old, or, on the contrary, automatic application of the rules to all objects predating a certain date of historical importance to the country, for example, the specific status of artefacts in Greece predating 1453 or 1830). Should objects be protected on an individual basis or, on the contrary, is it possible to "classify" them in groups?

The question of museum collections also arises. Should these also be governed by protection arrangements of this kind, or are the specific provisions covering them (in particular, the *domanialité publique* rules) sufficient? Not all countries decide the same thing in this area. For example, in France it is rare for a museum object to be also classified as a historic monument, which is not the case in Spain).

Lastly, there is the issue of religious objects: should they automatically be governed by special rules? For example, in Sweden, all religious objects are automatically protected under provisions on cultural heritage and cannot be removed.

3.2. Protection mechanism

As it is often difficult to know of the existence of such objects, the starting point for protection procedures may, therefore, be the carrying out of an inventory by public authorities with inspection rights, or the appearance of such objects on the art market or during export inspection (see below). Protection, therefore, requires a certain procedure to be followed which allows owners to present their arguments. The question also arises of possible compensation, because of the legal consequences that such protection can have on freedom of transaction.

It must be possible for emergency measures to be taken in cases where the length of protection procedures could result in serious harm to the heritage.

3.3. Legal rules governing protected objects

At first sight, such protection presupposes a minimum number of measures. Regarding the requirement for safety precautions, the competent authorities must be able to impose the implementation of preventive conservation measures, such as placing the most valuable church objects in locked cabinets to protect them from theft and fire, and possibly moving objects to suitable premises. This can present real problems, particularly for church objects that are both protected as cultural artefacts and used for religious services. What can be done, for example, in the case of a revered religious icon at risk of damage by smoke from candles?

In the event of work being necessary, protection involves, as a minimum, prior authorisation by the competent authorities and, where relevant, the obligation of using specialised staff to carry this work out (art historians, restorers, etc.).

Regarding movement of goods, limitations can be placed on access of such objects to the art market, either by prohibiting their sale (the object remains indefinitely in the hands of its owner) or by limiting their sale to the national territory by prohibiting their exportation, in some cases with public authorities having first option to purchase. In this event, the inability to sell at international market prices may result in loss, which can be indemnified by compensation or compulsory purchase.

Finally, there is the question of the protection of such objects. First, specific criminal rules can be adopted, with corresponding specific criminal sanctions; the rule of *imprescriptibilité* can also be applied to these objects (meaning that they cannot be acquired by prescription), which enables the owner of a stolen artefact to recover it at any time, this being a separate matter from the possibility of compensation being made to purchasers acting in good faith. If it is accepted that such objects may also belong to collections governed by *domanialité publique* rules, they may be classified as public property and, simultaneously, come under a specific protection system, making them both inalienable and unable to be acquired by prescription.

3.4. Tax system

As a result of the considerable costs involved in the upkeep of such objects, it is accepted that amounts spent on their preventive conservation and restoration are tax-deductible for their owners. Similarly, exemption from inheritance tax is possible, when movable property is confined to an area where it is safe and can be seen by the public. Various tax concessions related to patronage may also be introduced (see above).

4. The Romanian case

As a contact science, an interface defining itself within a wide range of shapes and aspects, and as a general state of affairs, "museology" proves stability and is characterised by traditionalism, without spectacular changes. Moreover, the political changes which occurred in Romania after 1989 found the network of museum institutions and the specialists totally unprepared. This caused real shocks and dramatic consequences: there was a serious reduction in public interest for unvarying and unattractive museum products, built upon political criteria determined by communist ideology; public bodies were labelled as ideological; there were conceptual and structural defects resulting from administrative ossification and bureaucratisation; and the impossibility of offering motivating salaries resulted in a massive migration of specialists to the academic and research fields. Thus, the political changes of 1989 found museums in an unprepared state, with unsatisfactory management, a lack of expertise and affected by ideological factors.

The serious conceptual crisis affecting the museum system emerged soon after 21 December 1989, thus changing the destiny of the dedicated bodies and many specialists. A long transition period made the effects of the crisis even worse and that went on until 1993-1994 when the first more energetic reactions occurred which aimed to settle this predicament and there were some signs of improvement.

Naturally, museums, together with the teams of experts – whose number saw a spectacular increase in Romania, from approximately 900 work places in 1990 to approximately 4000 in 2003 – got through the crisis, identifying solutions and achieving most of the targets: institutes were maintained, as well as their professional re-orientation and specialisation. The period 1994 to 2000 was characterised by a number of projects, most of them insufficiently documented, by political changes and turmoil.

The entire museum system – 658 institutes – followed the same path, reflecting in a direct way the political and economic changes encountered by the country as a whole. It was not until 2000 that one could identify signs of stabilisation and normalisation, reflected particularly in the indicators presented below.

4.1. The legislative issue

The main problem that the reformers within the museum system[7] were confronted with, in a macro-cultural context, as part of the cultural institutional system implicitly relating to heritage, was the legislative issue. After the Law on Museums and Public Libraries (1932) was repealed in 1948, the Romanian museum field no longer benefited from special provisions, as "museology" was previously associated with mass culture during the socialist era. A correction was brought through Law 63/1974 on Protection of the National Cultural Heritage, yet ignorance of the law, on the one hand, and the very short period set to achieve its objectives did not allow for its proper finalisation. In particular, there was a lack of financial resources. Moreover, on 5 January 1990 that law was repealed and replaced with Decree No. 90 which proved to be unsubstantiated and unreliable with regard to the protection of museum institutions during the transition period (the museums network remained diversified and unco-ordinated).

In the post-December 1989 legislative void left by the general conditions in the country, museums continued to function but suffered much disruption and decay. They were often confronted by huge problems, such as a severe shortage of development, research and valorisation funds. As a natural consequence of this, the institutions' ability to promote, support and valorise the natural and cultural heritage was seriously compromised. Some regulatory Acts issued by the Ministry of Culture referred to the "export regime of cultural goods" (Orders Nos. 403, 415/1992, 106/1994, 2003/1999 and 1284/1996) and those of the Ministry of Finance (Orders Nos. 72/1993, 2013/2000, 26/1995) as well as the Governmental Ordinances Nos. 26/1962, 68/1994, 523/1997 and 74/1998 sought to regulate, at least in part, the activities and characteristics of museums.

---

7. The network of museums and collections is regarded as part of the network of cultural treasury institutions (along with archives and libraries with rare and old books, institutes for historical monuments and decentralised services) belonging to the protection system for cultural heritage.

Yet they did not have general beneficial consequences for the entire field, which is so diversified and has numerous particularities. The major problems for museums – the network and its development; profiling, upgrading and modernisation programmes; the need for the institutes to upgrade technologically; restructuring of themes and exhibitions; services to the public; preventive protection; museum research; professional training; and specialist management – could not be approached in a coherent and logical manner until the end of the 1990s. The causes of this were essentially economic decay and a political discourse filled with contradictions, which involved even the most traditionalist museums, causing discontinuity and conflict.

4.2. Achievements of Romanian museums 1990-2000

However, in the above-mentioned decade several exceptional institutes were founded. These include the Museum of the Romanian Peasant in 1990 (EMY Award, 1996), the National Museum Cotroceni in 1991 (EMYA Mention, 1994) and the Sighet Memorial in 1994. At the same time the National Peles Museum was reopened to the public, while repairs and modernisation works were started in other major museums.

The establishment of a new co-ordination structure started in 1990 through the Department for Museums and Collections which led to the reorganisation of the sector. Furthermore, the National Specialised Commission acted to restore the autonomy and individuality of museums, as well as several specialised representative bodies: the ICOM National Committee of Romania; the Association of Ethnographic Open-Air Museums (AMEAL); the Association of Natural Science Museums; and the Association of Curators and Restorers.

The decade brought some clarification and allowed for the identification of certain directions for development. Thus, the autonomy of museums was emphasised and structural models were produced. In most districts the great museum complexes were reorganised and adapted to the new conditions. As a result, new museums with better established profiles and with a wider range of activities emerged. Individualisation of institutes allowed for a more precise identification of the internal research and valorisation programmes. Museum reorganisation of basic exhibits started, yet it was confined to the small museums where the actual costs could be covered. After 1996 even museum protection witnessed a certain growth. At the end of the past decade, the Law for Protection of the National Movable Cultural Heritage (No. 182/2000) was adopted. This offered a more logical approach to museums, as well as protection structures for heritage. Likewise, the regulation referring to insurance of cultural goods under temporary export was adopted (Ordinance No. 44/2000) and amended by Law 143/2001, which made an important contribution to recovery.

Major changes have occurred since 2000, indicating greater stability and a higher level of interest in this sphere.

4.3. Recent legislative solutions and systematic reforming

The first decade of the 21st century saw the start of a new approach to the issues of museums in a more direct and contextual manner. At the same time, the perspective of the sectors closely related to museums was addressed: archaeological heritage, historical monuments, research and conservation/restoration.[8] In addition, several rules, methodologies and guidance documents were produced to ensure a new institutional status. "Museology" in Romania has benefited from these moves in recent years and there has been an increase in heritage development funds for purchase and for major investment. A number of relevant examples are the following: the rehabilitation of the National Art Museum (closed in 1989) was finalised between 2000 and 2004 and major development works were undertaken at the Museum of the Romanian Peasant, the National Village Museum "Dimitrie Gusti", the National Bran Museum, the National Museum "Brukenthal" Sibiu, the Museum of Natural History "Grigore Antipa", the Museum Complex "Astra" Sibiu, the Museum Complex Goleşti and others. Restoration and reorganisation of the National History Museum has begun, with an estimated finish date set for three years time.

In the case of new museum buildings with modern architecture, examples range from the Museum Complex of Natural Sciences in Galaţi, the Museum Complex of Natural Sciences "Ion Borcea" and the Museum of Archaeology, History and Art "Iulian Antonescu" Bacău to the Museum of Contemporary Art in Sângiorz Băi. These achievements are evidence of a high European standard in museums. The foundation and opening of the National Museum of Contemporary Art in October 2003 in Bucharest was a very large project.

A number of new museums have also been established in recent years including the National Museum of Maps and Old Books (2003), the Memorial Museum "Vasile Grigore", the Hunting Museum at Posada (2001) and the District Museum Argeş (2004). Museum research has also been integrated into the national research system.

Substantial progress was made when Internet connection was implemented in more than 150 museums and personal computer (PC) operation was introduced into the public services. This has enabled the organisation of information shops in the major museums. We should also not overlook international exchange of exhibitions, Romania having made a sustained contribution to the presentation of its own heritage in the great European and American centres, as well as in China, Japan, India and Africa. Inter-museum dialogue has intensified, with Romanian museums taking part in the "Culture 2000" project, cultural itineraries and other international projects.

The main work concerning long-term museum orientation is the publication of the Law for Museums and Collections (Law 311/8 July 2003), which establishes a modern framework for institutional development, the classification of institutions and museum regulations.

---

8. An important series of legislative measures were passed between 2001-2004 to provide a coherent set of laws: Law No.182/2000; Law 422/2001, Law No.378/2003, Law 462/2003, Law 311/2004.

Constructed in the light of the European regulations in the field, and also taking into account Romanian realities, Law 311 defines the new museum philosophy, including operations, financing, organisation, ownership regime and appropriate classification of museums as national, district, regional or local as well as private. Regulations concerning the establishment and closure of public museums and collections have also been set up. The instituted hierarchy aims to develop the network of museums according to the basic structure, while establishment of certain regulations envisages a coherent evolution of the network according to the particulars of the heritage and requirements for its cultural and natural representation. The new law has harmonised the relationship between museums and public collections, bringing significant encouragement to private initiatives.

4.4. The work of museums

Museums are very involved in the conservation and active protection of archaeology. About 80% of all archaeologists in Romania work within museums. Large teams of archaeologists are organised to undertake all necessary preventive archaeology, for example related to highways, railways stations and telephone lines. The relevant companies pay for this work which can assist the budgets of museums at local and national levels.

Demographic museums are very involved in rural development projects. They rescue many old houses and artefacts and new modern open-air museums will be opened in the next two or three years.

Museums also deal with industrial archaeology and Romania has organised the 4th International Workshop on Industrial Archaeology in 2004.

4.5. Conclusions

Significant progress has been made in the museum field in recent years both through legislative measures and the establishment of museums. However, new rules for the management of museums are still needed as is the recruitment of people who can establish first class museums and deal with all types of authorities.

It is also necessary to encourage a new philosophy so that museums are for the people. The public must be encouraged to visit and for this reason it is necessary to organise interesting exhibitions and regular programmes. Mentalities do not change over night – but action in this direction has begun in the field of archaeology.

It is also important to develop joint programmes with countries neighbouring Romania and good co-operation has commenced between Bulgarian and Romanian museums.

5. Summary of questions and views

The following issues of debate and responses were raised in relation to the presentation of papers on Theme 6:

Issue 1 – The ICOM Code of Ethics for Museums is important in setting minimum standards of professional practice and performance for museums and their staff. With regard to standards in a general sense, are there any ideas on unification? Countries in transition want to know if they are moving in the right direction.

> *Response*
>
> The only real standard is the ICOM Code of Ethics for Museums, but this only contains recommendations. At the level of the EU there are no specific rules.

Issue 2 – In Bulgaria, there is a problem in that museum experts are paid at the lowest level. In Greece, the situation is quite different. We cannot attract new staff, but we have rich collections that we have to manage 24 hours a day to maintain the standard that the public requires.

> *Response*
>
> To assist the staffing problem, an example may be given in relation to France. A huge number of students work on voluntary placements in museums, especially as part of their university courses. The only obligation, given that these placements are unpaid, is that the university should provide social insurance cover (particularly for accidents at work, etc.). A placement agreement is, therefore, drawn up between the student and the museum, in which the university undertakes to cover the student against accidents at work.

Issue 3 – In Romania, it is required by law that collections are insured (for all risks). But it is uncertain where the resources will come from for this purpose. Art collections are the greatest in number. We ask for donations of works instead of raising money. Also private owners can have their works of art conserved (at a cost) instead of making donations. We also obtain additional money from companies. In Romania the state will only pay 20% of costs – the other 80% has to come from the museums themselves for instance through sales, exhibitions and publications.

> *Response 1*
>
> The museums policy pursued in western Europe for more than 20 years is based largely on the investment of a lot of *public money* (state and local authority). We need to realise that museums were a sector that was quite badly neglected for a long time, and huge amounts of public money have been spent, particularly in France, Spain and Germany, among others, partly out of national funds, and partly through considerable local government involvement. Lastly, money has also been invested in museums via structural funds. This money has been spent essentially in three directions:

- to maintain or erect buildings: there are examples where interior architects have been hired to improve internal design in order to encourage young people to come (with the support of teachers and trainers);
- to establish a new kind of museology;
- to make greater use of collections for the public, through cultural tourism and education (a lot of work with pupils to draw young people into museums); a vast number of things have been done, particularly agreements with the Ministry of Education and teachers on secondment to museums to work with their education services.

There has also been quite a large amount of *private money* injected into museums through sponsorship. Hiring out rooms to companies for formal dinners, for example, has been very successful and has brought in a lot of money. Other examples are the creation of so-called "spin-off products" (books, CD-Roms, calendars, reproductions, ties, handkerchiefs, scarves, statues, etc.). In 20 years there has been a complete transformation in museums, from places that religiously preserved the heritage to places that are truly open to the public and have a genuine museum strategy for expanding the heritage and exploiting it economically.

Response 2

In Romania, like other former communist countries, we have lost our young visitors to museums. But we are trying to encourage their return through setting up associations of "Friends of Museums".

Issue 4 – In Serbia the concept of an "eco-museum" has developed but the legal provisions for this type of heritage (immovable, movable, intangible) and for who manages these museums are not clear. It is difficult to classify such museums. There are similar problems in some western European countries such as Italy.

Response 1

There are not many in Italy or France. This is an idea that has grown up either in your countries, or in some Nordic (northern European) countries. In the case of France, eco-museums generally belong to private-law associations. These are associations which may receive a number of public subsidies but do not generally fall within the category of public museums. The statutes of such associations usually provide some long-term guarantee for collections of movable objects. In the case of immovable property, the situation is a bit more complicated since buildings have often been removed from different places and brought together in a kind of open-air museum. There is nothing in itself to prevent either the buildings being protected globally, as an architectural whole, or each building being protected separately. If you have a very fine house listed as a historical monument in Alsace for example (where the concept of open-air museums has been developed in relation to wooden houses), it could well be relocated with others into one place. This would enable all these houses to have the same legal status as a listed monument or a protected area. But this means some legal acrobatics.

Response 2

In Romania there are eco-museums. Private owners of property can organise themselves as a museum. There is a good tradition of open-air museums and these arrangements are good for tourists. For example, the state has financially supported the restoration of a water system in a textile mill, which the owner now opens to the public to show all the water installations in working order.

Issue 5 – The movable and immovable heritage of Bulgaria is in a very sensitive situation. The immovable heritage can turn into movable. For example, Roman mosaics can be taken from sites and sold by criminals.

Issue 6 – Regarding the status of museums, in Bulgaria we follow the United States legal approach – non-profit associations must be registered officially and they can get tax deductions if they register. However, the registration process is often very expensive for some non-profit organisations (sometimes they have to register in two systems which results in high administration costs). There is some assistance from local authorities, but this avenue tries to retain museums within the public museum structure. How is the issue distinguished in other countries – do non-profit organisations get tax relief?

Response 1

In France, whether a museum should remain in the public sphere or be a non-profit organisation depends on figures. All non-profit organisations in France must register with the state or local government. In the United Kingdom trusts have the same requirement to be non-profit-making.

Response 2

By comparison to the immovable heritage, there are now over 200 building reservation trusts registered with the Charities Commission in the UK. These often work on a revolving fund which means they buy old buildings to conserve and restore/rehabilitate, then sell them. The "profit" is then put into buying another property to work on. The process is not for profit as such but rather the charitable activity of rehabilitating historical buildings in need of action. For further information on trust, non-profit associations and associated tax relief measures, the report of the German National Committee of ICOMOS entitled "Legal Structures of Private Sponsorship" (1997) is particularly useful, as it gives information and examples from all over the world.

Response 3

In Romania only five private museums are given tax relief.

Response 4

In general, museums are "public property" – and not for profit. However, in France there are museums for profit, and also in the United Kingdom, such as Madame Tussaud's Wax Museum in London.

Theme 7 – The circulation and restitution of cultural goods

1. Introduction

The question of a market in cultural objects is a sensitive issue, especially in countries where earlier legislation did not usually regard private ownership of such objects as possible. What is attempted here is to define the rules applicable to objects belonging to private individuals, where it is held that only private persons may possess objects that may be traded (e.g. the issue of the status of collections in public and private museums, protected items and Church property as discussed in Theme 6).

If it is accepted that a market in such objects exists, it will be run either by antique dealers (dealers in cultural objects) or possibly by auction houses.

2. Regulations to be adopted for professional dealers (antique dealers and auction houses)

So that objects can be traced, it would appear very important for dealers to keep a record. This may contain various headings and be subject to control by the police and judicial authorities, which is where it gets its name in France as the "*livre de police*".

It may or may not be regularly checked and approved by the legal authorities and should contain at least a brief description of each object sold and details of the identity of the seller and the buyer (a simple statement if this person is known to the dealer or, if not, a photocopy of an identity document). Such a formality is necessary primarily to prevent unlawful transactions and money-laundering (traffic in *objets d'art* being one of the main activities used for this purpose). Moreover, such a record would obviously make investigation simpler in cases of theft.

Since the 11 September 2001 attack in the United States, a number of regulations have been adopted at community level to combat money laundering. There is also an obligation to declare any suspect money or transactions.

As for the art market itself, a number of solutions are possible in terms of access to the profession.

Generally, there are no restrictions on access to the profession of antique dealer or expert: in other words, anyone can claim to be a specialist in such and such a period, and there is certainly no particular reason to create a regulated profession. The market itself will weed out the poor performers.

The question is a little different in respect of auction houses – the largest in the world are in New York, London, Paris, Geneva and Hong Kong. In fact, different methods may be used to distort the free play of an auction, and it may be highly appropriate, and desirable, to impose strict rules. In the Anglo-Saxon countries, anyone may set up as an auctioneer and open an auction house, but it is often the case in these countries that strict discipline is in fact exercised by professional associations and institutions, which have instituted rigorous codes of ethics. In other countries, there is some degree of regulation of the profession. In Belgium, for example, auctions must be held in the presence of a ministry official. In France, under the latest law of 10 July 2000, although any company may be approved by the regulatory body (the committee on voluntary sales of furniture at public auctions), the auctioneer managing the sales must have formal qualifications (in law and art history), and the company must itself provide guarantees of good name, financial probity (to prevent misappropriation of funds) and transparency of sales (for example prohibiting the company from selling property belonging to it or from buying at its own auctions).

It is possible to introduce a "right of pre-emption", which can in practice only apply to sales at public auctions. In such cases, the state is authorised, acting on its own behalf or on that of other local bodies or museums, to buy an item for a public collection at the price of the last bid. The rights of the seller are not infringed because the price is that which the last bidder would have paid. This means that a sales catalogue must have been sent to the public authority concerned.

The regulatory authority will, of course, control the market by means of a disciplinary procedure that may impose heavy administrative penalties (suspension of a sale or withdrawal of approval), subject to there having been a fair hearing in accordance with the rules set out in Article 6 of the European Convention on Human Rights.

3. Regulations on the circulation of cultural objects

Separately from these mechanisms, a state may or should introduce internal rules to control the circulation in cultural objects. This is obligatory for the states that are party to the UNESCO convention of November 1970, Article 6 of which requires the establishment of a mechanism to control the export of cultural objects. This is also obligatory for the states that are members of the EU – this, therefore, being one of the elements of the Community *acquis* – since the regulation of 9 December 1992 requires states with customs borders outside of the Community to put in place checks on the 19 categories of cultural objects defined according to criteria applied in Great Britain (the so-called "Beverley" criteria) such as their nature, age and a threshold value, numbered by reference to the Common Customs Tariff. For example, any art paintings that are more than 50 years old and with a value higher than €150 000 would be subject to exportation control outside of the EU.

Member states can, therefore, check that an item has a "passport" – a unique customs document with a photograph – which complies with the requirements of the regulation and is duly stamped by the competent authority of the member state of origin of the item (usually stamped by the Ministry of Culture and by the customs authority, since customs duties apply to exports outside the EU). At that point, a state has a number of choices in implementing the control of the external frontiers provided for in the regulation. For example, the French customs authorities which work along the Atlantic coast on the monitoring of cultural objects leaving EU territory should verify that the cultural objects are included in these 19 categories and that they are accompanied by a passport with a photo and a statement allowing the export of the object signed by the originating member state.

Once such external border controls are put in place, and Article 30 of the Treaty of Rome is respected (limits on imports and exports of national treasures) then states are free to do as they wish. The three following scenarios are possible:

- A. They do not impose any control on cultural objects which do not fall within these 19 categories. In such cases, notably in France and Italy, this refers to the following types of objects.
    - i. Certain items may not be exported (national treasures: objects in public collections and protected objects (see Theme 6).
    - ii. Some items are subject to export control and these, for reasons of simplicity, are treated the same regardless of whether they are exported outside the EU or within the EU. Control within the EU may take any form provided, firstly, that it is proportionate to the free movement of goods and secondly, in view of the Single Market, that it does not involve customs duties. In France, for example, items falling within the categories mentioned above which are more than 20 years old may only be exported once an export licence issued by the Minister of Culture has been obtained for them, and has been formally validated in the case of items over 100 years old. If the item is of such interest in terms of the cultural heritage that it is indispensable for it to be kept within the country, the government may object to its export for a period of two and a half years. During this period, the government must offer to buy the item from the possessor at the international market price (at a fixed price in the case of disagreement after legal expert opinions have been sought). If the government cannot raise the funds, it no longer has the right to object to the export of the item. If, on the other hand, the possessor rejects the final offer, the government may object definitively and without compensation to the export of a cultural asset which has become a national treasure.
    - iii. Items below certain thresholds may be traded entirely freely both within and outside the community subject to VAT formalities. In order for this mechanism to function, heavy penalties must of course be prescribed (for the purposes of dissuasion: particularly through confiscation of items exported illegally), and police and customs services must be effective in this area, which calls for specialist expertise (e.g. in France the Office de lutte contre le traffic des biens culturels). This mechanism operated in France is similar to one adopted in the United Kingdom.

B. In other countries, such as Germany, control is less strict. Like all other member states in the EU, Germany must, of course, control the export of listed cultural objects outside the external frontiers. Beyond this, it simply forbids the export of several hundred items on a detailed list, which presupposes an exact knowledge of each item concerned (the situation is comparable in many northern European countries). This attitude is a result of the fact that the majority of cultural assets in Germany are objects from the Church and that Germany considers that the Church is rich enough to ensure by itself the protection of its own heritage.

C. On the contrary, a very different strict mechanism is possible – as is the case in Spain. In addition to the obligations under the European regulations, all items of cultural interest are subject to export control, and the government can object to their export without time limits and without compensation. In this case, control is obviously much greater. Thus, all assets considered as Spanish historic cultural heritage would remain subject to export control. Regardless of whether they are going to another member state in the EU or to another continent, such as the United States, all cultural assets are subject to rigorous control, not only paintings of a value higher than €150 000.

4. Combating illicit trade and restitution of cultural assets

Illicit trade in cultural objects is one of the largest forms of trafficking in the world, being used in particular to launder illegal money. Hence, EU member states are bound by legislation on combating money-laundering (Tracfin), which has been reinforced since the attacks of 11 September 2001. In order to combat this traffic, provisions need to be introduced within each state, particularly in the area of criminal law. It is, therefore, important to punish the possession of stolen objects very severely, and to initiate the prescription period not at the moment of the initial offence but at the date when it ends (continuous offence).

4.1. Two bodies of law may apply

At the international level, the UNESCO Convention of 14 November 1970 provides that member states must take appropriate steps to seize and restore objects stolen from a museum or public, civil or religious institution, thereby limiting its field of application, by compensating bona fide possessors and covering the costs associated with restitution. This still raises delicate questions since it is possible for organised traffickers to give the impression, by means of multiple owners, that the last owner in the chain is bona fide. Restitution becomes very difficult since in this case it must be accompanied by compensation.

For this reason, the Unidroit Convention on Stolen or Illegally Exported Cultural Objects, signed in Rome in 1995 and currently in force in 21 states, obliges purchasers and dealers in the art market to exercise due diligence. Compensation is only possible "provided that the possessor neither knew nor ought reasonably to have known that the object was stolen and can prove that it exercised due diligence when acquiring the object", which reverses the burden of proof to the disadvantage of dealers. This wording has often raised numerous objections from this point of view, and the states that are the main players in the art market (especially the United States, the United Kingdom and France) have not ratified the convention.

At the European level, on the other hand, the EU adopted a certain number of texts in so far as it considered that the suppression of customs controls between the member states and the institution of the Single Market in 1993 were likely to facilitate the illicit traffic of works of art. Besides, the diversity and the complexity of the national laws were such that it could take years to obtain restitution. For example, in the case of France and Italy, which are countries very close from a legal and linguistic perspective, it took years before the Renaissance tapestries, which had been stolen from the Palais de Justice in Riom, a city in the centre of France, and had been found a few months later with a Milanese antique dealer, were returned to the Embassy of France.

The EU Council Directive 93/7/EEC of 15 March 1993 on the return of cultural objects unlawfully removed from the territory of a Member State, has, since then, taken into account all the discussion and work that went into the *Unidroit Convention*. In particular, it establishes the following mechanism that applies to national treasures (either because they are listed in the inventories of museums, libraries and archives, or because they fall within the 19 categories set out in the appendix, which are the same as those covered by the regulation, and are specially protected by the state).

4.2. A distinction should be drawn between two types of case

A. Where a member state is the requesting state (as a result of consulting an auction catalogue, for example) or is alerted by the authorities of a member state that one of its "national treasures" is on the territory of another EU member state, it may request restitution subject to the following conditions:

- the item was exported unlawfully (theft or failure to apply for an export licence in accordance with national legislation or the regulation of 9 December 1992) after 1 January 1993;

- the item is considered by the member state as a "national treasure" – the export of which is prohibited;

- it must have been exported unlawfully, i.e. the purchaser or the host country could not provide proof of the authorisations or passport which accompanied the object. (The EU directive reversed the burden of proof a little: it is now up to the purchaser to show that he/she was diligent.)

In this case, the requesting member state contacts the relevant national authority designated by each state and refers the matter to the appropriate court. This in its turn must order the return of the item to the state of origin, provided that the conditions set out in the legislation are fulfilled, and may decide to grant fair compensation to any person who the court is convinced exercised the "diligence required" at the time of acquisition. Once this compensation is paid by the member state of origin, the item is restored to it. The question of the status of the item (confiscation by the state or restitution to the owner if the latter reimburses the compensation paid to the state, or indeed security measures to prevent further thefts) depends on the legislation in each state. In the case of France, the state returns the object to its owner in so far as they have paid the compensation.

For example, if a French cultural asset is sold in London following an illicit export, the British court must order the return of the item to France, and France will pay, if necessary, an amount of compensation to the owner who exerted necessary diligence when acquiring the item.

B. Where the member state is not the requesting state, that is, where another member state has referred to it an application for restitution, it must comply with the following obligations:

- to appoint a single competent authority to handle this type of case and to which member states may apply;
- to put in place procedural rules to ensure that applications for restitution are effective (e.g. organising a summary application procedure permitting an emergency court to forbid the sale of an item at auction and to grant time for the requesting member state to produce the evidence for a trial on the merits.

The legal system of each state, therefore, has some room for manœuvre, provided of course that it complies with the directive.

Thus, if a cultural asset was stolen in Germany and then found on French territory, the German state asks the French state to take conservation measures (via a court to avoid infringement of the right of ownership), which would temporarily block the item on the national territory to prevent it from leaving the country and being stolen again. The procedure continues then in front of the French courts, under the same conditions as the procedure presented in the first case, and the object is then finally returned to the German state which pays an amount in compensation, if necessary, to the owner if he/she has acted in good faith.

In practice, the EU Directive of 15 March 1993 has been transposed where there was not yet a sufficient body of law, although some member states had already introduced such a provision when applying the UNESCO Convention. As a result, very few cases have gone to court, but it has proved effective as a preventative: it has created an awareness of the issues associated with illicit trafficking in Europe. It has made restitution of cultural objects easier, usually at the stage of police or judicial investigation: where it has appeared that such and such an object had been stolen in country X or Y, the authorities of state Z have immediately returned the said object. This presupposes, however, that sufficient evidence can be produced for items declared national treasures and, therefore, subject to restitution: hence, once again, the need for an exact record.

Thus, for example, the Swedish police authorities quite simply returned cultural items that had been stolen in Finland back to Finland without following the European Directive, that is, without going to court and without paying compensation.

These provisions pre-suppose, however, for those goods declared as "national treasures" and, therefore, suitable for restitution, that the states are capable of providing adequate evidence and insist, once again, on the need to have a precise register/inventory of the national movable cultural property.

5. The Albanian case

The current law on cultural heritage in Albania dating from 1994 is trying to develop the legal basis for the preservation and conservation of heritage and also to regulate the relationships between individuals, organisations, central and local government. It may be necessary to go further and make a law that will provide greater management and protection to the cultural heritage and each institution, as well as some evaluation. The existing law is probably insufficient to cover the wide range of problems concerning property in Albania.

In essence, the 1994 law was only an attempt – but it tried to resolve old conflicts: to clarify concepts on ownership and cultural heritage on the one hand, and on the other, to settle how to handle the cultural heritage, mainly in relation to real estate. But there are other forms of ownership that need to be considered – for the movable heritage in particular. There is a need for a new registration process, which was not fully considered before. There is an intention to complete this process and to provide an actual procedure for the circulation of heritage values, regardless of various kinds of ownership rights, and also to computerise the list of heritage objects, which was not provided for and not adopted by the national law in Albania.

5.1. Problems with the previous legal regime

There is a need to go further and to consider the necessity of categorising. The old law (dating from 1974 and earlier) did not do this. There was no categorisation nor was there the possibility of recording, having a database or writing passports for every type of movable asset. This is clearly an important issue to safeguard the movable heritage.

The old law also did not include a considerable number of property categories of cultural heritage, both movable and immovable, and in failing to do this it risks loss, decay or damage. Moreover, the old law did not include or adopt measures on the important issue of financing. Financial measures are very important for the developing market economy.

It was not possible to speak of auctions and the movement, buying and selling of cultural goods in socialist times. But this is an issue today. Because there is a lack of current solutions, problems have arisen.

The old law was only partially competitive. It must be stated that by refusing private ownership of cultural heritage property and not fixing rules on movement and on the obligation for each object to be registered, the classification rules were not providing the right situation. This was an obstacle in a real sense. It was also partly the mentality – it was not seen as necessary. That creates a different risk – a moral risk concerning ownership.

In 1991, and especially in 1997, objects, part of our cultural heritage, were stolen and smuggled abroad. Actually, most of them were simply exported and not identified. This fact shows that the law must act and it could not act because it did not provide legal clauses for movement, computerised listings and authorities. On the contrary, they were dealt with as uncontrolled objects or objects of craftsmanship, which are under the authority of other sections. The joint commission for identification and licensing lacked professional ability in most cases and it was not performing its role.

5.2. The new legal regime

So, regardless of the owner – we now protect. In the first part of the 1994 law, there are general provisions classifying objects of cultural heritage into material and non-material. Now there are specialist officials dealing with this and this classification has been recognised as being important. In one chapter of the 1994 law, the institutions in charge of identification, protection, documentation and research of this cultural property are mentioned. These include the establishment of a General Department of Cultural Heritage, a National Authorisation Commission, a National Centre of Cultural Property Inventory and an Institute of Finance of Culture.

The law specifically mentions issues of ownership – transfer, expropriation, registration and documentation, as well as other issues. Albania is in the process of establishing and identifying national property, of studying the varieties of properties, the top level of property, what is national, what is most important, and so forth. It is part of the process – we cannot bypass the rights of registration, we try to protect these values regardless of the owner. So, there is a system – regardless of the owner we protect.

In most cases movable objects are protected by several generations or by large groups of people. In this context we are developing a draft law for the benefit of society – particularly in relation to objects of "unique value" which have major importance for our history and our national and cultural heritage. There is a need to go further than is foreseen in the current law – new solutions are needed regarding the problems of legal relations between the owners and the state concerning the protection, preservation and the movement of objects both within and outside Albania. There is a problem internally because ownership is transferring and changing, shifting from one owner to the other. This creates a risk – that we will lose track of the changes.

In the last ten years, the responsibility and care of local authorities has not been at its highest level. But, the law has introduced the idea of putting both the object and people under cultural surveillance. It is part of the procedure of investigation and criminal procedure. There are offences regarding cultural heritage values, but they are not really fixed or classified as yet.

The "market" for buying and selling cultural objects in Albania is important because it is in its early stages. It is an important issue not only as a concept but also with regard to how to treat the problem – but the process is, to some extent, in vain.

Provisions for compensation for compulsory purchase exist in a general sense in Albania. The right to pre-emption – to buy an item for public collections – is quite new and modern as a concept in Albania. It could be developed in Albania, but it depends on the cost – the country's budget is small – and it would be difficult to buy a painting at a cost of US $12 million for example.

Albania is also trying hard to control the illegal export of cultural goods and is a member of the UNESCO Convention of 1970. A passport with full details of each object is required for any protected object that is to be exported (including temporary export for exhibitions).

Defining the "national treasures" is a priority for the government and is part of the ongoing process in the country. It is part of a huge anti-trafficking policy that was begun successfully three to four years ago. An example of this was when a lorry carrying cultural objects was stopped at the border. The owner of the vehicle said that the objects proposed for export were not "national treasures". In fact, a commission of Albanian experts was established to decide this case. This was an important development – but in this instance the objects were found not to be of national importance, or "national treasures". So, it is now recognised in Albania that the classification of cultural objects is important.

5.3. Conclusion

Progress in improving legal measures commenced with the new law of 1994. Prior to this, registration of objects was not fully considered. Albania is still in the process of developing a registration system and it is recognised that new solutions are needed with respect to the relationship between private owners and the state concerning the movement of goods within and outside of the country. The concept of an art market is very new. New offences have been created as well as surveillance procedures and the requirement of a passport for the export of goods – which helps to prevent illegal trade in cultural goods – as a part of an anti-trafficking policy. The defining of "national treasures" remains a priority for the government in this field.

6. Summary of questions and views

The following issues of debate and responses were raised in relation to the presentation of papers on Theme 7:

Issue 1 – The free movement of cultural items in the EU is a very important issue for Bulgaria to consider and for all countries in the pre-accession stage for the Union. It is important for these countries to harmonise their legislation with European standards. For many years we have been preparing a law on trading in antiques. As yet we have not finalised this. When this is achieved we can start to have auctions. The Bulgarian judiciary has no grounds in law to register individuals or small traders for trading in cultural assets. Therefore, there are contradictions in our legislation.

Response

Four points:

i. The first important thing to bear in mind is that there is no principle of free circulation of cultural objects in the EU. This is a completely false idea. On the contrary, Article 30 of the Treaty of Rome allows for derogation from the principle of free circulation, particularly in the case of what are known as "national treasures". Hence, the Treaty of Rome allows each member state to take the steps which it deems necessary, subject to control by the Court of Justice where appropriate, in order to protect its cultural objects. This principle was reaffirmed when the Single European Market was established.

ii. The second point is that there are two types of cultural objects. On the one hand, there are the cultural objects that are known about, particularly those in museums, archives and libraries, together with religious and private objects that enjoy protected status, for example as historical heritage. For the purposes of providing proof and restitution, it is very important to have a precise register of these known objects. To give an example, when the 1993 European Directive came into force, France launched the "Movable Property Heritage Plan" because considerable attention was then given to immovable property, but little to movable property. A certain sum of money was, therefore, spent to create databases which listed exactly all the objects (around 300 000 in France) which were protected, in order to provide proof (by means of photographs, descriptions, etc.), that they were on French territory on 1 January 1993.

Many legal systems require notice to be given to a government department whenever ownership of a listed object changes. Very simply because this enables the authorities to know where the object is; it was in the hands of owner A, and it has passed to owner B, and so it can be established where the object is at any time. On the other hand, there is a difficulty in that there are huge numbers of objects that are not known about: objects that are in private hands because they have been there for years, because they are the result of illegal trafficking, or for a whole host of unknown reasons. Either these objects will leave without anyone noticing, or they will be recognised one day when they appear in the art market or when application is made for a licence to export them. Objects thought lost since the French Revolution have been discovered in this way. When this happens, it needs to be clear what can be done. If the objects are protected, and there is a wish to add them to the national collections in museums, the issue of funding arises.

iii. The issue of funding to buy back works of art arises everywhere: US $12 million paintings are leaving Albania, just as major works have left France because France did not have the funds to buy them. For example, a few years ago (between 1995 and 2000), as a result of pillaging during the Greco-Turkish war of 1920, the last Byzantine copy of the Treatise of Archimedes was found in France. It had been picked up by a Frenchman in a Byzantine monastery in 1920. When the owner applied to export this object, France refused and, in accordance with French legislation, the owner asked France to buy it. Since France did not have the necessary funds, the manuscript was sold at Sotheby's in New York for US $2 million. In order to avoid this type of problem, a system of sponsorship has been introduced in France to allow companies to fund part of the purchase of "national treasures" so that they can be added to public collections.

iv. Lastly, it is important to stress the importance of controls over illegal trafficking. In France not long ago, the customs stopped a lorry-load of sculptures on their way to Belgium, not at the border since they no longer have the right to do this, but 15 km inside the country. Quite effective penalties were applied under French law. The first was a fine of €450 000, which is a substantial sum and might act as a deterrent. Secondly, since the items were regarded as prohibited goods under the Customs Code, they were confiscated and handed over to museums.

That said, we should not be under any illusions. In the case of archives, if you have a letter from Napoleon, you can put it between a couple of shirts in your suitcase and take it out of the country. No one will notice. There are, none the less, some successes, although the most optimistic customs estimates suggest that they manage to stop just 20% of illegal traffic, the scale of which is immense. Once again, therefore, it is really important to draw up an exact register of cultural objects in order to combat trafficking effectively. The key issue is the need for registration.

Theme 8 – Archaeological sites and research

1. Introduction

This paper deals with the legislation necessary to protect the archaeological heritage *in situ* and to regulate archaeological investigations and excavations. The intention of this paper is to provide some guidelines on legislative matters concerning the protection of the archaeological heritage and also to demonstrate some decision patterns (integrated conservation) from which the protection will benefit and at the same time balance the protection of the heritage against other public interests.

The guiding principles in this paper are taken from international standard setting instruments such as conventions and recommendations but they are also inspired by legislation from different member countries of the Council of Europe.

2. Scope of legislation

Legislation is the necessary means to regulate the behaviour of civil citizens. But it is also used to delegate power to specific authorities and to establish public institutions and divide power and duties between them.

It is the first, and only partly the second of these functions, which is of direct interest to the citizen in his or her everyday life. The scope of the legislation must, therefore, be decided in order to have simple and understandable legislation. Reiterating the points made in Theme 1, the primary role of legislation is to regulate the behaviour of public citizens. Ideally, any civil citizen of society should be able to grasp what the legislation is for, what it requires to be done and what should not be done. The provisions that regulate the behaviour of the citizens should not be mixed with provisions that regulate the public bureaucracy. Many of the draft laws examined by the Council of Europe's legal task force have been found to be blurred by numerous and complicated institutional set-ups, which could be better regulated in by-laws that do not have to pass by the legislators in order to reorganise administrative structures. Only where independent agencies are entrusted with powers to regulate the behaviour of private citizens is legislation needed to empower the agency.

The geographical scope of the legislation to protect the archaeological heritage should also be considered. The protection of underwater cultural heritage in the zone defined in the UN Convention on the Law of the Sea (1982), Article 303, paragraph 4 and Article 33 requires special provisions in the national legislation of coastal states. Unless special provisions are provided, the underwater cultural heritage protection will only apply in territorial waters.

In relation to the continental shelf and exclusive economic zone, as well as the area beyond state jurisdiction, the UNESCO Convention on the Protection of the Underwater Cultural Heritage (2001) stipulates rights and duties of coastal states as well as states of residence and flag-states of persons and vessels engaged in activities directed at underwater cultural heritage.

3. Specific issues concerning the archaeological heritage

3.1. Definitions and inventories

Definitions of the protected archaeological heritage should make it clear what is protected. They should also ensure conformity with international standard setting instruments such as the Valletta Convention (1992), Article 1.

The archaeological heritage consists of both immovable items – monuments, sites, man-made structures and stratigraphical features – and movable items. The legislation will have to take the peculiarities of both types of heritage into account. The legislation on immovable items is often similar to environmental and planning legislation providing regulation of landowner's rights to exploit their land. This is the main subject of this paper. The legislation on movables concerns conservation and curation of archaeological items excavated or found and deals with regulation of ownership or traffic, for example.

There are two extremes of definition clauses in current legislation. One is a broad and general definition combined with a designation procedure that ensures an evaluation of the monuments or sites before they are offered protection by the law. The other is an exhaustive or non-exhaustive enumeration of types of monuments and sites that are afforded automatic protection by the law. These extremes are often modified in the national legislation to take into account the benefits and problems they carry.

The designation procedure is costly and will often have to be carried out when a site or monument is under pressure by development or neglect. This could make the designation a very politically interesting decision. This extreme will, therefore, put emphasis on an early inventorisation of the heritage in order to make the decisions before the heritage comes under pressure. The designation is often combined with a legal requirement to establish the cultural value of the monument or site. This has led to many cases of litigation where landowners or other parties with an interest in the property or the land on which it is situated contest the evaluation of the public agency in charge of the designation. Such litigation has taken away public resources from the tasks they are really designed for and there is a tendency in modern legislation to use automatic protection under a blanket definition without reference to cultural significance or value.

The automatic protection will protect monuments and sites without consideration of their cultural value. This means that there will be a need for a procedure to allow interventions on protected heritage of less value. It also means that it will sometimes be difficult to defend the general protection of archaeological heritage because many of the specific decisions are about heritage with less cultural value. This extreme therefore puts emphasis on an early inventorisation of the heritage in order to identify the heritage that should be refused protection under the law.

The remedy for both extremes is apparently inventorisation, which is reflected in Article 2 of the Valletta Convention.

In order to complete the inventories, the legislation should oblige citizens to report finds to the archaeological authorities. The obligation should also rest on developers obliging them to stop their construction work when they discover archaeological heritage during their work.

In order to serve as a planning tool as well as a tool for decisions on the cultural value of sites and monuments, inventories should include both protected and unprotected monuments and sites. In some countries, the protection is varied according to the type and value of the monument or site. Less important sites or sites which have no appearance in the landscape may only be afforded protection against destruction by development while other sites may also be protected against deterioration caused by farming or other types of land use.

In some cases, as for example reporting of historic shipwrecks, a system of rewards for the reporting may be envisaged.

The inventories should be developed to live up to the standards set by the International Core Data Standard for Archaeological Sites and Monuments, 1995.

3.2. Treasure trove and ownership

There are long traditions and a great variety of solutions of ownership and treasure trove in different countries.

In most countries, the landowner will also own the monument or sites on the land, but there will be restrictions on his/her use and right of disposition of the monument or site (see below).

The legislation should have provisions for compulsory acquisition of monuments or sites of special importance or that needing particular careful land use practices. On the other hand, legislation should also have incentives for the landowner to take special care of monuments on his/her land. Such incentives are sometimes included in the agricultural grant systems.

Ownership of movable archaeological items varies. In some countries, it follows the ownership of the land on which it is found even if it is found during an excavation funded by public money; in other countries the finder becomes the owner, if there is no other owner (the Law of Finds in common law countries such as the United States); and in some countries, archaeological objects belong to the state (treasure trove).

In most countries, however, there is a system for public requisition of archaeological objects. This might entail compensation according to market value or a reward system based on circumstances, such as the metal value or the way the finder has treated the object.

3.3. Ancient monuments and sites and protective zones

Both monuments and sites should be protected against any interference. This means interference by new development as well as archaeological excavations. The legislation should provide that licence to interfere can be given only if there is an overriding public interest or private interests of very great importance are implied. In these cases, licence to interfere should only be given on the condition that a proper archaeological investigation and documentation is provided for by the licence-holder. The costs of the investigation and documentation as well as the costs of conservation and curation of artefacts found during the investigation should be paid by the licence-holder.

A buffer zone around monuments and sites should be provided by the legislation. The size of the zone could either be fixed by law or could be a flexible zone provided by law but fixed by the authorities in each case. The legislation should state which kind of development requires special authorisation in the zone. This type of regulation is found in several laws on archaeological heritage protection such as the Swedish law.

3.4. Archaeological reserves

The archaeological heritage is a finite, non-renewable resource and should be managed carefully so that it can last as a scientific source in the future. This makes it necessary, as the primary option, to leave remains preserved *in situ*. Excavations should, therefore, only be permitted when they are absolutely necessary to answer a scientific, archaeological problem or when unavoidable decay, erosion or development threatens remains.

It also makes it necessary to create archaeological reserves where the remains, whether visible or hidden in the ground, are left undisturbed for future archaeological investigation, preferably by new non-intrusive methods developed sometime in the future. The reserves will have to be created and managed carefully to preserve the remains in their proper context.

Archaeological reserves may be acquired and managed by the state or other public institutions, which will require provisions in the legislation for expropriation of land for this purpose.

Even without the creation of archaeological reserves the preservation of archaeological remains should be an integral part of land-use policies. In some cases, the legislation could provide for incentives to farmers and foresters to use methods or produce crops that do not harm the archaeological strata in the subsoil.

3.5. Integrated protection

The legislation should provide for consultation procedures. This procedure should be carried out at an early stage in the planning of development projects in order to make mitigating measures possible. The procedure could encompass the possibility for the authority to carry out consultation of existing records, field survey, sampling, probing and investigations to determine the cultural value and conservation conditions of archaeological heritage affected by the planned development. The procedure should be directed at providing documentation on which an agreement can be made as to possible changes in the planned development project or the excavation of the heritage before the construction work starts.

Where an agreement cannot be reached, the archaeological authority should even be granted the power to veto development plans that would harm very important archaeological remains. The veto may release compensation to the private owner for the delay in the realisation of his/her project or – in the case of prevention of the development – compensation according to normal rules for expropriation. A veto may also result in the involvement of governmental bodies at a higher level in making decisions by balancing the archaeological interest against other public interests in the planned development.

The archaeological authorities and developers have set up the procedure of mitigation as a voluntary procedure or a code of conduct for developers in some countries such as the United Kingdom. It seems that such agreements can be effective even without a legally binding status.

Where development projects affect archaeological remains and mitigation cannot prevent the eventual destruction of the heritage the legislation should provide for the necessary time to carry out excavations to record the heritage and conserve the artefacts. In principle, the costs of the excavation and the publication of the results should be borne by the developer at least when the excavation could be foreseen during the planning procedure. This stresses the need for inventorisation and for statements by the archaeological authorities designating "areas of known or perceived areas of archaeological importance".

Provisions in the legislation should also be considered that allow the authorities to require that parts of monuments and sites, in or under current buildings, are conserved *in situ* as it could further contribute to the value of the environment and buildings. In these cases, the costs of providing public access should be shared or borne by public funding.

3.6. Underwater archaeological heritage

The underwater environment is often a very good conserver of archaeological remains. This means that the underwater archaeological heritage should be considered as an archaeological reserve and managed accordingly.

The legislation will have to take the special conditions into account. In freshwater systems, this means that there should be provisions for the control of water levels so as to avoid the lowering of the water table, which would expose the heritage. Also, control of all other activities should be considered.

In the marine environment, special considerations have to be given to the rules of international law which affect the state's power to protect the underwater cultural heritage, mainly the rules regulating jurisdiction.

Coastal state jurisdiction gives the right to protect the archaeological heritage within the territorial sea just as on land. The legislation should extend its protective provisions to the marine area of the state, that is, to the territorial sea, and should also provide for protection against dredging, landfill and other construction works as well as protection against erosion created by marine traffic and fishing methods affecting the heritage. It should also have provisions for regulating diving activities and for creating reserves where diving, anchoring and fishing is prohibited.

The United Nations Convention on the Law of the Sea (UNCLOS, 1982) has provisions on the protection of the underwater cultural heritage. In Article 303 it obliges states to protect the heritage and to co-operate to achieve effective protection. It also extends the coastal state's right to protect the underwater cultural heritage to a zone outside the territorial sea up to a limit of 24 nautical miles from the coast or from the baselines from which the width of the outer territorial sea is measured. Until now, however, very few states have extended their jurisdiction over cultural heritage to that area.

Legislation should also provide for the protection of the underwater archaeological heritage in connection with exercising their rights to exploration and exploitation of natural resources on the continental shelf so that these activities do not harm important wrecks or other underwater heritage sites.

In some states, the regulation of underwater heritage protection is engulfed in salvage law. This is, however, not in accordance with international recommendations such as the ICOMOS Charter on Underwater Cultural Heritage 1996 as it encompasses economic incentives to "salvage" cultural heritage and not to protect it or perform proper excavations. The International Convention on Salvage (1989) has provisions which make it possible to exclude salvage law in respect of historic shipwrecks. But even without a formal reservation, a state is free to regulate the protection of the historic shipwrecks with the exclusion of salvage law.

The UNESCO Convention on the Protection of Underwater Cultural Heritage (2001) provides for a consistent system for the protection of all underwater heritage including in inland waters and freshwater systems. The convention defines the rights and obligations of coastal states, flag-states and states of residence regarding activities directed at the underwater cultural heritage. It sets up a system for international co-operation to best protect the heritage where it gives the coastal state specific roles in regard of its continental shelf and exclusive economic zone. So far, it has been ratified by Panama and Bulgaria.

3.7. Maintenance and restoration

The legislation should have provisions for the maintenance of archaeological monuments and sites. It should define the duties and rights of owners and authorities to remove unwanted vegetation and create the proper environment around the monuments and sites. This is especially important where the monuments and sites are in private ownership. The provisions should give the authorities access to the heritage and to take the necessary measures. Maintenance should aim at both preservation of the heritage and promotion of the heritage by enhancement of the sites and monuments and their surroundings.

Restoration should only be carried out by professionals under the supervision of the competent authorities as it entails interference with the archaeological strata and structures. The provisions of the legislation should ensure this and give the restorers access to the property to do the work.

3.8. Public access

The archaeological heritage belongs to the general public. Wherever feasible, public access to the monuments and sites and to collections of archaeological items should be envisaged and supported by legal provisions. In many countries the access is provided by voluntary agreements between the landowners and the archaeological authorities or by private or semi-private foundations like the National Trust in the United Kingdom. At the same time, legal provisions should make it possible to regulate the access to protect the heritage. Access to private land may entail compensation according to procedures of expropriation when access is forced upon a landowner but may also be part of a voluntary agreement.

The legislation should make it clear that public access does not include the right to interfere with the heritage. Legislation should also forbid the use of metal detectors on archaeological monuments and sites.

3.9. The archaeological profession

The archaeological profession is differently organised in different countries. In some countries, only the state may undertake archaeological excavations, while in other countries they are made by other public institutions, such as universities or museums, or even private persons or companies. The latter countries have developed systems of contracts stating for each investigation the conditions and destination of records, for example. The main principle should be that records of all kinds should be kept together and that finds should never be dispersed in an irretrievable way.

The important thing is to make sure through legislation and licence procedures that archaeological excavations can only be carried out by skilled archaeologists and that the records – both data and material records – are made available to professionals and researchers. Excavators should also be obliged to publicise the results of their investigations and finds suitable for display should be in collections open to the public. Further guidelines for the policy in this field can be found in the ICOMOS Charter for the Protection and Management of the Archaeological Heritage (1993) and the ICOMOS Charter for the Protection and Management of the Underwater Cultural Heritage, adopted in Sofia in 1996.

3.10. Enforcement measures

The first point to make is that it is difficult to enforce laws that are not generally understood by the public.

Implementation of legal protection would ideally be possible without legal sanctions. This ideal should be pursued as far as possible through information and public enhancement of the archaeological heritage. In fact, there are fewer than 10 punitive enforcement cases per year in Denmark. Educational measures should be considered, as well as public access and even participation.

The archaeological services' regular and frequent visits to landowners and supervision of the monuments and sites should also be seen as a means of implementing and enforcing the protection. However, the legislation should provide for proper penal and economic sanctions for breaches of legal protection.

Fines should be set at a magnitude that would outweigh the possible economic benefit that could be obtained by breaking the law. The costs of documenting, by archaeological methods, the damage as well as the costs of the possible restoration of the monument or sites to their former appearance should also be borne by the intruder.

4. The Bulgarian case

The archaeological heritage is a considerable part of the national and international cultural heritage. By nature, archaeological sites are a limited and non-recoverable resource. Because of this, there has been a greater emphasis on the establishment of a system of legal regulations for its adequate protection in recent years. This is aimed at preventing different destructive factors and in order to preserve the archaeological heritage for future generations in its most original mode as far as possible. Such a strategy is inspired by the presumption that with progressive invasion in the process of archaeological investigation through new methods and technologies, it will be possible to obtain much more and fuller information about the nature of ancient cultures.

4.1. European standards for archaeology

The main principles for preservation of the European archaeological heritage are formulated in different reports, recommendations and legal documents, elaborated mainly on the basis of the Valletta Convention of 1992.

On the basis that archaeological monuments are specifically to be regarded as a non-recoverable information resource, it is persistently recommended that they are preserved in the most possible authentic state. Implementation of this requirement relies on the creation of national and international legal standards, in conformity with the character of the archaeological heritage. The general recommendations refer to the establishment of a protection system for the archaeological heritage against different kinds of risks. The main negative factors in this respect are construction and development activities, illegal excavations and the process of archaeological research itself. While destructive activity caused by new constructions or illegal intervention in archaeological monuments is an old problem, which has been discussed for a long time, in respect of measures for its restraint, the excavation of archaeological sites has only been rated as a serious dangerous factor in relatively recent years. A similar tendency is related, on the one hand, to the development of investigation methodology and, on the other, to the development of archaeology as a science. The accumulation of a large quantity of archaeological material and the transition of it to a higher level of interpretation, gradually decrease the need to uncover new archaeological sites or unexplored parts of already known ones. By entering into a wider sphere of inter-scientific methods in archaeological research, archaeology is becoming more and more dependent on the rapid development of new technologies.

In the context of this situation, the idea of preserving the archaeological heritage in its original state is correctly and more persistently being established, thus giving the opportunity for future generations to obtain more information using more developed ways and means. The main recommendations in this respect include the legislative standardisation of requirements for "minimum intervention" in archaeological structures, by giving preference to non-destructive research methods. On the other hand, the requirement to issue licences for archaeological research only in the cases where it is of a considerable social or private interest is being promoted, and also where the holder of a licence will undertake a complete archaeological research assessment with all relevant documentation.

4.2. The situation

The establishment of an appropriate legal regime for preservation of the archaeological heritage in each separate country should take into consideration recommendations and trends in European legislation, but most of all it should be in conformity with specified and concrete conditions. The status of the archaeological monuments in Bulgaria does not always allow for conformity with these trends. The existing legislation has already created, to a great extent, mechanisms for preservation of cultural heritage, through the establishment of relevant responsible institutions for cultural monuments, as well as through the adoption of respective normative documents that regulate the statute and treatment of archaeological sites. The Law of Cultural Monuments and Museums (LCMM), which has been in force since 1969 and has been amended and added to over the years, defines the archaeological sites in Bulgaria as exclusively state property, thus limiting any intervention in them without permission from the competent authorities responsible for their preservation.

According to a letter of declaration of the National Institute of Cultural Monuments No. 545 (27 February 2001), all archaeological sites are cultural monuments of national significance and are under the protection of the law, according to Article 12, paragraph 1.b."a" of the LCMM. Archaeological research of sites situated in the territory of the Republic of Bulgaria is regulated mainly in terms of institutions and persons authorised to undertake on-site research. The main requirements of the holders of licences/permits for on-site archaeological research are to have Bulgarian citizenship and a high standard of education in archaeology with a minimum of two years experience in scientific management of other archaeological sites (Article 14, paragraph 1 of the Regulations for undertaking of on-site archaeological research in the Republic of Bulgaria, *State Gazette* 12/1997).

Within the Archaeological Institute and Museum (AIM) under the Bulgarian Academy of Science a specialised Council for Site Research, involving experts from different institutions related to archaeological research, has been established. The proposals for granting of licences for on-site archaeological research are considered in the relevant scientific units of the AIM before being put forward to the Council for Site Research. The existing normative requirements for holders of a licence for undertaking excavations are not so much of a methodological nature, but mainly concern the requirements to create scientific documentation in the process of archaeological research.

Implementation of the processes required by European standards as mentioned above concerning the process of archaeological research has come up against objective obstacles in the existing conditions in Bulgaria. The hard conditions of the transition period during the last 15 years has led to the collapse of the operating system of standards, while on the other hand an adequate new system, corresponding to the new situation and consistent with the recommendations of European standards has not yet been created, at least regarding the destruction of the archaeological sites in the process of their research. Currently, Bulgarian archaeology is facing the situation of having to choose between the lesser of two evils. The lack of proper controls over new construction and accelerated treasure-hunting activity have led the scientist to the unavoidable choice between full or fractional research of every site in danger, when the appropriate financial resources are available. Standardisation of archaeological research is impossible until the above two factors have been controlled. The process of loss of archaeological information as a result of the interventions of developers and treasure-hunters is of such an extent that keeping ahead of them has become the main momentum for archaeologists. Urgent measures for restraint of these activities are indispensable, as well as the creation of effective relations and co-operation between the responsible cultural heritage institutions and the executive power bodies.

Of course, conformity with related European standards is to be recommended in the context of the creation of new legislation to regulate the preservation of archaeological heritage in Bulgaria. It is essential to create stricter requirements for drawing up archaeological documentation and publication of results of the research, as well as the setting up of a system of norms related to archaeological research methods. The standards for archaeological research should be based on the principle of "minimum intervention" in the archaeological substance, but only in conformity with the particular situation and the level of risk to the monument.

4.3. New criminal proceedings

The recent amendments and supplements to the Criminal Code of 2004 aim to resolve the gaps in legislation, bearing in mind government priorities in the area of preservation of cultural and historical heritage. These changes allude to the prevention of and sanctions for violations of archaeological cultural monuments and provide criteria for the legal protection of valuable movable items discovered on archaeological sites, particularly in relation to the plundering of sites and the selling and export of such finds. Paragraph 2 of Article 278b introduces new levels of "aforethought" in perpetration of the crime, where different kinds and different amounts of penalties are provided, the most severe being imprisonment for a period of three to six years and a fine of 5-50 000 Bulgarian leva (BGL), as well as confiscation of the object of the crime in favour of the state. Additional remedies against damage, destruction or export of cultural monuments are introduced in Articles 278 and 278a of the Criminal Code.

4.4. Private collections

In Bulgarian legislation on the protection of cultural and historical heritage the status of private collections is not considered or regulated. Because of this all such currently existing collections remain unknown to the public, as well as to science. There is a need to create rules in the standard regulations to exclude any possibilities of criminal activity regarding the transfer of movable archaeological items. As a first such step towards this, the Law on Cultural Monuments and Museums requires the registration and cataloguing of the private collections with the state and municipality museums (Article 5 of the amendment law to the LCMM, *State Gazette*, 55/2004). This provision was adopted in 2004 and came into force on 1 January 2005. However, a more detailed consideration of the use, presentation, exchange and sale of movable cultural items in such collections is necessary.

Because of the lack of appropriate legislation, some illegal auctions exist, through which some movable cultural valuables with a high scientific, cultural and historical value are being sold. Once such sales have been regulated, the state would have the opportunity to make preliminary redemptions, and thus to enrich the stocks of state museums. This would also contribute to the archaeological knowledge of the territory of the country, by including it in the scientific process, irrespective of the collections' ownership. This is indispensable also because the number of existing private collections is unknown, as well as the quantity of movable cultural valuables which they consist of.

4.5. Concessions and finance

One of the principles of preservation of cultural and historical heritage is the exposure of archaeological monuments *in situ*. In the majority of cases for single archaeological objects/sites, this is impossible or almost impossible, because they become the target of an illegal intrusive activity. Until now, archaeological sites that have been created as open-air museums have not had enough financial aid for their maintenance. This leads to substitution of the original with contemporary materials during current conservation and restoration activity.

The legal regulation of concessions for archaeological cultural monuments and reserves is also regarded as necessary as this could help the state to finance the process of their preservation. It would also allow for development of cultural tourism linked to archaeological heritage. The use of legal agreements through concessions in relation to archaeological sites would decrease the chance of illegal excavations occurring and would actually serve to assist their physical protection. The creation of concessions is deemed necessary for the purposes of preservation of the cultural and historical heritage until such a time when the Bulgarian state will be able to undertake the financing of protection-related activities.

4.6. Conclusions

The main negative factors for the archaeological heritage continue to be linked to development activities and illegal excavations by treasure hunters. Urgent restraint of these activities is required – through new legal provisions. A new Criminal Code dating from 2004 provides new preventative measures and sanctions for violations but it will take time to see how effective these will be.

Archaeological research has also created damage to sites but there is an increasing recognition of the need for "minimum intervention" through the use of non-invasive techniques.

There is an important issue to be resolved concerning the status of private collections and a first step has been made through legislative amendments dating from this year. However, more detailed provisions are needed to control illegal auctions and to deal generally with the exchange and sale of movable items.

The funding of archaeological research and preservation remains a difficult issue. The use of "concessions" has had some impact in that they help to control illegal excavations and assist in the preservation of archaeological sites.

5. Summary of questions and views

The following issues of debate and responses were raised in relation to the presentation of papers on Theme 8:

Issue 1 – It is important to share thoughts and ways of resolving problems. Five issues should be raised in the context of Bulgaria.

   i. The unregulated excavations conducted by individuals – they are an unavoidable evil. An example can be given of an archaeological reserve where machines have been used to clear the land of artefacts.

   ii. There is a lack of co-ordination between excavations and conservation and a lack of funding – how do we raise resources for these activities? We need to anticipate the possible sites that might be ruined by the unregulated activity of individuals. Therefore, do we need more regulated investigation? But conservation cannot always follow as archaeologists are not able to make records (see iv below).

   iii. The archaeological heritage is owned by the state. Therefore, in an area where there are "invaluable" monuments it is assumed that the remains belong to the state, but the land is in other ownership. Landowners remove (or find) and sell remains from their land. We need to explain that these items belong to the state and resolve the problem.

   iv. There is a delay in publishing findings from archaeological investigation. Archaeologists move from site to site but do not have the time to publish (despite the fact that this is required by law).

   v. There is a lack of integrated mechanisms between conservation/preservation and urban and regional planning. The state is not an equal partner in the race between development and archaeology.

Response

   i. Whilst the problems in Bulgaria are severe, it is not only a problem in Bulgaria but elsewhere as well. It is very difficult if there is unregulated investigation in designated archaeological reserves. Therefore, we should ask the question – do we establish reserves (which notify where the remains are)? In other countries the view may be that people who want to profit from unauthorised activity can obtain information on where remains are – therefore, by establishing reserves, do we make the information available?

ii. The lack of co-ordination is a problem in many countries. An example from the Netherlands relating to the underwater heritage: sunken boats are investigated and then the remains are burnt afterwards because it is not possible to conserve them. But this is contrary to good archaeology. In Sweden they have tried to resolve this.

iii. On the question concerning the "invaluable" heritage, development and construction or other new uses for land should be so profitable, so desirable, that they should pay for the investigation. This means that we may have to use preservation "by records" rather than preservation "*in situ*".

iv. Concerning publication problems, it is a problem all over the world – a genuine problem. Much rescue archaeology does not seem to produce new knowledge – only more on what is already known. Therefore, is it worth doing? Should we only publish findings where new knowledge is gained – but this is difficult to anticipate. A European group of archaeologists has established a code of ethics based on the idea that a new permit to investigate should not be issued until findings from an earlier licensed investigation have been published. But this is not usually enforced. This is an option, however, to deny further permits until the findings are published.

v. The lack of integration is a problem. It is vital for archaeologists to understand the way that developers work. Do not be idealistic. Confidence must be built between the two sides. The problem is especially in countries-in-transition that have not yet developed integrated systems of working.

Issue 2 – What are the rules that govern archaeological sites and transparency?

Response

This is a very national problem – and can vary from country to country. It can be a national curator, an archaeological museum, or similar. There are no general rules. The general idea of the Valletta Convention is that it should be the state that has responsibility for policies for the granting of permits for archaeological investigation and that these should require publication. Such basic rules should be understood by the whole archaeological society.

Regarding finance this is also an issue that varies from country to country. It is better to issue a licence when it is known that there are financial resources for this. But the decision to issue a licence should not be based on the question of finance. Investigation should be to resolve a recognised research problem or because society needs the land for another purpose (such as for new development requirements).

Issue 3 – In Romania, archaeology is in a good situation. In 2007 Bulgaria and Romania became members of the EU, which, it is hoped, will bring money. We must prevent and we must protect. To assist this process we have established a group of 20 people in the

National History Museum who examine proposals for new roads, fuel stations and other developments that could have an impact on archaeological remains, which assists the process by anticipating problems.

We need to link with the Council of Europe and other European bodies in the hope that this will bring more finance. Perhaps we should now change our archaeological philosophy. We have 400 archaeologists in Romania. They all want to do excavations, but it is not possible financially to do this. Moreover, there is also the cost of preserving artefacts in museums. We also believe it is necessary to publish in foreign languages.

Issue 4 – A further comment on the Bulgarian situation concerning illegal investigations – it is important to be able to react in time. Permits are very significant. For development proposals on large sites there must be a permit. It is important to link the development permit with an archaeological investigation. In some countries, the number of archaeologists has increased as a result of this (for example in Belgium and the United Kingdom).

Issue 5 – In the United Kingdom, the identification of areas of "perceived archaeological importance" in development plans means that development will only be granted consent subject to a condition requiring archaeological investigation. This has resulted in developers having to pay for such investigations (and an increased number of archaeologists as a result). Contracts for archaeological investigation are usually based on the British Archaeologists' and Developers' Liaison Group Code of Practice which was the basis for the Council of Europe's European Code of Good Practice "Archaeology and the urban project" (2000).

Part 3

Operational conclusions and key issues

Operational conclusions and key issues

The state of the cultural heritage policies in relation to countries participating in the *Regional Programme for Cultural and Natural Heritage of South-East Europe*, taken together with the debate on legislative reform, as presented in this book, has culminated in a number of operational conclusions and key issues for further consideration:

1. Coherence and clarity in legal language, guidance and advice

It is not uncommon for legal texts to be written in a form of language that is understandable to the specialist and professionals working in the particular field of interest. However, there are often calls for legal language to be simplified into a plain form that is understandable to those members of society that will be affected by the provisions of law. This situation has been confirmed from the experience and consideration of legal drafts for the reform of law in the field of cultural heritage.

Moreover, with the changes in society, "countries-in-transition" must accept a greater participation of the public in the management of the heritage, in their common heritage. This issue is central to the question of human rights.

The process of transition in this area requires a balancing between public and private interests, which, in turn, requires a process of education and awareness-raising. In order for the public interest to be properly served and for society to be a stakeholder in this process, the process of cultural heritage protection and management needs to be clearly explained. Aside from the question of law and the institutional regimes in this field, the public should be made aware of the issues. This logic points to a requirement for greater information, so that the ordinary citizen is able to understand and contribute in an intelligent and informed manner.

At a government level, this means that all relevant ministries should be made aware of the role of heritage in society, in terms of the culture and identity which bind society, but also in relation to the potential functional, economic and social context of the heritage. From a horizontal level, this must pervade through to the vertical level from central government down to local government level where the public will have a greater voice and where systems of management and control may be more connected with members of the public.

Guidance notes should be developed to put the context of heritage management within the overall spheres of economic and social sustainable development. These must link the cultural heritage with other issues: cultural tourism, business development, housing provision, environmental protection, urban planning and so forth.

The law must be explained in its own context and within other spheres that have an impact on society. The integrated process demands a more holistic approach.

This, therefore, points to the need for "policies" that put the law in context and that are presented for public consideration and awareness, allowing the possibility for greater understanding and harmony with the policy objectives of the government and specialised institutions in the field of cultural heritage.

It is, therefore, recommended that new laws in the field of cultural heritage should be explained by guidance notes and specific "policy notes" to clarify the application and context of the law and also its relationship to other laws (for example the link between a law on cultural heritage and a law on urban planning and specific land use/development plans).

These could take the form of specific explanatory notes detailing different procedures. For example, an explanatory note on how to obtain consent for works to a protected building could explain the process in plain terms, including how documents should be prepared, the information that is required, the period for decision-making and an appeal process.

Similarly documents should be produced to explain the obligations placed on owners and occupiers of heritage property (both immovable and movable), the process of enforcement action and the sanctions and penalties that may be incurred by not following the law. This will help to find solutions to the problem of illegal building and unauthorised activity.

Design guides and technical notes should be developed to inform enterprises and individuals on conservation, restoration and rehabilitation processes. The process of developing such information should be shared between ministries where relevant and also at the institutional and local government levels. Information on the recorded and protected heritage should be available for public inspection and the institutions should provide an advice service to clarify enquiries from the public.

Moreover, one of the challenges presented by the process of globalisation is the development of, and the possibilities for, access to digital information. In the "information society" there is a need to ensure that everyone has reasonable access to knowledge including in relation to the cultural heritage and its legal and management regimes. The technology to enable web-based information products has allowed for the development of new tools for networked professionals, non-governmental organisations, teachers, tourism industries, businesses and individuals. The Internet offers a new challenge for all countries to disseminate information and provide access to information on cultural property to further good practice by decision makers, applicants and other interested people.

These possibilities should help to encourage civil society participation in heritage policy as indicated in the conclusion of the summary of the present state of the cultural heritage (the first part of this publication), promoting a dialogue with developers and other interested parties. It should be remembered that new laws will have little meaning except for the specialists in the field without such open consideration.

Central to the issue of the law and its relationship with the public is the issue of the purpose of the law. It must, therefore, be reiterated that, apart from the good practice of education and other awareness-raising approaches, legal provisions for the cultural heritage should be directed towards the people affected by the provisions and separated from the public bureaucracy that has the responsibility of managing the process. This means, at the very least, that the law should separate the issues that concern the regulation of actions by the public from those that regulate the delegation of powers to specific institutions. Where these are contained within one law they should be placed in separate chapters. Otherwise, the procedures for regulating the bureaucracy should be provided through separate regulation (norms) or secondary legislation.

The Council of Europe conventions concerning the cultural heritage provide an exemplar to this approach. The Delphi (movable heritage), Granada (architectural), Valletta (archaeological) and Florence (landscapes) conventions give clear ideas on the type of procedures that are required to control the activities of the public – but do not spell out the procedural rules applying to institutions. A greater awareness and understanding of these and other conventions as well as the recommendations of the Council of Europe is required when developing legal procedures, as they highlight the key issues for regulating the actions of citizens but not the bureaucracy.

Developed along the lines suggested by the conventions and other recognised standards and recommendations, a law should provide greater clarity to the ordinary citizen. Furthermore, the "explanatory notes" associated with the conventions highlight the need for explanatory information to advise on what is meant by adopted legal provisions.

Guidance and policy must, therefore, go hand-in-hand with the approval of new legislation to encourage understanding and enlightened participation in cultural heritage protection and management.

Key issues – A law should be understood by all members of society who may be affected by its provisions. This additionally requires accessible information, guidance and the provision of advice to aid this process. This will assist in encouraging civil society participation in the development and application of heritage policy.

2. Methodologies for selection, categorisation, identification and valorisation

Many delegates from different countries have raised concerns regarding these issues during the Sofia debate.

The approach to selecting items for protection should be separated from the management and control process for subsequently designated items.

The first step must be to define a set of criteria for the selection of items for protection. These should be clearly set out and published so that members of the public are aware of the criteria and are given the opportunity to make a case for specific items to be designated. The law should provide this opportunity and guidance notes should be issued to explain, in straightforward terms, the main categorisations of items that can be designated. This implies a need for a simple set of criteria such as those indicated in the conventions of the Council of Europe and the guidance that has been developed to assist the reform of law (*Guidance on the development of legislation and administration systems in the field of cultural heritage*, Council of Europe, 2000). Moreover, a simple set of criteria such as those indicated in the Granada Convention (conspicuous historical, archaeological, artistic, scientific, social or technical interest) with explanatory notes should assist this process.

It is important not to be too extensive as this leads to confusion, but each country should decide an appropriate solution. Furthermore, as indicated by the explanatory notes to the Granada Convention, the relevant authority (the relevant minister, ministry or institution as determined by law) should be responsible for deciding whether the criteria are met. An exemplary approach has been shown in the methodology adopted in Bosnia and Herzegovina, in that an independent commission makes the decision as to whether a specific item is put forward for designation by an official body or an ordinary member of the public, according to the defined and published "Criteria for the Designation of Property as National Monuments".

This debate has raised issues concerning identification and valorisation of the cultural heritage. The term "identification" implies the need to survey, declare or otherwise identify, according to established criteria, which items can be subject to protection measures. The relevant conventions refer to this process (Article 9.c Delphi, Article 2 Granada, Article 2 Valletta and Article 6.C Florence) and give examples of the types and categories of assets that could be designated (Appendix II Delphi, Article 1 Granada, Article 1.3 Valetta and Article 2 Florence) (further discussion of this issue is included in the *Guidance on the development of legislation and administration systems in the field of cultural heritage*, 2000). It has been accepted through the previous debates that countries do not need to use the exact terms and categorisations used in the conventions as long as the approach is in harmony with the conventions. However, a thorough understanding of the ideas presented will help to ensure there is harmony with the approach advocated by the Council of Europe and by other internationally recognised standards.

Moreover, while different types of assets are considered in relation to the architectural and archaeological heritage (as immovable heritage) as well as the movable heritage, there is a need to recognise that some immovable assets include items of a movable nature. This will require cross referencing in the identification process (for further information see *Guidance on the development of legislation and administration systems in the field of cultural heritage*, 2000 and Recommendation No. R (98) 4 on measures to promote the integrated conservation of complexes composed of immoveable and moveable property).

The action of identification presumes a process of recording the identified information. Once items have been designated, there is a requirement to record them and, according to law, to determine appropriate courses of action for their management and safeguarding. There is no conclusive approach regarding this recording process: some countries use an inventory just to identify items of recognised interest with a separate register of protected items, while others use the inventory as a formal system of registering items for protection.

The identification and registering process is another case example where the use of digital information systems can be used to provide reliable data on heritage assets already protected or requiring protection. Moreover, as indicated in the conclusion of the summary of the present state of the cultural heritage (the first part of this publication), the development and use of such information systems could help to provide solutions for finalising or updating inventories, and documentation systems in these transition countries should be explored. (Details on the role, use and types of inventory, including as a means of protection, can be found in the Council of Europe publication *Guidance on inventory and documentation of the cultural heritage*, 2001.)

More significantly, knowledge is required of the different methods of identifying and protecting the cultural heritage adopted in western European countries (where there is greater involvement by the public, more activity by private enterprises and a consciousness of a living heritage) in order to compare it with the methods traditionally used in the South-East European countries. Historically, the heritage in the countries-in-transition has been managed by the state more as a "museum" heritage with the state and other public institutions undertaking most of the work. This has largely led to a restoration approach, fuelled by the valorisation process.

Valorisation is different to *identification* as it implies that a detailed scientific and conclusive investigation is required, based on a well-founded convincing study, in order to validate that specific items meet the criteria to merit protection. Such a detailed study tends to focus on the heritage to determine what may have been its original form.

For the archaeological heritage it is now recognised that such detailed investigation can result in irrevocable damage, hence the emphasis now placed on non-destructive techniques and "minimum intervention" (see explanatory note to the Valletta Convention in relation to Article 1). Similarly, in relation to the architectural heritage, the Granada Convention emphasises "conservation" meaning maintenance, restoration (where there is sufficient evidence of an earlier state), rehabilitation and management of properties and not specifically "restoration" back to what may be thought to be an "original form" which can often lead to conjectural work. Moreover, the Council of Europe has emphasised the need to use this heritage for socially useful purposes, in other words as "living heritage" (as has been discussed during this debate). A detailed investigation will tend towards a restoration approach (a "museum" approach) rather than a conservation approach that could consider beneficial use, socially or economically.

More significantly, the valorisation approach requires a detailed and lengthy assessment as to whether an item meets the selection criteria. Apart from encouraging the restoration approach, this has other problems. It means that significant financial resources from the already limited budgets of the relevant institutions are taken up by such studies. Evidence has suggested that there is a reluctance to give up this type of role for fear of job security, apart from an ideological difference in opinion about the best approach to adopt. To some extent this is an issue of inertia – some institutional officials are unwilling to change their traditional roles and also unwilling to adopt new approaches that envisage a management approach to the heritage rather than a purely protection approach (or otherwise are unable to make such changes for budgetary reasons).

Many of the professionals within the state institutions in South-East European countries have traditionally held a monopoly in investigation and subsequent restoration projects. The reluctance to change from this position stems from a number of reasons, for example pride in their work, potential job insecurity, a belief that the private sector cannot be trusted. Accordingly, the traditional approaches continue and the reluctance to accept the heritage as a "living heritage" is maintained. However, lack of resources and limited budgets mean that it is very difficult to carry out necessary works and the heritage becomes even more at risk.

This indicates a need to remove the institutional monopoly on the management of the heritage and to develop a partnership approach with owners and the private sector, particularly as the restitution of private property interests increases.

Thus, an identification approach has been advocated, in favour of immediate valorisation, through the use of rapid surveys to determine whether an item meets the defined criteria for selection. This should speed up the process of designating protected assets. Once identified, heritage assets can be managed and protected under relevant legal provisions (duty to maintain, control over works, etc.). Moreover, any proposed actions by private owners would require appropriate consent procedures (e.g. alteration for a new use in a historic building, demolition or restoration).

In western European countries it is more normal for applicants for consents to be required to justify their proposed works, which may include a detailed assessment of the particular characteristics/interest factors/values and how these would be affected by the proposed works. Thus, for example, it is for the applicant proposing the works to justify any interference in a protected historical structure and for the relevant authorities to determine at this point in time whether sufficient detailed assessment has been made of the special characteristics of the asset and, accordingly, whether the proposed works should be granted consent. There is a need, therefore, for the management of the heritage to be opened up to the private sector (an issue developed in Theme 3 of this debate) and for owners and enterprises to accept responsibility in justifying their proposals. This type of approach has been advocated with respect to the development of archaeological sites – the European Code of Good Practice "Archaeology and the Urban Project" highlights the need to create partnerships between different players: public authorities and planners, designers and developers, and archaeologists, but ultimately developers pay for the damage or for mitigating against the damage that may be incurred (the "polluter pays" principle).

In addition, to assist this process "management agreements" could be developed for particular assets of the immovable heritage (such as large-scale buildings, archaeological sites, landscapes and other complex cultural heritage entities). These could be used to define the characteristics that are important, to provide a better and improved understanding of assets, to define the nature of works that would or would not require consent and to provide guidelines on alteration, maintenance and conservation. It would further help to provide a more effective partnership between owners, managers, local authorities, specialised institutions and other interested parties concerning designated assets through positive long-term strategic management.

Other identification methods have also been highlighted to encourage better management practice, such as the use of condition surveys and registers to determine which heritage assets are at risk (from disrepair, lack of use or the threat of development proposals). Again, this could take the form of a rapid survey and digital information systems can be used to record this information so that heritage assets can be better managed with a view to determining where priority action is needed (for example, expropriation or persuading an owner to agree to the voluntary sale of a protected building, or in relation to the provision of subsidies or other financial or fiscal assistance). Moreover, for owners who are unable to take appropriate action to safeguard protected assets (for financial or other reasons), a register of such assets could be used as a marketing vehicle to find new owners who are prepared to take appropriate action.

This could help in getting the public and relevant authorities to recognise the role played by the heritage in society and making them more aware of the responsibility to preserve it, whilst recognising its potential economic and social role.

Key issues – Identification should be distinguished from valorisation. A swifter procedure for designating assets through defined selection criteria will assist the management of the cultural heritage. Digital information systems should be used to finalise and update inventories on protected assets. Such systems can be used to prioritise action following rapid surveys and resultant registers of heritage assets at risk or under threat for various reasons and also to "market" such assets to attract potential investors. These actions will help to develop a new management approach to the cultural heritage, in partnership with private owners and the public in general.

3. Linking the cultural and natural heritage

The European Landscape Convention has raised the profile and concept of "cultural landscapes" and the cultural environment linking the cultural and natural heritage. This debate has highlighted and recognised this link but identified that the tools for co-ordination of activities between the two spheres are still in their early stages. Moreover, there is a need to develop systems of management and protection that do not create a conflict between the relevant authorities and institutions dealing with the cultural heritage and the natural environment respectively. This will require the development of a suitable system of landscape categorisation and mapping techniques such as by GIS. Currently, as identified in the presentation of policies in the first part of this publication, different authorities deal with the cultural heritage as opposed to the natural heritage. This shows the need for a new process within the concept of integrated conservation in which different authorities will have to co-ordinate activities for protection and management.

Key issues – A system of categorisation, protection and management of landscapes encompassing the cultural and natural heritage must be developed according to the principles laid down in the European Landscape Convention. This will require different authorities and institutions to work together to introduce and develop the concept of cultural landscapes.

4. Cultural impact assessment

This debate has raised the question as to whether some form of impact assessment, for example of new development and construction activity on existing heritage assets, should be required. Through an integrated process of management it would be necessary to consider any material considerations relating to the impact of new work on the heritage resource before consents are granted. This is the normal approach in western European countries and implies a co-ordinated approach if different authorities are involved in the process.

Moreover, for EU member states, the European Council Directives 2003/35/EC and 97/11/EC, amending the earlier Directive 85/337/EEC, require the introduction of a procedure for the assessment of the environmental effects of certain public and private projects. This is largely in relation to major and complex projects that could have a significant impact on the environment including the cultural heritage, natural areas and landscapes of cultural interest (for example, the impact of the development of a major road in relation to an important archaeological site). As most countries in South-East Europe are working towards membership of the EU, and following membership would be required to introduce relevant regulations in this field, it would be good practice to start developing relevant procedures now.

Key issues – The impact of new activities on the heritage must be assessed through co-ordinated approaches. For the immovable heritage this must be undertaken by an integrated approach to the management of the cultural heritage in which all interests will be fully considered.

5. Integrated conservation and sustainable development

This debate has raised several further issues concerning the development of integrated conservation systems (identified in the Granada, Valletta and Florence conventions) and sustainable approaches to the management of the heritage (embracing the four pillars of sustainable development: economic development, social cohesion, environmental protection and the prudent use of natural resources).

From the discussion of the present situation of cultural heritage policies, it must be reiterated that the challenge to improve the necessary means of action for such approaches requires the reform of laws in the context of the market economy, better co-ordination and co-operation between relevant authorities on the implementation of laws and policy, devising and implementing strategies and funding mechanisms, and increasing training, education and participation by the public.

Integrated conservation encompasses the two objectives of *conservation* (protection, conservation and enhancement processes) and *integration* (rehabilitation, revitalisation and co-operation). An essential part of this process is the link between the management of the heritage and the control of development and land use. This requires a co-ordinated approach to consent systems. Moreover, consents for any activity directly connected with, or which would affect, the heritage will require systems of co-operation between relevant authorities to determine the impact of proposals. This process must be informed so that land use and development plans have policies for safeguarding, and importantly, utilising the cultural heritage so that it becomes a "living heritage". This further implies the need for information on the cultural heritage to be recorded. This then requires a process of mapping of heritage assets and the development of joint policies at the national level (linking such issues as finance, revitalisation strategies and urban and regional planning with the heritage).

Knowledge can be gained from many countries in western Europe that use map systems for recording the heritage. Geographical information systems (another form of digital information) can be used in this context. Examples have been given in relation to the Survey of Architectural Values in the Environment (SAVE), whereby individual surveys of areas are developed into heritage atlases in Denmark; intensive and extensive urban assessments, which are being developed in the United Kingdom to assess the archaeology of historical centres; archaeological and heritage atlases are being developed in France; and in the Walloon Region of Belgium the mapping of heritage properties is undertaken. These systems are used to inform urban and rural planning processes.

It is important to consider the development of co-ordinated policies on new development/ construction affecting archaeological sites (whether protected or not) and other aspects of the cultural environment (protected building, areas, landscapes, etc.). National policies on spatial planning, land use, environmental protection and enhancement and economic development should be dovetailed with national policies on the cultural heritage. This implies the need for a more holistic and global approach and the setting up of inter-ministerial arrangements to facilitate this.

Information, advice and guidance should be provided for the public, private owners and potential investors, not just to identify obligations but also to encourage participation in the development of heritage policies and to encourage investment and the reuse of heritage assets.

Moreover, social issues can also be considered in the integrated process. This debate has highlighted examples of heritage funding strategies based on a partnership approach (involving heritage institutions, local authorities and business) centring on areas of heritage importance (such as historical city centres and towns) suffering from economic and social problems (deprivation) and focusing on the restoration, conservation and rehabilitation of heritage assets (particularly to provide homes and businesses). This reinforces the concept of identity with the local heritage, endorses the concept of the "living heritage" and is a sustainable approach. In this respect, examples have been given of funding mechanisms and coherent programmes to support the preservation of the cultural environment as a factor of sustainable development. This again requires a co-ordinated approach involving law, policy and partnership arrangements at national and local government levels and with other public institutions and the private sector.

The development of sustainable strategies should integrate all aspects of the cultural heritage (architectural, archaeological, movable, intangible and include the concept of landscapes) with other environmental, economic and social goals including revitalisation strategies, housing, business and tourism, education and training, cultural identity and religion. In this respect, the heritage can be a factor in improving the "quality of life" of citizens. However, it must be reiterated that the implementation of long-term sustainable strategies will require a firm political commitment.

The starting point for such action and for developing appropriate integrated mechanisms is to define goals to be achieved and to develop indicators that can be monitored over time to measure the progress towards reaching these defined sustainable development goals. These can then inform policy and the development of co-ordinated strategies.

Key issues – It is a priority for relevant public authorities and institutions to recognise the important and potential role of the heritage in society in economic, social and environmental terms. This requires a more holistic and global approach and co-ordinated involvement of a broader range of relevant authorities. Laws should be amended in the wider field to bring them into line with the current transition to market economies and the means of action necessary to organise integrated conservation systems (applying to all immovable heritage assets), and for building sustainable communities, need to be improved.

6. Funding mechanisms

Central to the issues considered in connection with integrated conservation and sustainable development, is the development of appropriate funding mechanisms and fiscal provisions to ensure investment in the heritage.

At present, all countries in South-East Europe have limited budgets in their transition phase and the cultural heritage is not regarded as a primary area for support. This has resulted in reduced budgets for the ministries and institutions responsible for the cultural heritage, not just in terms of staffing but also in supporting investment in heritage assets. The general situation is that public funds are limited to public property, and private owners have to cover their own costs.

Despite this situation, there is evidence that some countries have provided, through law or other means, limited measures of financial support (in Bulgaria tax incentives are provided, but in practice do not operate as the state budget is controlled by the International Monetary Fund; in "the former Yugoslav Republic of Macedonia" funding programmes for integrated community development and institutional development are assisting the heritage; in Romania tax incentives are provided for preventative conservation and restoration work for cultural objects; in Bosnia and Herzegovina religious and foreign sources have partly offset inadequate public funding).

Apart from these limited examples, charging for the commercial exploitation of the heritage and the granting of "concessions" provides some opportunity for the private sector to invest in the heritage and for the relevant authorities to raise additional finance. However, there are several problems associated with the concession mechanism: it is too often regarded as the primary method of raising finance; it is uncertain whether the money raised will be redirected into subsidy/revitalisation programmes to assist investors and private owners; it is a way of avoiding the heavy cost associated with public investment; the conditions negotiated are not always ideal; and it may be manipulated to retain property in public ownership. The exception is in Croatia where the income raised from a charge on the commercial use of images associated with the heritage and application of a "monument rent" on the use of heritage property for business premises is redirected into state or municipal budgets to support preservation action by owners. Other countries should learn from this experience if they fully implement subsidy or other assistance programmes.

Clearly the question of land tenure is related to the finance issue. Setting in motion systems of renting out cultural property will prolong public control over land. The restitution of property interests is in varying stages throughout South-East Europe, but a large percentage of property still remains in public ownership. This situation will gradually change. However, restitution of property ownership has its own problems in that the owners of recovered property usually do not have sufficient financial resources to invest in their properties, whilst at the same time they are often set onerous obligations in terms of maintenance, conservation and restoration. Therefore, incentives will have to be developed to encourage investment by private owners and from other sources.

In several countries, studies into the economic and social value of benefits gained from public investment in the heritage have proved positive in terms of tax revenues, homes and businesses created as well as employment in specialist craft trades and the leverage of significantly more investment funds from the private sector. Governments should be made aware of these studies so that the argument for developing subsidy and incentive programmes can be made. Moreover, revitalisation programmes and tourism strategies should be co-ordinated within integrated strategies for the heritage.

Key issues – Restitution of property ownership will increase the role of the private sector in the management of the heritage. Financial support measures will increasingly be required to encourage investment. An exchange of information is required concerning the benefits of investing in the heritage from an economic and a social perspective, apart from the benefits to be gained in relation to heritage assets. A co-ordinated approach to funding should be adopted, recognising that the heritage has a role to play in the economic and social sustainable development of society, thus requiring the development of revitalisation programmes as envisaged under the integrated conservation concept. The perspective of potential investors in the cultural heritage also requires further examination in order to encourage participation and the generation of additional financial resources from private sources.

7. Institutional reform and partnership with the private sector

The review of the present state of cultural heritage policies has already identified that while most countries lack personnel in some specialised areas, a decision as to whether specialised restorers should remain in the public sector or be "privatised" remains outstanding. This issue was also raised in Theme 3 of the debate and Sections 1 and 2 of these operational conclusions.

In fact, institutional reform raises a number of issues not just in terms of human resources, training and education, but also in relation to the areas of operation of relevant authorities and official institutions and the co-ordination with parallel authorities in different but connected spheres (for example, in relation to environmental protection and the natural heritage, urban and regional planning and economic development). Moreover, the gradual transition to developing market economies, changes in land tenure and property restitution emphasise the need for a rebalancing of the roles of the public and private sectors.

Progress in this area has been slow, as much due to the limited budgets available to make changes as the resistance to and fear of change itself. However, it will be necessary to adapt to new and developing circumstances. The present structure of national and regional institutions in most South-East European countries largely retains the ideology of the previous political era.

It must be reiterated that the management and control of the heritage should not be the sole remit of the public sector in an open society. It is necessary to draw on the experience of western European countries, in which private owners, their advisers (including both architects and archaeologists) and contracting organisations play the major role in conservation and other work to safeguard the heritage and rehabilitate it for continued use in society (to create a living heritage). It will be necessary to reconsider the traditional role of institutions and move towards a more managerial approach.

It is also important to redefine the present regional structures of specialised institutions and to consider the decentralisation of activities, linking in with municipal responsibilities (such as in relation to the co-ordination and integration required between land use planning and the heritage). Linking to Section 1 of these operational conclusions, there is an increased responsibility for official heritage services to provide accessible information mechanisms and advice to guide the transitional process and participation by society.

At the ministerial level there is a need to develop joint policies and work closely with other ministries (spatial planning, investment and economy, environmental protection, etc.). Similarly, there is a need to develop joint working relationships with institutions in different fields (such as for the designation and management of cultural landscapes, the integration between land-use planning and cultural heritage and cultural tourism strategies, etc.).

Key issues – Institutional reform must acknowledge the potential of the private sector in conservation and restoration work. This implies a move towards a more "management" rather than "control" approach by official institutions. New and existing staff will require training and retraining to adapt to new circumstances, particularly in relation to the provision of advice and supervision of work. In the transition phase, the opportunity should be taken to streamline existing official services and to develop a more co-operative approach with the private sector (owners and investors as well as ordinary members of the public). Institutional services must adapt and integrate with other levels and fields of administration (ministries, institutions an d local government).

8. Sanctions and enforcement measures

For a successful law, there is need for both positive measures (financial support, technical assistance, etc.) and negative measures (appropriate protection policies backed up with administrative and legal sanctions). It is important to ensure that there is a balance between the management and the control of activities.

As indicated in the review of the state of heritage policies, solutions must be found to the ongoing problem of illegal or unauthorised activities that are detrimental to the immovable heritage. Promoting a dialogue with developers and investors will assist in resolving this problem but this does not dispense with the need for penal measures (fines and imprisonment), set at such a level as to act as a deterrent, and other enforcement and coercive activity (for example, "stop" provisions in the case of damaging activity, repair and reinstatement orders, etc.). Expropriation powers should generally only be used as a last resort as it will imply a burden of compensation for the relevant authorities.

Effective enforcement and policing services should be developed to prevent or halt damaging or illegal activity. The process of institutional reform should consider this aspect, which implies the formulation of appropriate legal powers, a new form of official service and the training of new enforcement officials backed-up with appropriate powers (rights to enter premises, preventative and remedial orders and other measures).

Such a service could be linked to municipal authorities (or other relevant authorities dealing with development activity) rather than heritage services, but this will require a further level of integration and co-operation between different authorities.

Key issues – Effective policing powers, legal and administrative sanctions and an enforcement service must be implemented as part of the process of institutional reform. This will require a further level of integration with different authorities (police, specialised services, local authorities, etc.).

9. Museums and the movable heritage

The ICOM Code of Ethics for Museums remains as the minimum standard for professional practice and performance of museums, which all South-East European countries should aim to adhere to.

However, the museum networks in most South-East European countries have suffered in the transition period. When circumstances permit museum services need to be more inviting and to entice the public back. Opportunities to raise awareness should be explored through educational programmes, exhibitions, publications, the media, improved interior design and layout. The development of collections may be aided by tax incentives in combination with expropriation measures and pre-emptive first options to purchase cultural objects.

Restructuring is taking place in some countries but progress varies. Shortages of financial resources and staffing remains but opportunities for increasing volunteer staffing may be a partial solution (with sufficient will and training). Sponsorship should be encouraged and opportunities to make revenue from the sale of products (books, cards, reproductions, compact discs, etc.) should be explored. The facilitation of non-profit organisations in the museum sphere should also be encouraged with the consideration of tax incentives. Opportunities should be created for joint programmes and exhibitions between museums in different South-East European countries, particularly where there is a shared identity and heritage.

Concerning the circulation of cultural goods, the issue of illicit trafficking remains an outstanding problem in most countries. The concept of a legitimate "art market" is still at an early stage of development in South-East Europe. Awareness of the Unidroit and

UNESCO conventions is important in this sphere. The reform of law should, therefore, require that art operators in this market have a duty of care and must notify the relevant authorities if there are serious doubts as to an object's origin (which could have been stolen from museum collections or which could otherwise be protected).

Registration is the key to knowledge about cultural objects. Private dealers must be obliged to maintain records of objects passing through their hands. More significantly, in order to provide proof of origin (and ownership), to allow for restitution and for customs and officials to be able to track cultural goods, it is important to draw up a precise register of protected objects in order to combat illicit trafficking effectively. This provides a further avenue for the development of digital information systems (databases) for recording and management purposes. Furthermore, it must be reiterated that protected "national treasures" must be defined and registered (for EU member states this means that they will not fall under the presumption of free circulation of goods).

Key issues – Museum services should be restructured and developed by various means: for example creating new revenue sources, tax incentives, sponsorship opportunities, improved design and awareness-raising. Cultural objects must be safeguarded by effective and precise registration. Digital information systems should be developed and used in this sphere.

Part 4

The next stage

The next stage

The review of the state of heritage policies and the operational conclusions on legal reform have highlighted that there are many differences concerning legal and institutional systems for the cultural heritage in the countries of South-East Europe, all of which are at different stages of development. There has been a general consensus in favour of an improved methodology for the protection and management of cultural heritage and of the need to move away from the ideology of the past towards a more inclusive and integrated approach, recognising the value of the heritage in society. The concept of sustainable development and the contribution of the heritage in this sphere is a new field of consideration – in its early stages in terms of understanding and implementation, but this should not deter investigation of sustainable solutions.

This debate has made a major contribution to the reform process. There is a need for a functioning network and capacity building to exchange ideas to further assist this process. The Council of Europe will undertake to organise, with different host countries, a programme of activities drawn from the requests of country delegates and the operational conclusions of this examination. The issues for subsequent consideration will be based on the following subject areas, for which a number of themes have been *provisionally* identified:

- the use of digital information systems;
- cultural landscapes;
- integrated conservation systems;
- cultural heritage and sustainable development;
- financial policy and funding measures including revitalisation programmes, the use of the heritage as an economic resource and the perspective of investors;
- human resources for the management of the cultural heritage.

1. The use of digital information systems

Threaded through the operational conclusions to the debate on legal reform are several references concerning the possible use of electronic information systems for databases, registers and other information methods to assist in the management of the cultural heritage. A debate on this theme would seek to further explore the current use and development of digital information systems in South-East European countries and examine the roles and types of systems already developed and in operation elsewhere.

A number of systems may be examined including:

- information web-based portals for facilitating access to knowledge, information and advice on policies and the use of the cultural heritage including technical guidance and other information;
- core data standards and indices for the archaeological and architectural heritage;
- object ID for recording cultural property;
- inventory and registration databases in operation;
- cultural landscape categorisation using geographical information systems (GIS);
- heritage atlases and mapping using GIS systems to inform both heritage managers and integration with other systems (planning and revitalisation programmes, etc.);
- control systems for registering and controlling the movement of cultural goods (for market operators and heritage and customs services);
- "heritage at risk" registers (to record and set targets for architectural and archaeological monuments and sites that are under threat and to monitor action);
- cadastre/land registry systems for recording property ownership, land tenure and restitution;
- networking in relation to other related disciplines.

Apart from examples of various systems, further related issues could be examined such as how technical infrastructure should be developed (linking different areas of public administration) and the need for relevant public authorities to ensure broad access to digital information systems, including the promotion of ethical, non-discriminatory public access and the adoption of "user rules" and data protection procedures.

2. Cultural landscapes

As of 1 November 2007, 28 countries have ratified the European Landscape Convention since its opening for signature in Florence on 20 October 2000. This convention has now come into force as 10 ratifications was the qualifying condition for this. Moreover, while a number of member states have not yet signed the convention, some non-signatory countries have taken a lead in developing the concept of cultural landscapes.

Work has been developed by the Council of Europe, the EU and various partners and country organisations and agencies, for example the Pathways to Cultural Landscapes project involving 12 participating projects in different countries in Europe concerning cultural landscapes.

A debate on this theme would seek to explore key issues for understanding and recording the cultural landscape, as well as access issues, sustainable management and protection:

Cultural landscape characterisation

- examination of research into the cultural landscape with reference to the different and varied methods of characterisation and landscape types utilised in different countries as a first stage in the process of studying and understanding;
- exchange of information on approaches adopted and standards defined.

Geographical information systems

- the opportunities for utilising GIS databases as a tool for research, developing models in planning and public awareness;
- exchange of experience and standardisation of systems.

Preservation and protection

- defining protected areas;
- co-ordination of protection (between existing institutions for cultural heritage and environmental protection);
- balancing preservation and protection with economic and social needs.

Sustainable management and use

- positive management through farming, forestry, cultural tourism and other uses;
- consideration of settlements and building uses;
- balancing economic and social needs of local people and tourists with preservation.

Physical access

- development of access infrastructure through signs, pathways and other means to allow access for local people and tourists.

Virtual access

- development of digital presentations via the Internet, compact disc presentations and other non-physical means of access including information centres and museums.

3. Integrated conservation systems

The principle of integrated conservation is now firmly embedded in the Council of Europe conventions on immovable heritage (Granada, Valletta, Florence and Faro conventions).

A debate on this theme would seek to explore the measures required for developing integrated conservation systems:

Administrative measures

– provision of an appropriate department or project co-ordination team with administrative, technical and professional staff to deal with conservation issues, to act in close co-operation with the relevant authority responsible for urban and regional planning/local authorities, owners and investors;

– development of integrated conservation programmes and the revision of planning and other regulations, promoting rehabilitation rather than demolition and new development which enhances heritage areas or by the control of new development through restrictions particularly in relation to design, dimensions, materials and impact on sensitive heritage sites (including archaeological sites);

– mapping of areas to indicate all aspects of the cultural environment worthy of protection or under threat (risk registers) and the provision of protection zones;

– planning and implementation of projects by experienced practitioners, technicians and skilled craftspeople;

– involvement of training agencies and education providers and the training of people in relevant expertise and skills.

Social measures

– to enhance the social fabric and living conditions at all levels of the population, particularly the less affluent ones, using multidisciplinary teams to make studies of areas and develop solutions likely to be acceptable to local authorities and to the public, including the provision of affordable housing in rehabilitated buildings, the avoidance of gentrification and property speculation, and involvement of the public, residents and business in the preparation of integrated conservation schemes.

Financial measures

– co-ordination of different funding agencies, allocating specific budgets and the provision of financial aid including the leverage of private investment.

Awareness-raising measures

– facilitation of community participation in the development of schemes, plans and decision making and the provision of information and education to assist this process.

Specific examples of integrated conservation operating in western Europe include

- partnerships between public and private sectors;
- urban rehabilitation programmes;
- development in areas of archaeology;
- co-ordinated management of rural cultural landscapes.

4. Financial policy and funding measures

A debate on this theme would seek to examine the heritage-funding problem: the shortage of financial resources and how to deal with this.

Methods of raising finance to support state budgets or otherwise to support the heritage include

- the role of foundations, trusts, sponsorship and private philanthropy;
- bond issues;
- lotteries;
- concessionary use of heritage property;
- revenue charges on heritage property;
- tourism levies.

Creation of a favourable setting for the initiation of projects

- the role of studies into the economic and social benefits of investing in the heritage;
- incentives for putting buildings to use;
- support from planning and urban development policies;
- administration mechanisms/project co-ordination;
- rental policy.

Financial incentives

- subsidies;
- tax incentives;
- loans;
- combined measures.

Legal conditions

- public guarantees;
- leasing systems.

Use of suitable programme management structures (integrated rehabilitation/ revitalisation approaches)

- revolving funds (often based in localised areas, but sometimes nationally);
- heritage-led regeneration/rehabilitation schemes;
- housing improvement programmes linked to areas of older housing;
- public-private partnerships.

5. Sustainable development

A debate on this theme would seek to explain what "sustainable development" means in practice by reference to developed national strategies that have been put in place, in which a global approach is taken – linking the spheres of responsibility of all government departments/ministries in building sustainable communities. From this standpoint, a more detailed consideration of the role of heritage as a factor in sustainable development can be examined with reference to examples from different countries.

Further relevant issues include the development of indicators for a sustainable heritage so that, from established baselines, targets can be set in achieving sustainable goals. This should inform policies and strategies which can be reviewed in the light of the monitoring (measurement) of progress. Such indicators could encompass, for example, the following (and other) issues:

Understanding heritage assets

- data on the number of individually designated assets, heritage areas, sites and other cultural environment resources (such as landscape categorisation);
- data on heritage assets in public or private ownership.

Managing the heritage

- data on the development of national policies and their integration at local administrative levels, on the maintenance of inventories, on heritage assets at risk and the maintenance of condition registers, on the number of determined applications for consent for different types of works, on the development of integrated conservation management plans, on the provision of design guidance/frameworks/briefs for individual assets and areas, etc;

- statements on the significance of key heritage assets;
- performance measures for institutions/heritage services;
- assessment of available funding resources, of the social and economic benefits derived from the heritage, of progress in enhancement schemes, of training and employment in craft skills and professional services and their development, etc;
- assessment of enforcement and remedial orders.

Communication
- advice to owners and occupiers on heritage assets at risk, on repairs and maintenance, on funding, on the submission of applications, etc;
- publication of research reports, organisation of events and exhibitions;
- awareness promotion.

Using the heritage for the benefit of society
- data on the rehabilitation of heritage assets (for example: for new homes or businesses);
- assessment of community participation, membership of heritage organisations and forums, volunteers, visits to heritage sites and museums;
- assessment of school qualifications in history and higher education qualifications in heritage-related disciplines, of educational visits to heritage sites and museums;
- assessment of attitudes to the cultural heritage and progress in enhancing the cultural environment.

6. Human resources and institutional reform

A debate on this theme would aim to explore how institutional regimes could be reformed, bearing in mind the transition to market economies, land restitution, the need for integrated mechanisms, community participation and involvement in the management and preservation of the heritage by private owners, enterprises, developers and investors.

New services will need to be introduced to include advice and information, and heritage inspector, supervisor, and enforcement services.

The training and education of conservators, architects, archaeologists, heritage managers, information system specialists and other professions as well as traditional craft trades and enterprises is also a relevant consideration in the improvement of human resource provision in both the public and private sectors.

The role and development of private sector professionals and construction enterprises in the field of conservation and restoration work will need to be further assessed including existing provision, the scope for their development and educational programmes (and qualification standards) to support such activity.